The Water Sellers

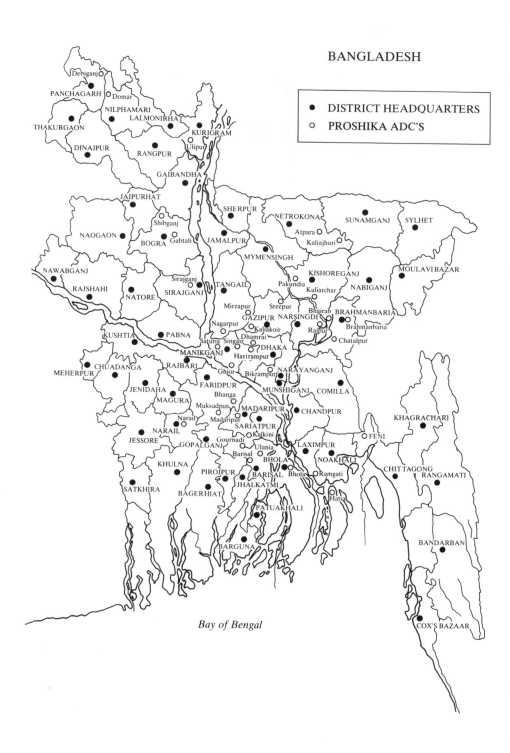

BANGLADESH

● DISTRICT HEADQUARTERS
○ PROSHIKA ADC'S

The Water Sellers

A Cooperative Venture
by the Rural Poor

Geoffrey D. Wood
Richard Palmer-Jones

with
Q. F. Ahmed
M. A. S. Mandal
S. C. Dutta

KUMARIAN PRESS

Published in the United States of America by Kumarian Press, Inc.
630 Oakwood Avenue, Suite 119, West Hartford, Connecticut 06110-1529 USA
ISBN 0-931816-83-1 (U.S.)

Published in the United Kingdom by Intermediate Technology Publications Ltd.
103-105 Southampton Row, London WC1B 4HH United Kingdom
ISBN 1-85339-084-4 (U.K.)

Printed in the United States of America
Printed on acid-free paper by McNaughton & Gunn, Inc.
First Printed in 1991

Cover design by Laura Augustine
Edited by Susan Palmer-Jones
Typeset by Rosanne Pignone
Proofread by Beth Penney

Library of Congress Cataloging-in-Publication Data

Wood, Geoffrey D., 1945–
    The water sellers : a cooperative venture by the rural poor / Geoffrey D.
  Wood, Richard Palmer-Jones with Q. F. Ahmed, M. A. S. Mandal, S. C. Dutta.
        p.   cm. — (Kumarian Press library of management for
  development)
    Includes bibliographical references and index.
    ISBN 0-931816-83-1
    1. Irrigation—Bangladesh. 2. Water-supply, Rural—Bangladesh.
  3. Agriculture, Cooperative—Bangladesh. 4. Rural poor—Bangladesh.
  I. Palmer-Jones, Richard, 1946– II. Title. III. Series.
  HD1741.B35W66   1990
  333.91'0095492—dc20   90-21202

---

95   94   93   92   91   5   4   3   2   1

Contents

Tables

Figures

Bangla Terms

aman	main monsoon rice season/crop (broadcast (B. aman) or transplanted (T. aman))
aus	summer rice, usually lowland with early rains
baid	low-lying soils in Mudhupur Tract
bari	residential area of extended family
bheels	low-lying areas in which flood waters are trapped
bhumihin	landless
bigha	land measure, usually one-third acre
boro	dry season/rice crop grown in the dry season
braus	hybrid rice season combining winter rice and *aus*
chala	upland soils in Mudhupur Tract
dhone	traditional irrigation with canoe-shaped scoop
gorib	poor
haor	low-lying tracts of land with long flood period
khas	untitled land allocated by the Government of Bangladesh
krishi	farmers
kurmis	field staff
KSS	farmers' cooperative (originally from Comilla model)
madrasa	village Islamic school
matbar	acknowledged senior leader in a village
maund	a unit of weight measurement, approximately 37.3 kg
para	residential subarea of a village
parishad	council (at different administrative levels)
prantik	marginal peasant
rabi	late autumn/winter crops of pulses, oil seeds and vegetables
samity	group level organization
sardar	village leader
shalish	informal village court
thana	old term for subdistrict unit of administration
union	sub-*upazila* unit of administration
unnayan	development
upazila	sub-district unit of administration

Units

1 hectare	2.47 acres
1 bigha	1/3 acre
1 maund	37.3 kg. = 82 lbs.
1 US $	Tk33.3 (1988)
1 £	Tk56 (1988)
t	ton
ha	hectare

Abbreviations

ADAB	Association of Development Agencies in Bangladesh
ADC	Area Development Center
AST	agricultural sector team
BADC	Bangladesh Agricultural Development Corporation
BAU	Bangladesh Agricultural University
BBS	Bangladesh Bureau of Statistics
BIDS	Bangladesh Insitutute of Development
BKB	Bangladesh Krishi (Farmers) Bank
BRAC	Bangladesh Rural Advancement Committee (NGO)
BRDB	Bangladesh Rural Development Board (formerly IRDP)
BSCIC	Bangladesh Small and Cottage Industries Corporation
CARE	Committee for American Relief Everywhere (NGO)
CIDA	Canadian International Development Agency
CUSO	Canadian University Services Overseas
DSSTW	deep-set shallow tubewells
DTICP	Deep Tubewell Irrigation Cooperative Program
DTW	deep tubewell
EZE	German development assistance foundation
EIG	employment- and income-generating
ETP	evapotranspiration
FAO	Food and Agricultural Organization

FYP	Five-Year Plan
GDP	gross domestic product
GBP	Grameen Bank Project
GOB	Government of Bangladesh
HYV	high-yield variety
IBRD	International Bank for Reconstruction and Development (World Bank)
IDA	International Development Association
ILO	International Labor Organization
IRDP	Integrated Rural Development Program (now BRDB)
KSS	*Krishi Samabay Samity* (farmers' cooperative)
LOTUS	Landless Operated Tubewell Users Service
LLP	low-lift pump
MIDAS	Micro-Industries Development Association
MoA	Ministry of Agriculture
MPO	(Water) Master Plan Organization (GOB)
MTFPP	Medium-Term Food Production Plan
NGO	Non-governmental organization
NOVIB	(Dutch development assistance foundation)
PROSHIKA	*Proshika Manobik Unnayan Kendra* (Center for Human Development, NGO)
RD1	Rural Development 1 program
RD2	Rural Development 2 program (World Bank-sponsored)
RLF	Revolving Loan Fund (Proshika's Credit Service)
RPP	Rural Poor Program (within BRDB)
SIDA	Swedish International Development Authority
STW	shallow tubewell
Tk	Taka (unit of currency)
UK-ODA	United Kingdom Overseas Development Administration
UNICEF	United Nations Children's Fund
USAID	United States Agency for International Development

Preface and Acknowledgments

THE RESEARCH THAT formed the basis for this book and the data supporting it are described in detail in the report *Social Entrepreneurialism in Rural Bangladesh, Water-Selling by the Landless,* which the authors produced for Proshika in 1988. Readers wishing to examine our localized data in greater depth are referred to that report. Only data that we felt to be essential have been included in this book, much of it in the Appendixes, where the basic technical information can also be found. Terms that appeared in Bangla in the report have been translated into English here, except for those without any direct English equivalent; these are listed in Bangla Terms.

The book is a collective effort with contributions from Proshika's R & D Cell; two staff members from the Bangladesh Agricultural University in Mymensingh (the departments of Agricultural Economics and Irrigation and Water Management), Dr. M. A. S. Mandal and Dr. S. C. Dutta; two staff members from UK universities; Dr. G. Wood (Bath) and Dr. R. W. Palmer-Jones (Oxford and now East Anglia); and the Director of Proshika, Q. F. Ahmed. This, however, is only part of the collective effort, since the groups themselves have taken on the primary burden of the experiment and have willingly provided much scarce time at the end of long working days as well as during them to answer endless questions and maintain records. Furthermore, the Proshika *kurmis* (field staff) have been extensively involved in assisting the groups in implementing the program and in collecting data. Both groups and field staff have also taken part in many planning and review sessions at the Area Development Centers (ADCs) and in Proshika's planning headquarters at Koitta, Manikganj. Among many others who have shown interest in the approach, the continuing support of the Ford Foundation since 1980, through its representatives in Bangladesh, has been important to the development of the program. This support has taken the form of grants, guarantee deposits to the Bangladesh Bank to facilitate lending to the groups by the Bangladesh Krishi Bank and recoverable loan support to Proshika's Revolving Loan Fund (RLF). It has also taken the form of considerable technical support from three program officers, Dr. M. Hanratty, K. Marshall and A. Bottrall, who have participated in planning and review sessions and have visited group irrigation schemes in the field extensively. The authors would like to thank Susan Palmer-Jones for prodigies of editing under the adverse circumstances of authors who had moved on and were often in distant places.

Introduction

WATERSELLING BY THE landless is a concept that aims to empower the poor through facilitating their access to a crucial rural resource. Thus it is not merely an income-generating activity but also an attempt at agrarian reform.

This book presents the experience of an experimental program in which over 150 small groups of landless water sellers worked in association with Proshika, a Bangladeshi non-governmental organization (NGO), to establish an irrigation service. The policy context for this program had several dimensions.

The agrarian situation in Bangladesh is desperate. The country is one of the most densely populated rural regions of the world, with an average of nearly 1,500 people per square mile and a total population of approximately 100 million. The population growth rate is one of the world's highest, at around 2.3 percent,[1] and its ramifications pervade the agrarian structure. While families grow larger, the landholdings that support them remain the same size or, worse still, are reduced to tiny fragments by the multiple inheritance system. Peasants already living below subsistence level are disposessed through mortgage and debt. The availability of land for sharecropping has declined (especially for supplicant, marginal peasants on the best land in the more abundant seasons). The number of landless has increased. Ironically, in this deteriorating situation children are valued all the more as income earners and providers of old-age security. There has been a depressive effect on wages, except perhaps in the peak seasons of new production. The old patron-client dependency, which offered minimal security to labor in the past, has been undermined as an increasing reserve army of labor contributes to the commercialization of labor relations.

In 1980, when the program described in this book was started, an estimated 91 percent of the population lived in rural areas and approximately 80 percent appeared to be directly dependent upon agriculture for their income. The ownership of land was becoming increasingly concentrated, with 11 percent of rural households owning more than 52 percent of all cultivable land while over 30 percent owned no land at all. The latter, together with those owning less than half an acre, constituted about 50 percent of the rural population. The situation was accompanied by high rural underemployment and a decline in real agricultural wages.[2] In 1980, the *per capita* annual income was reported as equivalent to US$130 (World Development Report 1982). If the concentration of incomes in urban areas is taken into account, however, then the average rural income becomes considerably lower. It was estimated that 62 percent of rural people receive only sufficient income to satisfy 90 percent or less of the necessary daily intake of calories. By the end of the 1970s, the production of major agricultural crops was only 7.3 percent higher than in 1970 (Clay 1978; ILO 1977).

It has been argued elsewhere (Wood 1981) that, certainly in the period up to the end of the 1970s, rural class relations in Bangladesh were characterized by the use of capital in the sphere of exchange (renting, moneylending and trading) rather than by production. This, in the absence of profitable opportunities in agriculture or manufacturing, effectively raised the level of absolute surplus value accruing to certain classes but did not contribute to the generation of productive agricultural capital. The result was a form of polarization in which the numbers of landless and the levels of rural unemployment rose dramatically, creating a problem of effective demand for the required expansion in agricultural output, especially foodgrain.

Rising landlessness is not so great a problem if alternative rural employment opportunities are available. Unfortunately, this has not been the case in Bangladesh. Due to the annual population growth rate, approximately 45 percent of the population is below the age of fifteen. The rural labor force is increasing at about 4 percent a year—almost 1 million men and women. This increase far exceeds the number of additional employment opportunities available in agricultural and other sectors. The World Bank estimated in 1980 that, during the first half of the 1980s, approximately 2.3 million new entrants to the rural labor force would not be able to find gainful employment.

The rapid increase in unemployment directly affects agricultural production. Limited employment would mean that a substantial segment of the rural population must limit food purchases. If production increases outpace demand, this could result in low producer prices and the growth of large, government-financed food surpluses under conditions of persistent malnutrition. By now, it is hoped that the expansion of employment programs in rural works and income-generating projects has had some positive effects on overall rural purchasing power.

The response to these problems in Bangladesh was contained in the advice given to the government by the World Bank (IBRD 1979) and incorporated by the government into both its 1980–85 Second Five-Year Plan (2FYP) and the longer Medium-Term Food Production Plan (MTFPP). Essentially, the strategy was based on a significantly expanded investment in agriculture and rural works, on conditions derived from the analysis in the "Food Policy Issue" World Bank Report. The report lists the physical constraints to the development of agriculture as scarcity of cultivable land, limited yield potential, climatic hazards, the need for dry season irrigation and improved drainage and flood protection. It attributed the slow growth of agricultural output to weaknesses in agricultural support services, inadequate provision of input supplies and constraints stemming from the agrarian structure. Any expanded investment was dependent on external aid. Both the World Bank and the United States Agency for International Development (USAID) were determined to liberate the rural economy from bureaucratic management and control by encouraging open-market systems of food and input distribution. The strategy therefore consisted of open-market dealing in food, phasing out fertilizer and other input subsidies (on various forms of irrigation) and a major emphasis on high-yield variety (HYV) technologies in rice and wheat. These efforts concentrated on the improvement of foodgrain supply with a noticeable lack of attention to the structure of demand for food. The strategy involved the untested assumption that a combination of support prices (through a generous procurement price) and open-market dealing in rural goods (inputs and food) would encourage the landholders to raise the productivity of their land, thereby increasing their marketable surplus to pay the full market price for inputs.

As noted above, richer landowners in Bangladesh have traditionally opted for higher rates of return on investing capital in nonproductive economic activities. But if the incentive assumptions behind the 2FYP for agriculture are valid (and especially under conditions where the supply of goods and services remained scarce), then we could expect sharecroppers to be dispossessed at a faster rate and small owner-cultivators to become more dependent on credit (usurious or institutional) in order to compete successfully in the market for inputs. Where small farmers failed to obtain cheap sources of credit at the right time, the productivity of their land would remain stagnant or decline. A consequence of such tendencies would be a rise in the rural landless population. These potential outcomes therefore constitute risks for both production and equity objectives, involving further increases in landlessness and indebtedness, further additions to the underemployed labor force and further reductions in the levels of effective demand for agricultural food products.

The 2FYP therefore envisaged an annual average increase in foodgrain output of 6.5 percent (the government of Bangladesh (GOB) and World Bank 1982), to be achieved principally through developing minor irrigation and doubling the supply of fertilizer. The irrigated area was expected to double from 2.6 million acres to 7.2 million acres, representing 32 percent of the maximum feasible cultivation area of 22.5 million acres. The greater proportion of this increase (45 percent according to MTFPP) was to be through shallow tubewells (STWs), with deep tubewells (DTWs) at 32 percent and low-lift pumps (LLPs) at 20 percent. Despite the problems experienced during earlier programs of organizing farmers' irrigation cooperatives around DTWs (problems that still persist in contemporary programs), the technology is regarded as unavoidable in areas with low water tables. The increase in LLPs was technically limited by the availability of additional surface water resources.

Irrigation in the previous plan periods (1973–78, 1978–80) had developed at a slow rate. This was attributed to the low level of equipment use in the field due to an over-generous subsidization policy involving heavy public-sector costs and inefficient, corrupt implementation. A policy of privatization was therefore adopted. This policy represented the attempt to deploy lines of credit, based in the first instance on US$40 million from the International Development Association (IDA), to sell STWs and LLPs to any farmer, contractor, rural entrepreneur, group or collective who could appear in the market with the collateral on which a loan could be extended. No quotas were established initially, even for the farmers' cooperatives (Krishi Samabay Samitis (KSSs)) of the Bangladesh Rural Development Board (BRDB).

The proposals noted above for the 2FYP caused some anxiety within the Ministry of Agriculture. Its Planning Cell was asked to consider the broader, institutional implications for the rural poor of a rapid increase in the scale of capital investment in agriculture. Wood contributed a paper[3] with a pessimistic prognosis on labor absorption even under the most optimistic trickle-down scenarios. The paper referred to the problems of rural underemployment and the potentially depressive effects of weak purchasing power, among the net rural purchasers of foodgrain, upon the price incentive for producers. But under the proposed conditions of privatization and withdrawal of subsidies there were, as Wood's paper pointed out, a range of possibilities for the productive inclusion of the poor in these expanding economic opportunities. Such possibilities might address production objectives as well as equity ones. Rural works and irrigation were also discussed (not only the minor, mechanized irrigation technologies but surface water and gravity flow systems). Rapid expansion of the mechanized, minor irrigation sector was envisaged. In this context, the proposals for the landless to enter the market for these assets caught the immediate attention of the senior personnel in the Ministry of Agriculture, who wanted to integrate production and equity objectives where possible. Some of this analysis and the proposals deriving from it were presented to the February 1980 Consortium meeting in Paris and were incorporated into the Minister's speech to the April 1980 Regional Food and Agricultural Organization (FAO) conference in New Delhi. The Ministry was therefore keen to see if these principles could be translated into a program of action. Through the Ford Foundation's support for the Ministry's Planning Cell, Wood was invited to prepare a project outline in August 1980. In this, he was assisted by Dr. Martin Hanratty, program officer, the Ford Foundation, by Dr. Dan Jenkins, an agricultural engineer with USAI;, and by continuing discussions with senior personnel within the NGO Proshika. Throughout the exercise, support and encouragement was forthcoming from the then Minister of State for Agriculture, Dr. Iqbal Mahmud, and the then Secretary for Agriculture, Mr. A. Z. M. Obaidullah Khan. The Ministry officially approached the Ministry of Rural Development and the Integrated Rural Development Program (IRDP, now BRDB) to develop a program of landless provision of irrigation services through some of the landless groups that had been formed alongside the more familiar farmers' cooperatives in the seven *thanas* of the Rural Development-1 (RD1) program sponsored by the World Bank. These negotiations proceeded, with inevitable delays, as the IRDP was changing its status to BRDB and a new Irrigation Management Cell was being created. Many within IRDP were skeptical about using the cooperative strategy and IRDP personnel in the systematic mobilization of the rural poor. In the meantime, the Ministry of Agriculture reacted positively to the suggestion from Proshika that it engage in a parallel experiment on the basis of the project outline.

Proshika is an NGO established in 1975 as a project of Canadian University Services Overseas (CUSO), funded by the NGO division of the Canadian International Development Agency (CIDA). In 1976, Proshika became a Bangladeshi organization, with CUSO acting as an executing agency on behalf of CIDA until 1984, when formal links ceased. CIDA has been Proshika's principal funding source. Other principal sources of external funding are: Swedish International Development Authority (SIDA), EZE (a German development assistance foundation), NOVIB (a Dutch development assistance foundation) and the Ford Foundation. Proshika also operates a bus company whose profits are invested in Proshika's development activities. Proshika originally consisted of two operational wings based in Dhaka and Comilla. Over time, differences in approach and methods between the two wings developed, and in mid 1981 two independent organizations emerged: Comilla Proshika and Proshika Manobik Unnayan Kendra. The latter, henceforth known as Proshika, developed this program of establishing irrigation assets in the hands of the landless as the basis of a landless provision of irrigation services.

The name Proshika is an acronym of three concepts: *proshikan* (training), *shiksa* (development education), and *kaj* (action). *Proshika Manobik Unnayan Kendra* is then translated as Proshika—a Center for Human Development. Proshika is established to increase the level of socioeconomic self-sufficiency of landless workers (men and women), marginal peasants and other poor people in rural Bangladesh by:

- forming groups to build up their unity and organization,
- providing knowledge and skills through human development and skills training, and
- assisting the groups through loans and technical support to develop employment and income-generating activities.

By 1989, Proshika had mobilized almost 14,000 groups (of which 2,500

are women's groups), with an average membership of 20 family representatives in 2,500 villages through 36 Area Development Centers (ADCs) distributed across 19 of the new districts. It currently employs 55 central program staff and 400 *kurmis* (field staff), 255 male and 145 female, working
through the ADCs.

In the national context of numerous landless peasants and indebted
small tenants with little access to institutional credit, agricultural services
and inputs, the employment and income-generating (EIG) opportunities
outside agriculture have been restricted to rural works programs and petty
trading. The former have provided some temporary, seasonal relief at
basic, individual, subsistence levels; the latter is characterized by low
turnover and exploitative debt relations in order to obtain materials and
working capital. In this situation, Proshika sees a strong link between the
local unity of the poor and activities that, in providing a degree of material
independence, assist the poor in counteracting the structures responsible
for their poverty—wage rates, tenant shares, interest rates, concentrated
access to land, water (drinking, irrigation and fishery), other means of production, means of transportation, production skills, education and health.
In this sense, Proshika's activities have to be seen as mutually reinforcing.
They consist of the following:

- group formation,
- conscientization (through informal processes of development
  education),
- training (activity skills, management practices, literacy and health),
- social action (on wages, tenant shares, occupation of *khas* land, leasing *bheels* and ponds for fishing and provision of pure drinking water
  through hand tubewells), and
- income generation (livestock raising, vegetable growing, roadside
  forestry, sericulture, apiculture, fishing, milling and so on).

In pursuit of these aims, Proshika is committed to experimental action-
research projects that involve institutional innovation. As far as possible its
methods are participatory, with initiatives arising from open discussions
between group members and the field staff. Ideas and programs are never
imposed upon the groups, though sometimes the ideas and enthusiasms of
the groups may not be supported by Proshika. In the case of irrigation,
groups observed the expansion of mechanized irrigation equipment in the
countryside and themselves raised the possibility of their own purchase of
these assets. Proshika personnel could see the enormous significance of
engaging the landless directly in agricultural production through the ownership for the first time of a principal means of production—water. It would
be an activity distinguished from other, more self-contained, income-generating activities because it would involve direct and continuous interaction
with landowners, commercial classes and officials, and at the same time

would offer opportunities for leverage in other economic and political spheres in the locality.

Proshika initiated this approach through two mechanized minor irrigation technologies, STWs and LLPs. A tentative beginning was made in the *boro* season of 1980–81, with sixteen groups deploying STWs and ten deploying LLPs, concentrated in the Bhairab and Chatalpar ADCs respectively. Proshika was prompted to move quickly into the program through a fear that the demand for this imported equipment from richer landowners and agrarian entrepreneurs would be high under the conditions of open-market dealing and liberal credit, and that after a few years the technology would have been monopolized by these classes. Landlords would become waterlords. There was considerable experience with irrigated HYV rice and wheat production in Bangladesh through the DTW irrigation cooperatives and the rental of LLPs from the Bangladesh Agricultural Development Corporation (BADC—a parastatal extension of the Ministry of Agriculture), but there was little experience of irrigation management through STWs. And STWs tended, initially, to be located in new areas of HYV production where DTWs had not been suitable because perennial monsoon flooding was likely to damage the permanent installation. LLPs were usually located in areas where private contractors had previously rented them from BADC. This meant that little experience of irrigated HYV production was available among the groups, Proshika or the farmers. This was also the case in the private sector generally, and some observers (those, for example, from the Bangladesh Water Master Plan Organization (MPO)) have subsequently argued that the reliance on market forces and liberal credit irresponsibly stimulated an introduction and use of these technologies that was inefficient both in terms of location and management. The scatter diagrams of the current location of STWs reveal an anarchic pattern of competition with DTWs, especially in the northwest, with implications for command area size and reliable aquifers. These diagrams also reveal that a principal criterion of their distribution seems to be proximity to railheads rather than hydrological and soil conditions. The 1980–81 winter rice season was therefore truly one of action research for Proshika and the groups in Bhairab. The groups and the farmers were the teachers, giving their time generously in extended debriefings during the season and afterward.

The initial year's lessons were transferred to the 1981–82 winter rice season,[4] and the findings and analysis from this period will be summarized in chapter 2. Further questions clearly had to be asked concerning the broader social objectives of the program alongside the need to monitor financial and economic performance of groups as they continued and new groups as they started. The program was expanded modestly and always at a slower rate than that requested by groups, who were eager to seize the opportunities offered by participating in irrigation in this way.

In January 1984, a further period of research was proposed, involving collaboration between Proshika and the Department of Agricultural Economics at the Bangladesh Agricultural University. The early floods of 1984, which destroyed much of the 1983–84 winter rice crop, necessitated some modifications to the research design in February 1985, and of course the floods significantly disturbed the program, causing much hardship to many of the groups. Farmers were unable to pay water fees, so costs for that season's irrigation could not be recovered.

Since 1980, there have been several attempts in Bangladesh, following Proshika, to establish an irrigation service provided by groups of landless workers and marginal peasants to farmers, who are either landowners or sharecroppers. In the 1987–88 irrigation season, 250 such groups, initiated by Proshika, were in existence: 160 STW groups, 71 LLP groups and 19 DTW groups. The DTW groups have started more recently from the 1985–86 season in association with the Landless Operated Tubewell Users System (LOTUS) run by the NGO Committee for American Relief Everywhere (CARE). Since the inception of this irrigation service by the landless, some other NGOs, such as the Bangladesh Rural Advancement Committee (BRAC) and the Grameen Bank Project have inaugurated similar programs. From 1984–85, the BRDB, through its Irrigation Management Cell and its Rural Poor Program (RPP), initiated a similar experiment, although it has encountered many problems due to the weakness of its group formation concepts and the lack of commitment to the program's principles within the Board itself.

The constraints on production were not only technical but social, embodied in the structures of tenancy, moneylending, tied labor and the related problems of effective demand stemming from precapitalist forms of servitude. The transformation of a major means of production such as water for irrigation must be considered within the context of all these aspects of the rural political economy. The danger inherent in the privatized minor irrigation strategy was the concentration of these relatively new, uninstitutionalized water assets in the hands of those who already possessed rural capital in the form of either land, moneylending or other commercial forms of accumulation. Such a pattern of control over water might ensure that large farmers obtained water to expand their production into another season, but the question was never asked whether the incentives to expand production actually existed for potentially progressive farmers in the absence of any provision to ensure a buoyant rural demand for the produce. Also, a privatized minor irrigation strategy might create a class of waterlords—a class with access to the technology that realized profits from the sale of water to those smaller farmers whose subsistence (rather than marketable surplus) really depended upon irrigation to intensify the use of their land.

This is clearly an example of wider problems concerning the relationship among production, distribution, effective demand and equity. The most familiar response to these problems in the subcontinent has been land reform, but equally familiar are the political and social limitations of such programs. The policy landscape is strewn with legislative debris. A broader concept of agrarian reform, however, might contain some solutions.

Basically, the argument consists of appreciating that rural property rights other than land exist and that, since land is the most institutionalized and custom-bound of these rights, its socialization or even modest redistribution is the hardest to achieve. But when agriculture is recognized as a system of exchanges between means of production and goods and services, landholding becomes only one right (until now the most significant) alongside others such as water, inputs, mechanized technology, energy sources, service institutions (including credit), marketing networks, means of transportation and communication. In the rural political economy of Bangladesh these other forms of property (that is, from whose control a rental income can be derived) are relatively uninstitutionalized and undeveloped by comparison with land. They are therefore more easily available for capture and control by landless and near-landless marginal peasants, especially through joint group action. This enables the landless to participate in the rural economy not as *supplicants* in the labor market, their value undermined by a surplus of labor or by personal ties of dependency, but as *owners* of commodities and services that have a more buoyant market value. Such a process can lead to a redistribution of assets and incomes, thereby stimulating effective demand and the expansion of production.

In the context of a highly differentiated and polarizing access to land, this approach to agrarian reform still encounters the entrenched vested interests in the countryside along with their urban, entrepreneurial allies. Landless or marginal peasants have little prospect of entering this market for non-land factors of production and services as *individual* entrepreneurs. As will be emphasized below, collective action by groups of landless and marginal peasants is an indispensable part of the overall strategy. There are, however, other social resources in favor of this approach when applied to irrigation, through the constraints on farmers' cooperation for water management.

The rights to both ground and surface water in Bangladesh are complicated by the fragmented structure of landholding. With few exceptions, plots are never large enough or sufficiently consolidated with others to achieve sensible economies of scale with lifting technologies dedicated to those plots alone. The same is generally true with plots adjacent to surface water courses, and is further complicated by the perceived rights of those with more interior plots. This has meant that farmers have been obliged to cooperate with each other, pooling their plots within the service capacity of a water source (that is, within the command of a water source), whether that source is gravity flow from canals, low-lift pumping from canals, rivers or ponds or mechanized lifting of groundwater through tubewells. The experience of farmers' cooperation for irrigation, however, has been dominated by conflict, unequal distribution, control by one or two families, the deprivation of tail-enders in weak social or geographical positions, default on capital and operating-cost loans, mechanical breakdowns, unrepaired equipment, underutilization and often, in the end, non-use of the installation.[5]

This set of circumstances contains an opportunity for the landless and marginal peasant groups to enter the irrigation service. On many occasions when initial agreements between the groups and the farmers were being made, farmers expressed their enthusiasm for this arrangement as a way of avoiding disputes among themselves by receiving water from an external source. Of course, this enthusiasm could be attributed to a transfer of risk from themselves to the groups. The landless groups might be expected to have an incentive, due to their poverty, in maximizing the returns to irrigation and therefore in providing a more reliable service than large, farmer-dominated sources, faction-ridden cooperatives or private irrigation entrepreneurs.[6] If the water supply was more reliable through this service, then other positive features for production and equity should appear. The command areas should be larger and nearer an efficient maximum. The equipment should therefore be more optimally utilized. Farmers would be prepared to invest more in secure irrigated farming, generating greater output and employment than comparable schemes under other forms of management. Smaller farmers should enjoy better access with impartial distribution of water in the command area. Increased employment would not only imply higher incomes from ownership of the irrigation assets but should also lead to a reduced dependence upon rural patrons, thereby increasing the bargaining power of landless workers and marginal peasants selling their labor in labor markets.

The program therefore has a number of interrelated irrigation, economic, social and political objectives. Most simply, it was intended to facilitate the acquisition and use of STWs and LLPs by groups of landless workers and marginal farmers to enable them to sell water to owners and cultivators of land. In this sense, it is an income-generating project for the rural poor. Behind this lay other purposes:

- to ensure that such groups share in the benefits from the enhanced productivity of land to which they contribute through their own labor and by providing the source of irrigation,
- to use water more efficiently and equitably by improving access to irrigation for small farmers who are usually the tail-enders in other systems of distribution for minor irrigation,
- to distribute productive agricultural assets more equitably between those with and without landholdings,
- to create additional opportunities for employment,
- to develop an income basis for the effective purchasing of expanded

foodgrain output (the World Bank report cited above now refers to "constraints upon effective demand for foodgrains" as inhibiting the projected annual growth in foodgrain production for the Third Five-Year Plan (3FYP)),

- to prevent landlords, rich peasants and rural and urban private entrepreneurs from becoming a new class of waterlords and monopolizing this increasingly important means of production,
- to demonstrate that other rural property rights than land can exist from which landless and marginal peasant classes can derive both rent and a corresponding enhancement of political status within the community, and in this way demonstrate the possibility of capturing other agricultural services (repair workshops, input supply, plowing operations, processing of agricultural products or marketing),
- to demonstrate that loans can be extended to poor people for productive use without depending on land as collateral,
- to improve through practice the independent access of the rural poor to institutions (banks, government offices, markets, dealers or courts) outside the patron-client ones within which they are currently oppressed, and
- in short, to contribute to an independent, material basis for autonomous, social action by the rural poor on a broader set of rights and opportunities within the political economy of Bangladesh.

We recognize the limitations upon any one NGO to develop a program and an approach to rural development of national significance. We wished to contribute to a wider policy debate on strategies for the rural poor in which other NGOs, government and donor agencies (bilateral and multilateral) are involved. There are principles here of agrarian reform and social action whose relevance extends beyond Bangladesh. The contents of this book are therefore of interest to a wider audience—of governments, political parties, trade unions, peasant associations, NGOs, donor agencies and applied research institutions.

Chapter 1 outlines the project in operation; the subsequent chapters examine its specific aspects in greater depth. Chapter 2 considers the initial criticisms the program encountered, summarizes the early experience that refuted or validated these criticisms and describes the research design and the constraints upon it. Chapters 3 and 4 look at the relationships between the landless and other social classes in Bangladesh and discuss the effects on these relationships of an alteration in status from landless peasant to co-operative entrepreneur. Chapter 5 deals with the question of whether the program improved the smaller farmers' access to irrigation services. Chapters 6 and 7 analyze the financial, economic and technical performance of the project. Chapter 8 surveys its effects on employment. Finally, chapters 9 and 10 provide an in-depth summary of what has been learned from the experience of the project and suggest its implications for the future, not only for the landless in Bangladesh but also for the rural poor, and organizations existing to assist them, in other Third World countries.

Notes

1. This under conditions where private gain conflicts with social cost (Arthur and McNicholl 1978).

2. Some observers now argue that this decline has been arrested, but their impressions are likely to be biased by the seasonal concentrations of higher wages (a temporary phenomenon, although there is evidence of an increase in the number of days of employment).

3. "How the interests of the rural poor can be included within the 2FYP," subsequently published in the Dhaka *Journal of Social Studies* (No. 10 1980:22–46) as "The Rural Poor in Bangladesh: A New Framework?" (Wood 1980)

4. The experience of these first two years was written up into the report *The Socialisation of Minor Irrigation in Bangladesh* by Wood (Dhaka: Proshika, 1982). In November 1982, this report was presented to a national seminar convened by the Association of Development Agencies in Bangladesh (ADAB), in which the NGOs BRAC and the Grameen Bank Project also presented their more limited experience from the 1981–82 season.

5. This scenario has applied especially to irrigation cooperatives using DTWs, because LLPs were more frequently hired by contractors on an annual basis from BADC at heavily subsidized rates. The DTW irrigation group experience is more relevant to the shallow tubewell (STW) technology, because similar organizational and technical principles apply, although on a smaller scale. There were some assumptions within the government and the World Bank that many STWs would be purchased by individual contractors selling water to other farmers on the BADC rental principle as used for LLPs. But cooperative arrangements were also envisaged despite the negative experience with DTWs.

6. The private irrigation entrepreneurs used equipment that was, in effect, highly subsidized through loan defaulting. The World Bank estimated agricultural credit recoveries for 1984–85 at only 38 percent. See World Bank Report No. 6049 (1986).

CHAPTER ONE

The Project

THE BASIC AIM of the project described here was to initiate an income-generating enterprise for the rural poor in Bangladesh. It was also thought that the project might serve as a model for use in other Third World countries where similar economic conditions prevail. The scheme in its present form was, of course, shaped to a certain extent by the context in which it arose, namely the social and political situation within Bangladesh. This background has been covered briefly in the Introduction. The following chapter sets out the framework of the project and the sequence of its operations.

The landless irrigation project within Proshika consists of groups of landless workers and marginal peasants owning mechanized, minor irrigation equipment and selling an irrigation service to farmers with plots of land in the command area of the water source. The groups are paid in cropshare, cash or, occasionally, a fixed amount in kind.

The project has concentrated until recently upon shallow tubewells (STWs) and low-lift pumps (LLPs), with deep tubewell (DTW) groups starting in 1985–86. The discussion here is focused on the STWs and LLPs, the former having greater prominence in the program.[1]

With a distribution of irrigation schemes over eleven Area Development Centers (ADCs) in 1981–82, rising to twenty-three in 1986–87, the groups have been working under different sets of ecological and socio-economic conditions. Thus many variations affect such factors as the following:

- agreements with cultivators,
- forms of payment,
- the value of the water fee as a proportion of the crop,
- the size of command areas and their cropping characteristics outside the winter rice season (not forgetting winter season wheat),
- irrigation practices,
- soil conditions,
- rates of pumping,
- owner-tenant composition of the farmers in the command area,
- the number of group members cultivating small amounts of land in the command area,

- the prices of paddy,
- the extent of group savings, and
- other local sources of finance.

The nature of many of these variations could not be predicted at the out-set. The range of possibilities had to be learned by doing, to some extent, through Proshika's methods of participatory action research. This helped to determine which combinations of variables best suited local conditions and was also valuable for transferring experiences between groups.

Several steps are required to establish the group irrigation service. The selection of a group is of critical importance. Groups associated with Proshika are selected by mutual consent of the groups themselves, the ADC field staff and the ADC and zonal coordinators. The groups selected are of course a small fraction of the total number of groups associated with Proshika, and many more than those currently participating have expressed a wish to enter the irrigation service market. A group's election is based on its previous collective experience of income generation and on some evidence of its solidarity—either under pressure from other classes in the locality or, for example, during flood or drought conditions.

Once a group has elected and been accepted to participate in the pro-gram, the group members begin negotiations with land-owning and share-cropping farmers who cultivate land in a potential command area. This area is defined by the following:

- suitability for irrigation (elevation, soil types, adjacent plots in a con-tinuous stretch of land unbroken by roads, embankments, canals or *bheel* areas),
- the likelihood of the group's access to it (that is, a suitable site to locate a boring or a LLP, either owned by one of the marginal peasant group members or to be obtained through rental), and
- the absence of seriously established claims on the same or a signifi-cantly overlapping command area.

These negotiations include, in the first place, a recognition of the group's rights to provide water in the area. This is particularly important in LLP command areas, where it is not difficult for a competing water-seller to locate a pump next to the existing one. It also matters in STW areas where competing well owners eager to sell water may encroach on the group's command area.

The negotiations are then extended into the making of formal agree-ments between the group and the farmers who intend to cultivate irrigated crops in the established command area. The agreements are drawn up on a semi-legal deed, using signatures and thumbprints. They vary slightly in content, to reflect local conditions, but all specify the following:

- the duration of the scheme (usually five years),
- rates of water delivery (once the season is underway, the distribution arrangements are usually serial, with three main channels in sequence each taking two days, leaving one day a week for maintenance—see appendix A for a technical discussion of water distribution),
- form and rates of payment (cash, cropshare or fixed-kind—if cash, proportion paid in advance or after harvest; if share, then agreement on a package of full high-yield variety (HYV) cultivation practices is necessary),
- deposits to cover operating costs where not covered by form of payment, and
- division of responsibility between farmers and the group members for the construction and maintenance of the main channels or drains and the feeder watercourses to the plots.

The next step is for the group to arrange the credit to meet capital equipment and operating costs. This is a critical component in the entire project, because the scale of loans required exceeds the level normally considered safe to lend to the poor.

An element of the program was to test the capacity of groups to interact with local branches of nationalized commercial banks and to test the ability and willingness of the banks to extend loans to landless workers and marginal peasants. This strategy was based on the assumption that any specialized credit scheme—whether non-governmental organizations (NGO), Grameen Bank Project, Bangladesh Rural Development Board (BRDB) cooperatives or other targeted arrangements—would always have limited utility to the poor, either in geographical coverage or in restrictions on use, and that in the long term, functional, generalized relations need to be established between the banks and the rural poor. Accordingly, an agreement was made between Proshika and the Bangladesh Krishi Bank (BKB—the main agricultural bank in Bangladesh with the widest distribution of rural branches), to the effect that its branches in the program localities would lend to the groups. To accept such an agreement, the BKB had to secure its loans in the absence of any collateral offered by the groups. The Bangladesh Bank, as the parent holding bank for all banks in Bangladesh, required guarantees before it would authorize such lending by the BKB. In 1980, lending such amounts to the poor was extremely rare and considered an unacceptable risk by many in government and among the donors and their experts. This is still the case, to a large extent, despite the evidence that the richer farmers are in fact the habitual defaulters. The climate of opinion has changed somewhat, however, with the recognition that unemployment leads to weak rural purchasing power, and many donors are seeking to induce the banks to lend to the poor (McGregor and Wilkinson 1986). In 1980, the formula involved the following:

- the deposit by the Ford Foundation of a guarantee fund in the Bangladesh Bank, representing 30 percent of the projected value of loans over a fixed period,
- estimated resale value of equipment if reclaimed in lieu of repayments at 50 percent (averaged over five years of repayment schedule), and
- 10 percent surety offered by Proshika from its own funds, matched by 10 percent surety from the BKB.

In this way, the BKB risked only 10 percent that, in the context of high default rates on the rest of its portfolio of agricultural lending, represented no risk at all. Senior personnel from BKB headquarters supported the program generously from both an ethical and a commercial point of view. It was therefore a substantial disappointment for these staff, as for Proshika, that after five years of recalcitrant branch behavior caused by bad headquarters–branch communications, lack of orientation to the program, frequent transfer of local branch managers, and deliberate obstruction by branch personnel who failed to provide adequate access and demanded bribes, Proshika and the groups reluctantly decided to terminate the agreement with the BKB. Instead, Proshika opted to extend the services of its own Revolving Loan Fund (RLF). This was already being deployed to assist groups with the funding of operation costs, especially in the aftermath of the 1983–84 floods. Floods losses had made it impossible for some groups to keep up with their instalments, thus preventing further releases of funds from the BKB branch to finance the following season's operating costs (such shortsightedness is a weakness of current commercial bank lending practices). The resultant enforced expansion of Proshika's RLF (although it was already due to expand to keep pace with Proshika's increased program of income generation across other sectors) has required organizational changes for Proshika headquarters in its management and monitoring practices. Fortunately, the introduction of microcomputers has reduced both the number of extra staff that might have been necessary and the length of time in which information can be recorded and retrieved.

A group secured a loan from BKB by presenting evidence of an agreement with the cultivators in the proposed command area together with supporting documentary evidence, provided by the local office of the Bangladesh Agricultural Development Corporation (BADC), of the feasibility of the command area. This BADC feasibility statement was soon discredited and has fallen into disuse. The staff of the local BADC offices used the opportunity to exercise leverage for bribes by delaying provision of the document, which, in turn, delayed the group's ability to apply for a loan. Such delays can crucially affect a group's performance. Furthermore, BADC local staff were not carrying out a proper assessment of the command area (elevation, soil type, competing installations) and after a time ceased to visit sites altogether. In some cases, the command area locations were inappropriate, especially on the soil-type criterion. This failure of BADC staff to carry out their technical assessment duties constituted a serious dereliction of duty and frankly is typical of the gross irresponsibility of that organization. The effects on Proshika were that yet another function that should have been performed in the public domain had to be internalized within Proshika's own structure. Twelve irrigation extension specialists are now being appointed.

To receive a loan, a group appoints a chairman, a scheme manager, a pump driver and a lineman. The chairman and manager, together with three other group members, have joint power of attorney. Together they sign the documentation for the loan and undertake the legal responsibility for it on behalf of the group. The figure of five is a compromise between, on the one hand, ensuring that responsibility, accountability and financial information is not confined to one or two individuals in the group, with all the burdens and temptations that responsibility would involve, and, on the other hand, recognizing the inefficiency of total, collective responsibility.

Having power of attorney involves the five members in joint visits to the bank. The lack of cooperation from branch staff compelled these group members in the different localities of the program to make frequent visits to the bank to secure the loan, often accompanied in the later stages by one of Proshika's field staff. This has been costly in time away from work, in the opportunity cost of forgone labor, and in traveling expenses. Travel time is not insignificant in rural areas, where many miles of walking might be required. These problems are of course removed with the operation of Proshika's RLF through the ADC.

With the loan acquired, the group is able to purchase equipment (the engine and pump unit, spare parts, tools, pipes, filters and so on) and an initial consignment of diesel. None of the installations in this program are yet electrified. Again, in the early period of the program, the equipment was purchased from the BADC unit offices at the *Upazila* because the policy of privatized dealing had not yet been translated into a sufficiently dispersed structure of private retail outlets. Where the BADC had a local monopoly of distribution, it was provided with further opportunities for causing delays as leverage for bribes. This situation has now improved in some areas where private dealerships have been introduced, acting as competition for the continuing BADC outlets.

The equipment and diesel supplies are then transported to the pump unit site in the command area, and a small hut is constructed to contain the installation.[2] Transportation time and costs are significant. Several modes of transport, involving trucks, boats, bullock carts, rickshaws and finally hand carriage may, on some occasions, all be necessary. The terrain from metalled road to site can be difficult and may cover several miles.

The moment when the equipment arrives at the site is the first physical reassurance for the farmers that an irrigation service is really possible in the command area. Until then, they have only the precarious evidence of agreement deeds and verbal assurances that the necessary steps have been taken. Because delays and postponements are common in Bangladesh, farmers are naturally reluctant to expend any labor in preparing plots or seedbeds until they are reasonably convinced that a regular supply of water is forthcoming. Also, after the dry months in the late *aman* season, the ground is often so hard that some water may be required to assist plowing. In some cases this may also apply to seedbeds, although these are usually located on a patch of low land, retaining some moisture, away from the command area. But, if we also assume that a lead time of approximately six weeks is required for the preparation of seedbeds and the maturation of seedlings ready for transplanting, then from the first season of an irrigation scheme it is vital that the installation be physically present on the site approximately six weeks before the date of transplanting and the start of regular irrigation. That date is determined by a local calculation on what usually happens to the plots in the command area with the onset of the rainy season. If early flooding occurs, the winter rice transplantation date must be early in the season.

In the first season of the program, 1980–81, the possible delays noted above caused a reduction in the potential size of command areas in Bhairab, as farmers were understandably reluctant to commit themselves to winter rice cultivation. This problem is exacerbated in areas unfamiliar with irrigated agriculture. Obviously, as the practice of irrigated agriculture extends across more areas of Bangladesh, this lack of confidence will decline. In succeeding seasons, Proshika insisted that the ADCs impose an abort date based on the calculation above. Thus, regardless of the reasons, if the equipment was not in position by that date, the irrigation service was postponed until the following year. In this way, the problem of incurring operating costs on uneconomic command areas could be reduced.

Before a group can provide early water on demand to farmers for plot preparation, two further stages have to be completed for STWs and one for LLPs. For STWs, a boring consisting of four-inch diameter interconnecting pipes and filter pipes has to be sunk, using a simple rig to move the boring pipes progressively downward into a pool of soft mud created by the prior sinking of a hand tubewell for the purpose. Occasionally, depending on geological conditions, more sophisticated but small-scale drilling rigs will be used. The borings are usually done by peripatetic teams under the supervision of a private contractor. Proshika has been able to establish some landless and marginal peasant groups into this business. A boring of 80 to 120 feet (the average depth) can be completed in one day if conditions are favorable. Problems can arise in finding acquifers, however, and occasionally two or more borings are attempted before the groundwater source is located. Proshika has restricted the program to geologically suitable regions, but random local problems can occur, especially with inadequate feasibilty assessments. In very rare cases, a command area may have to be abandoned and the equipment moved to a new location, which may also mean to another group.

The second operation, which applies to both STWs and LLPs, is digging the irrigation channels or drains.

Most of the STW groups have a similar layout, with variations corresponding to the elevation topography of the command area. Generally, three main drains are constructed. If the pump unit is located centrally in the command area on slightly higher ground, then the three drains will be set at 120-degree angles to each other. If the pump unit site is to one side, the angles will be narrower. The intention is to divide the command area into three approximately equal sections to enable a sequential distribution cycle. Each main drain will carry water for two days to deliver to adjacent plots, starting with the outer ones and moving inward, before diverting the flow to the second main drain, and so on. The command area for STWs can range from twelve to twenty acres, depending especially on soil conditions, with possible extremes outside the range under exceptional conditions. In some cases, the plots for a STW command area may not be contiguous, thus altering the standard pattern just described.

For LLPs, the pump invariably is located on one edge of a command area. A two-cubic-foot-per-second (cu.sec) pump unit can irrigate from thirty to sixty acres, depending on conditions, including distance and elevation variables. The variables of plot distance from installation and the elevation of the command area are more significant for LLPs than for STWs, but the soil type variable also matters. Frequently, a long, main channel carries the initial flow from the source (river, canal, pond or *bheel*) to the command area plots, which may begin several hundred yards away. Sometimes, the water flow is routed through some *baris* or a whole *para* before it reaches its command area destination. Only then will the flow be divided into separate main drains to obtain, as far as possible, a weekly cycle of water delivery to all plots.

The usual division of responsibility for drain construction is to leave farmers with the task of making the feeder watercourses from the main drain to their plots, except for those whose plots are immediately adjacent to a main drain. This involves farmers in negotiating with each other to route watercourses across neighboring plots. In the first 1980–81 season, the group members engaged in constructing the three main drains were quite reasonably paid a wage for their labor. In examining the cost structure for starting up a scheme, however, the roving Proshika troubleshooting team (joined by Hanratty and Wood) wanted to reduce up-front costs wherever possible, because the margins of return were not yet known beyond a series of hypothetical calculations contained in the original project proposal. It was then proposed, and is now standard practice, that all group members contribute voluntary labor for drain construction or contribute a cash amount if they are engaged in other employment that precludes their labor contribution. These drains are predominantly of compacted, raw earth, though there has been some experimentation with linings. Water loss, therefore, is an inherent problem, especially in systems with sandy soils and long distances (see appendix A).

The group is now in a position to begin the regular cycle of water distribution. There is some debate at this point among irrigation engineers on the optimal modes of distribution. Some argue that only in exceptional circumstances will a serial distribution actually constitute a technically optimum delivery of water, and that topographical and soil variations should entail distribution practices tailored to the specific characteristics of a command area. Others, bearing in mind the problems of human and social relations among the farmers and between them and the group, argue that a serial distribution, even if not technically the most efficient, minimizes conflicts among the farmers over equal shares of water delivery time. There are of course situations in which glaring differences in soil type undermine the credibility of the serial method.

Once the group is irrigating, there are further steps to follow to ensure a continuous supply and to collect fees. The most important requirement is to avoid, where possible, the mechanical breakdown of the pump unit, or any interruption in its operation. Obviously adequate and timely diesel supplies have to be sustained. Drums are usually stored in a member's house or at the site. Good relations with suppliers (that is, private dealers) are therefore important. These pump units require a regular replacement of some parts, such as filters, but other parts are prone to stress and require spares. The pump drivers have only elementary mechanical skills at this stage, although Proshika has organized mechanic training among some groups. Many groups do not yet have access to these Proshika mechanics, and must therefore establish firm agreements with the local, peripatetic, private mechanics.

The groups have to gain some proficiency in maintaining records so that the groups, as well as Proshika, can monitor performance, collect proper fees and keep accounts with the BKB and now with the Proshika RLF. It is obviously important that an accurate record of landholding in the command area is created and agreed upon with the farmers, especially if the form of payment is cash on a per-acre basis. But even if the payment is based on cropshare, the size of a farmer's landholding acts as an indicator of expected yield and a check on whether maximizing cultivation practices are being followed. The water fee currently ranges from 25 to 33 percent of harvested crop before threshing, depending on local negotiations that partially reflect soil types and elevation leading to variable requirements for water in different regions. At the time of harvest, when the share is made, it is too late to renegotiate a higher rate to compensate for a farmer's lack of investment or labor input, or for climatic constraints to production. This is the risk-sharing element in this form of payment. But good recordkeeping, which includes yields and shares received, enables the group to compare the yield performance both among command areas and among different farmers within the command area. They can then apply pressure in succeeding years on the less productive farmers. Of course the group members will also be aware of a farmer's total landholding and capital flow situation, recognize that smaller farmers may have capital/credit problems in maximizing inputs, and will seek to support such farmers by extending credit to them.

To avoid disputes over who owes what to whom, there has to be a record of payments actually made by the farmers. This is especially important where arrangements exist for advance payments by farmers to defray some of the group's operating costs, thereby reducing their reliance on loans. Proshika has encouraged such payments as a way of reducing risk to the groups in the event of climatic disaster such as the 1983–84 floods. The record also reflects practices in the private sector, where individual water users sometimes provide diesel to the owner of the pump unit before water is delivered to their plots. Obviously such advance payments are rarely made under cropshare arrangements, although the division at the time of harvest can be altered to reflect this.

Alongside the income records, accounts have to be maintained on costs. The groups record their costs in an exercise book. Initially, costs were recorded as they occurred in a diary sequence. From these, Proshika learned how groups preferred to present their cost headings, and these have now been streamlined in standard financial record sheets. In addition, passbooks have more recently been introduced to provide an agreed record among the groups, the Proshika field staff and the BKB (now RLF) of loans received and repaid, with dates. This information is also transferred to the standard financial record sheets. Because the major item in operating costs is diesel consumption, accurate accounts of diesel used are important. Initially, diesel was obtained from private dealers through cash payments by the groups funded out of loans or advanced payments from the farmers. Group relations with dealers were therefore positive compared to the problems dealers faced with private buyers of diesel for pump units, rice mills and transportation. Dealers are now prepared to offer diesel to groups on credit, and an agreed record of these transactions is necessary. In order to monitor and regulate the rate of diesel consumption, the groups also keep a record (a log manual) of hours of pumping and rates of diesel consumption per hour of running. The records include the use of mobil oil for lubrication. The log manuals enable the Proshika irrigation extension specialists to check on engine efficiency and make adjustments to running speeds where possible. Pumping rates also reflect variations in command area conditions (soil type, elevation and length of main drains), and the efficiency of the pump and boring in expelling water (see appendix A). The records enable these variables to be checked.

There are further steps to be undertaken and recorded before the annual cycle of a group scheme can be regarded as complete. If water fees are in the form of cropshare, as for the majority of the STW group schemes, then in each farmer's plot the harvested crop is divided into three or four equal piles (depending on whether 33 percent or 25 percent has been agreed upon) and the group is invited to select one of the piles and take it away as its share. (Group members are likely to have been employed in the total harvest by the farmers.) This pile is of course unthreshed, which means a threshing floor has to be organized in one of the members' houses. It also means that the group receives the straw as well as the grain. Usually threshing is done collectively by the group members, who in this program are still predominantly male and are assisted by the women in their families (there are currently three women's STW groups—two in Madaripur and one in Saturia).

When the grain is available, some options exist on its disposition. A major proportion of it must be sold to acquire the cash to pay costs and repay loan installments. But prices vary and are typically at their lowest at the time of the harvest. At the same time, there is often an urgency to sell at this time. When possible, the groups will sell the minimum required to meet immediate financial obligations on the scheme during this period and sell the required balance later when the price is higher. This complicates the process of accounting and monitoring economic performance for Proshika, and this complication is reflected in the problems of managing a data system for this kind of program. In some cases, the entire store of grain will eventually be sold and the cash used to cover operating costs in the following year, as a collective investment in another enterprise or to assist group members in times of domestic distress. In other cases, the proportion of grain not required to meet the group's financial obligations on the scheme will be distributed as kind income among the group members (see appendix B). This reduces their dependency on grain advances from patron employer/landlords, with important implications for their freedom of action within the locality. Other groups may retain a collective store of grain to assist members in domestic distress. One of the variables affecting these choices is group members' access to employment opportunities throughout the rest of the year.

The steps outlined above to establish the irrigation service have been based on the experience of groups operating irrigation schemes in the winter rice season. These steps represent most of the activities concerned with the program. There are, however, some additional features. First, it is possible in some cases to extend the winter rice command area by irrigating neighboring plots on which wheat is cultivated. Wheat requires much less water and less frequent irrigation. Its season is either completed before the winter rice season or marginally overlaps. For wheat, other payment agreements are made—usually cash, with a proportion paid in advance, or sometimes a direct purchase of the necessary diesel to deliver water to the farmer's wheat plot. Secondly, the command area can be intensified in some situations by providing supplementary irrigation at the beginning or end of the main, rain-fed *aman* rice season. Usually the *aman* plots concerned are upland (relatively) so that they flood later and dry out earlier. Again, the water fees are usually cash on similar arrangements as for wheat. The costs and income for these additional irrigation activities should be recorded in the same way as for winter rice, although the groups have tended to regard such opportunities for irrigation as a bonus that does not require inclusion in the scheme accounts. Occasionally, there may be a one-off (single-application) irrigation of *rabi* vegetable plots as well.

When the irrigation season has finally ended in all its forms, the pump unit for STWs is disconnected from the boring, the boring is capped and the pump unit (whether STW or LLP) is removed from the site and stored in one of the group members' houses for the duration of the rainy season. During this period, necessary repairs and overhauls should be completed. For STWs, the site hut is taken down (jute stick wall, roof sections and posts) and also stored in a member's *bari*. In many cases, the command area will then disappear partially or completely under floodwater until the end of the *aman* season—the irony of water in Bangladesh.

Proshika supports the groups during the annual cycle of the scheme. Three ADC support workshops are held during the season: at the beginning, approximately six weeks into the season, and at the end, after the harvest. All the groups involved in irrigation and associated with an ADC will come together on these occasions with the Proshika field staff (now including the irrigation extension specialist) and the ADC coordinator. The steps noted above and the variables affecting performance are discussed and experience is shared. New entrants to the program learn from the experience of other groups, and the field staff report on the experience of groups associated with other ADCs, because this knowledge is pooled at Proshika's central coordination and planning meetings, which are held in the Koitta headquarters during the year, with one especially focused on irrigation before the new season begins. In addition to these meetings, the field staff are in continual contact with the groups (not just the irrigation groups, and not just for irrigation discussions). The field staff are particularly involved with new entrants to the program, assisting whenever necessary. They were most needed for the transactions with the BKB and the BADC. The reliance of the groups upon the field staff, the ADC coordinator and the Central Program Coordinators within Proshika has been the major reason behind the withdrawal from the BKB arrangement.

Notes

1. There were 120 STW groups compared with 23 LLP groups in 1985–86. The STW groups are distributed among 19 and the LLP groups among 4 of Proshika's Area Development Centers.

2. In the first year of the program in Bhairab, these huts tended to be unnecessarily lavish and expensive, but the later huts were more modest.

CHAPTER TWO

Experience and Research

EVEN BEFORE IT started, this program had its critics, which was to be expected in the context of an institutional innovation that separated water from the landed classes and allied it to the landless. Such an idea challenged the preconceptions of many professions concerned with irrigation and the development of an agrarian economy. It ran into criticisms from radical activists as well as orthodox observers. The criticisms came, therefore, from different sources along different dimensions. It is useful to review those criticisms here, because they relate to the objectives of the program and the ability of the groups with Proshika to achieve them. To a greater or lesser degree, some of those criticisms have been upheld by our own research, although they often apply in specific cases rather than generally. They certainly constitute an agenda of concerns that have to be incorporated with the objectives of the program as a point of departure for its analysis.

1. Perhaps the most familiar and obvious criticism referred to the capacity of the highly illiterate landless workers and marginal peasants to carry out all the tasks required to provide a mechanized irrigation service. They lack the skills, capital and organizational capacity to run machines, manage water distribution and keep accounts. The general unfamiliarity in rural Bangladesh with irrigated agriculture and mechanization were unfavorable conditions under which to conduct such a social experiment.

2. Water was best managed by those with land, the users of it. Their rights to groundwater have always been presumed, and farmers must be allowed direct control over it. Surface water was admittedly complicated by the need to administer large-scale gravity flow systems over wide areas involving a great number of farms, hence the long history of irrigation bureaucracies in the subcontinent and other parts of Asia. This may have established the principle of publicly managed water, autonomous from immediate, individual-farmer preferences, but such an implied separation of control did not apply to the smaller-scale command areas served by mechanized low-lift pumps (LLPs).

3. The landless were too poor to participate in such a sophisticated economic activity, not just because they lacked skills and capital but because they lacked the collateral for loans and were too dependent upon the

landowning classes in the locality, either to obtain credit at reasonable interest rates or to negotiate water agreements. Mechanized irrigation involves many transactions, with landowners, contractors, dealers and officials, in which the landless are too weak to defend their interests. Income-generating activity for the landless should be confined to small-scale, self-contained activity in which turnover and risks are low.

4. This criticism was connected with one about appropriate technology. Some observers consider mechanized irrigation an inappropriate technology for all classes in Bangladesh because of the abundance of rural labor and the availability of traditional, labor-intensive systems of irrigation. Furthermore, mechanized irrigation encourages forms of production dependent upon chemical technologies (fertilizer, pesticide and herbicide) and biological innovation (hybrid seed varieties) that have long-term negative implications for the rural ecology and environment. There is something to these arguments, though the alternative choices in attempting to feed the population in Bangladesh are not clear. The more common version of the argument is that such technologies are inappropriate for the landless and the marginal peasants, who should be deploying small-scale, adapted technologies such as hand tubewells, rower and treadle pumps and so on. We detect here a highly reactionary perspective in which a dual-sector rural economy is being advocated, and where new agricultural capital is restricted to richer landowners capable of producing a net marketable surplus with trickle-down benefits to the poor, alongside a low-tech subsistence sector for marginal peasants legitimated by a veneer of liberal concern for their preservation. We strongly refute such attempts to ghetto the poor through a concept of technological forces appropriate only for them, although we recognize the strength of some appropriate technology arguments when applied to economic planning in the society as a whole. The technological transformation of agriculture in Bangladesh, however, has behind it international and national class forces too strong for the poor to resist on behalf of the society as a whole, and the poor cannot afford to be isolated from this transformation.

5. The whole proposition of trying to set up special, non-market conditions for the introduction of shallow tubewells (STWs) and an expansion of LLPs was anathema to those in favor of the privatization strategy for input distribution, utilization of inputs and marketing of output. The World Bank, in particular, was severely critical of any approach of this sort. The resident senior economist in 1980 intended to "flood Bangladesh with minor irrigation equipment," and the senior program officer for rural development revealed an intense and understandable frustration with the inefficiency of bureaucratic monopolies over input distribution and utilization. The farmers' cooperatives were included in this picture as extensions of the bureaucracy rather than as independent, private organizations. The Bank's initial position was to insist on no special quotas, not even for the farmers' cooperatives as a way of ensuring their entry into the mechan-

ized, minor irrigation market. Under these conditions, any suggestion of actually establishing a quota allocation to the landless was met with fierce resistance. The Bank's concern was to provide enough hardware and credit, on a first-come, first-served basis, to individual, entrepreneurial talent, whether rural or urban, willing to invest in agriculture under such conditions. A program designed to alter the social relations of production around agriculture and purposively redistribute the benefits from it did not conform to this scenario. Even in 1987, with the shift in Bank policy toward employment schemes for the poor and the involvement of non-governmental organizations (NGOs), the concept was still a dual-sector, rural economy with the landless excluded from participation in mainstream agricultural activity except as labor, and yet the Bank was prepared to contemplate an entrepreneurial model for landless income-generating projects outside agriculture. This entrepreneurial model derives from an analysis that the poor's lack of capital and skills can be remedied, while rejecting the analysis that poverty derives from a weak class position, in the rural and national political economy, for which conscientization and collective mobilization is required. With some modifications, the Bank's position is reflected in the general policy prescriptions of the government in Bangladesh—although we must recognize the valuable role of dissenters.

6. Further criticism called this approach to agrarian reform essentially revisionist, acting as a diversion from a more profound or radical strategy of mobilizing the landless and marginal peasants around wage and tenancy struggles and the occupation of unregistered property such as *khas* land, *khas* ponds and *khas bheels*.

7. The group ownership of productive assets such as mechanized irrigation facilities would act as a stimulus for petty commodity production behavior and attitudes. In this way it constitutes the privatization rather than socialization of the means of production. Group ownership might also undermine the broader principles of solidarity among groups (since any one group would have neighboring groups not participating in the irrigation service) and possibly within them, if the management of a scheme was dominated by one or two individuals in the group. This is one of the criticisms Proshika has to take seriously. There is some evidence from our examination of these issues that aspects of this criticism are well founded, as will be discussed in later chapters.

The conceptual basis for this type of radical criticism, however, has its own problems. Poor people in Bangladesh cannot be mobilized by words alone or by the prospect of a major collective push sometime in the future. Their problems are immediate in terms of both basic consumption and lack of political freedom through an entrapping dependency on local patrons for material survival. When people are trapped in the structures through which they seek survival, then mobilization in the abstract, directed merely towards opposing those structures, cannot liberate them. A material autonomy has to be developed as a basis of such liberation to the point where absolute survival is not on the line every time radical social action is contemplated. It is true that such a material autonomy may be achieved through a program of saving (a strike fund, in effect) rather than actual productive activity, if the employment opportunities are consistently available at wages sufficient to sustain savings and meet basic needs. But there is a further, more practical, problem with the rejection of income-generating projects. The occupation of these unregistered public assets is meaningless unless the means to use these assets also exist. *Khas* land is occupied only by cultivating it—plowing, puddling, transplanting and so on until the harvest. For this, all kinds of costs are incurred and some capital is required. Occupation must generate income, and the two cannot be divorced. The same is true of the other assets. The lease of a *bheel* is pointless without boats and nets, and if they are acquired only through the locally rapacious systems of moneylending, rental and control over the catch, then exploitation rather than liberation has been confirmed. The issue of units of ownership is important. How large does a collective have to be before entrepreneurialism gives way to socialism? And do large collectives reproduce their own bureaucratic and elitist oligarchies? Perhaps work on group and intergroup solidarity must be continual, recognizing that groups form shifting but relevant alliances with each other on many local issues.

Summary of Early Experience

This summary is based on data collected for the analysis of the 1981–82 season. It introduces the issues faced in the early stages of the program and shows how these guided the subsequent phase of research and the research design. Some aspects of the story introduced here will be pursued in later chapters, so the emphasis in this section is to identify the variables that affected performance rather than to integrate them into the chronological analysis of success and failure.

Of the 164 STW groups that started operating a service from 1980–81 to 1985–86, 120 are still in business. Of those that ceased to operate, 30 withdrew in 1984–85 after failing to recover from the 1983–84 floods (although the failure of these groups could not be entirely attributed to the floods). In the same period, 68 LLP groups started operations; 37 of these continue to offer a service. Many LLP groups discontinued because they had been operating on the basis of annual rental arrangements from the Bangladesh Agricultural Development Corporation (BADC). Floods and small command areas accounted for some of the failures. In many cases of failure, however, equipment and command areas have been shifted to more appropriate groups and locations.

Tables 2.1 and 2.2 summarize the STW and LLP landless/marginal peasant groups by region of Bangladesh for 1981–82. They indicate the scale of the program in different areas at that time and the distribution of success and failure as measured narrowly in financial terms. For the calculation of success, depreciation on equipment was excluded from the cost side, because some of the groups showed a net loss below the annual figure allowed for depreciation on equipment. Net losses that are marginal in this sense give only a slightly misleading impression of the capacity of the groups to meet all their debt-servicing commitments and the initial, one-off acquisition of essential capital equipment that is additional to the pump unit such as tools, drums, hut construction and high initial main drain construction costs. On this basis, for that season, 75 percent of the STW groups and 78 percent of the LLP groups emerged as successful. This certainly gave Proshika early grounds for optimism, although the floods in 1983–84 significantly modified the picture, along with other more structural problems.

Groundwater—STW Groups

Although there were some dramatic financial successes among these groups, especially in Saturia where one group actually paid off its five-year capital loan installment after one year, the average net return per STW group was much lower than for groups with LLP schemes (Tk1,256 compared with Tk6,906). We referred above to the lack of prior experience at that time of irrigated high-yield variety (HYV) agriculture in the locality of STW command areas. The following key variables accounted for the pattern of STW performance:

- size of command area,
- diesel cost as a proportion both of income and operating costs,
- rates of diesel use per acre, and
- the payment system between the water sellers and water users.

Other variables, the significance of which was less clear (although their presence could be detected in particular cases of strength and weakness) included the following:

- first season capital costs,
- salaries for group members engaged in scheme work (pump unit operators, linemen, drain construction),
- oil, grease and spare parts costs, and
- efficiency of the pumping equipment and availability of repair services.

Command area size and performance are closely associated. The average command area for successful groups was 14.6 acres, compared with 9.7 acres for unsuccessful groups. Overall, the average command area size was 13.4 acres, rising to 13.7 acres for the thirty-four groups that entered the irrigation service in 1981–82. This indicated significant learning from the first, tentative season of the program when delayed dates of boring and equipment installation resulted in suboptimal command areas in Bhairab. This achievement of a 13.7-acre average in the first season of entry indicated that, with correct timing on the date of installation, a group does not have to creep toward its optimal command area over a period of years.

The first variable that limited the significance of command area size was the form of payment between the sellers and the purchasers of water. Those groups receiving payment in the form of a 33 percent share of the harvested crop were the most successful as measured by gross income per group and acre, and by net return per group and acre (that is, after costs were taken into account). The high income per acre for groups with this arrangement seemed to indicate that the arrangement provides the greatest incentive for the farmers in the command area to maximize the productivity of their land. Other forms of payment, such as fixed-cash, fixed-kind (now very rare) and 25 percent cropshare brought successful groups relatively low net returns.

Diesel expenses represent the largest proportion of operating costs. Subsidiary factors influencing this variable are the rates of machine efficiency and types of soil. Within each region in 1981–82, a clear correlation existed between diesel cost as a proportion of income, diesel used per acre, average pumping hours per acre and performance. Because both successful and unsuccessful groups had similar diesel/total operating cost ratios (25 percent and 23 percent respectively), the significant ratio was between income and diesel costs. Groups in the region with the highest net return per acre had the lowest diesel cost/income ratios (18 to 22 percent), whereas those with the highest negative net returns had diesel cost/income ratios of 52 to 60 percent.

Surface Water—LLP Groups

In the 1981–82 season, the presence of eight groups renting rather than purchasing LLPs complicated the financial analysis. Our long-term concern is focused on the viability of purchased equipment, since the highly subsidized rented equipment is phased out under the privatization strategy. The renting groups were in a single-cropped area (deeply flooded during the monsoon) with a fifteen-year history of LLP irrigation. In such areas, where there is strong competition for limited water supplies and where water is even more crucial without a rain-fed *aman* in reserve, we had hoped that the groups might have been able to participate in rental agreements over a longer period. This would have allowed them time to capture water rights from established entrepreneurs by operating under the same favorable subsidy conditions, and would have helped them accumulate capital for a subsequent purchase. Lobbying to this effect, both with the government and the World Bank, has been ignored.

In the 1981–82 season, seven of the thirty-two groups using LLPs had problems. LLP groups were expected to appear immediately more financially secure than the STW groups because of the following:

- both rental and purchased equipment (at that time) were more highly subsidized,
- farmers in single-crop LLP areas were more dependent on and familiar with irrigated rice production, and
- the search for a command area could be more flexible as the equipment need not be permanently sited.

In Barisal, which is in the South of Bangladesh and therefore a tidal area, there were four unsuccessful groups with technical problems. Pumping here could only occur when the tide was in to hold up the level of the source (itself fresh water, of course). This acted as a constraint on the size of command area which, it was found, could be served as efficiently by 1-cubic-foot-per-second (cu.sec) instead of 2-cu.sec machines. The latter were shifted to other groups in the subsequent season. The failure of two other groups was attributed to low income per acre. Our data suggest that the groups were weak in bargaining over the water price with a large number of small non-group cultivators whose own margins on production costs were tight (perhaps this weakness of the groups contributed to small farmers' access to water). One of these groups also had major problems with spare parts from an old, rented machine. In the final, unsuccessful case, a very low command area (nine acres) appears to have resulted partly from the sandy soil and partly from interference by a rich, local farmer/contractor. Sandy soil requires more water and higher rates of pumping. There was a high water charge to compensate for this but it was not fully collected, because a dispute existed over command areas, with the contractor preventing the machine from serving the full command area. This is an example of the competition that can occur over command areas in a locality, especially when, as in this case, they are single-cropped with subsidized machinery from the Bangladesh Agricultural Development Corporation (BADC). Contractors in the past have been able to make large profits from monopolizing access to subsidized rented LLPs and charging monopoly prices in single-cropped command areas. Under these conditions, without continued access for the groups to LLPs on rental, it was often necessary to support a group financially during its attempts to capture or assert rights over the provision of irrigation (in a more equitable way at cheaper prices) in particular localities.

The remaining twenty-five groups using LLPs in that season were successful in producing positive net returns, and the twelve strongest were located in Khaliajuri, Mymensingh District in Northern Bangladesh. It has been a disappointment that eleven of these group schemes were subsequently discontinued, seven on account of the 1983–84 floods, when fees could not be collected, and the remaining four through management or mechanical problems. The very conditions for success at that time also contained the seeds of vulnerability. Khaliajuri is part of the *haor* area, a large tract of low-lying land in Bangladesh that is perennially flooded and therefore a single-cropped area. In these areas, cultivators have been accustomed to winter rice irrigation performed by the traditional *dhone*. As a result, the value of irrigation water has long been accepted by landholders. This history of irrigation (including fifteen years of contractors renting LLPs from the BADC) made farmers willing to commit land to command areas and themselves to long-term agreements, but the 1983–84 floods have undermined this confidence, especially in the deeper areas of the *haor* region.

The average size of these command areas was 37.9 acres, which might indicate underutilized capacity. But there were topographical constraints to expanding these areas. Most of the command areas were in effect extensions of existing winter rice land that had been *dhone* irrigated or was low enough to retain sufficient water. These areas resemble very shallow dishes, not necessarily circular, and mechanized irrigation is required for the sloping sides away from the low center. The size of these shallow depressions imposes a natural limit on feasible irrigation. Of course, despite the floods, traditional *dhone*-irrigated winter rice production continues, because it has relatively low investment and does not depend on a water operator's access to equipment, which can delay the start of the season and leave the expanded command area vulnerable to early flooding, as in 1983–84. The attraction of mechanized irrigation in low-lying single-crop areas therefore carries the corresponding risk of early flooding. But simply advancing the season if the late receding of floods delays plot preparation is difficult.

Soil quality was also a factor in determining command area size. Six out of the twelve command areas had a clay constituent, enabling irrigation over a wider area of less permeable soil for a given rate of pumping. In these six command areas, the average size was 41.6 acres, compared to an average of 34 acres for the command areas consisting of the more permeable sandy/loam mix. There was a strong correlation between the clay soil/pumping/diesel use variable and the net return per group. Groups with command areas averaging 41.6 acres, with a clay constituent and 15.6 hours per acre pumping rate had an average net return of Tk21,032. Groups in the other category had an average net return of Tk10,592.

Despite these overall positive net returns to the groups at that time in Khaliajuri, the water fee levels were low, representing approximately 17 percent of the crop value. The difficulty of raising the price or even of transforming it from a fixed-kind to a cropshare payment was that the prevailing rates reflected the previous charges under the subsidized conditions of BADC rental rates. Because the groups before the 1983–84 floods had achieved such positive net returns while bearing the real cost of providing water (through purchasing the equipment), it became obvious that private contractors had been profiting greatly from selling water during the rental era.

Social Implications of Landless Control over Irrigation Technology

Financial viability is a necessary indicator of material independence, but it is by no means sufficient for decreasing the dependence of the landless and marginal peasants upon landlords, moneylenders and employers. Indeed, financial success may be a misleading indicator of independence, if it is merely producing a different pattern of similar employment opportunities, or if cash surpluses are immediately absorbed in the partial honoring of usurious debt obligations. It is therefore important to examine the structural implications of the program. In this section, the intention is simply to note the questions that arose out of the experience of the 1981–82 season and how they informed the subsequent research strategy.

1. The groups stressed the effect of the irrigation service on their own status and confidence in the village community, precisely because they had demonstrated their ability to secure the assets, enter into agreements with farmers and institutions outside the village and organize service delivery.

2. The groups' solidarity was continuously tested in the relations with these external institutions and with the farmers. We noted above in the program description that there were setbacks, attempts at cheating, delays and requests for bribes and, of course, the unfamilar interaction with fuel dealers, spare parts distributors, mechanics, transport contractors and so on. At the same time, relationships within the village threaten that group solidarity. In the 1981–82 season, 48 percent of all the group members reported being in debt to local moneylenders, who are usually rich peasants with land in the command areas. Under such conditions, attempts by such landholders to seek preferential treatment through individual group members must be expected.

3. A structural issue beyond this must be considered. Are group profits from irrigation activity being used to meet unproductive debt obligations, partially or completely? Only in the latter case, with permanently severed debt dependency, can structural change occur.

4. Are profits being used collectively by the groups for further productive investment, or as a credit and strike fund, or are the profits dispersed to individuals for immediate and understandable consumption?

5. Are changes in the pattern and availability of employment affecting labor migration and the seasonal pattern of reliance on advances of foodgrain from landowner/patrons?

6. There seemed to be some confirmation of the earlier hypothesis concerning the value of fragmented landholdings for this kind of irrigation

strategy. Farmers with such landholdings can positively welcome someone else taking on the management of irrigation. In the process, they may lose autonomy over their production decisions, with their cropping cycles reflecting the needs of the plot's command area rather than the needs of the peasant family farm. Such a scenario represents a shift in the balance of social forces surrounding agriculture—the development of entrepreneurialism, in effect, as the activities in the agricultural system proliferate. Such a development also represents a wider set of opportunities for direct participation of the landless in agriculture if organized and supported. As argued elsewhere (Wood 1988), the water controllers in Bangladesh may have a much more consolidated asset than landholders in many parts of the country.

7. The socio-economic basis for the program did not consist of a simple antagonistic division between the landless and cultivating farmers, many of whom are small and/or tenant farmers. Indeed the groups themselves are not pure landless but include marginal peasants. The target-group terminology of "landless" in rural Bangladesh has to be modified by broader notions of poor kin and friends who occupy similar positions in village dependency structures, who may have land but only a precarious hold over it and who are therefore in the same dynamic of rural poverty, even though an individual's exact location in it may vary at any given moment. Today's marginal peasants are tomorrow's landless. It is the recognition that this dynamic occurs for some households and not others that brings such people together in a group, rather than an exact similarity of position. This is why target-group strategies as such are blunt instruments of rural development (Wood ed. 1985). In these circumstances, for the 1981–82 season, 30 percent of group members had some land in their group's command area. The landholdings are usually tiny and insufficient to sustain the family's consumption requirements, so wage labor has been a central part of their economic activity.

8. Therefore, the program seeks also to improve the access of such small farmers and group members with land to irrigate on the assumption that through their weak political position they suffer tail-end problems in water distribution. In the 1981–82 season, the importance of this issue was revealed by data on landholdings in the command areas. On the STW schemes, 32.5 percent of the owning cultivators held less than one acre, 54 percent less than two acres. For LLP schemes, the corresponding proportions were 43.5 percent and 59 percent. In total, 18.4 percent of cultivators in the command areas were sharecroppers. No detailed analysis of their access to water could be conducted at that time, but our concern for information prompted a closer analysis (see chapter 5). In the LLP schemes where the price of water had been bid down in the competition to secure control from contractors in already established sites, the economics of small farmer cultivation was improved. For both types of schemes, it seemed a fair assumption that the small farmers and group members

could interact on more equal terms in the water transaction. For share-croppers, the following two general issues apply to the whole minor irrigation strategy in Bangladesh:

- whether the enhanced value of irrigated land works to displace them, and
- the effect of irrigation (price structure especially) on tenant–landlord share agreements and therefore on sharecropper incomes.

The first question demands longer, time-series data, but evidence from Glaser's study suggests that larger farmers are entering the sharecropping market for the winter rice season to cultivate command area plots, thus displacing their own sharecroppers on such land and competing with them elsewhere. On the second question, several permutations exist for the distribution of water and input costs on the one hand and the product on the other, and this distribution pattern affects levels of production. It certainly seemed best for the sharecropper when the landlord shared in the water cost either directly, or indirectly, when a cropshare is paid to the water seller before the landlord–tenant division takes place. Some of these issues are pursued further in later chapters.

9. The 1981–82 season made it evident that the groups themselves had evolved different organizational responses to cope with the variety of relationships demanded by seeking access to the technology, delivering the irrigation service and receiving payment for it. With the smaller STW command areas and the smaller number of farmers, the groups operated these schemes independently of other groups. Indeed, there was a concern that the management of such schemes might be confined to a smaller group of group members, and this has happened in some cases. There were, however, occasions when groups allied into the joint management of a scheme, or when other groups assisted in disputes or in collecting water fees. With LLPs and their larger command areas and larger numbers of farmers, different functions emerged that often brought several groups together. One group may manage water delivery, another may secure the BKB loan and another may collect fees. The groups needed to show a more collective solidarity with the larger number of farmers (the most non-group cultivators in a LLP scheme was 105) both to secure the fees and to insist on a standard water delivery pattern. Such alliances also prevented a large command area in one locality from being monopolized by one group and avoided bitterness between groups.

This section has reviewed the early experience of the program, and has identified some of the issues that arose out of that experience and guided the design of a subsequent research agenda, which is reported in the later chapters. In addition to the irrigation of winter rice, options exist for the irrigation of wheat and the supplementary irrigation of *aman*. Higher returns on capital investment are also possible through using the machines for non-irrigating purposes such as milling, powering lathes in rural workshops, or transportation. It is also possible for these groups to move into other agricultural service activities (including the use of deep tubewells, which has started in association with the Committee for American Relief Everywhere/Landless Operated Tubewell Users Service, CARE–LOTUS, program). The final chapter will discuss these options further. This strategy for agrarian reform extends beyond this irrigation service based on STWs and LLPs.

While confident about the program's underlying principles, those involved with it sought further confirmation on the following issues, which are reflected in the subsequent research agenda:

- that the ownership of water can be separated from that of land,
- that the pattern of landholding and plot fragmentation lends itself to that separation,
- that landless groups with support can establish command areas and gain access to the technology,
- that these groups can use unsubsidized equipment to full capacity and derive an income,
- that they are creditworthy even without land as collateral,
- that these groups can maintain agreements with farmers and secure their fee income,
- that they can fend off attempts by some rich peasants and moneylenders to subvert them,
- that they can deploy income to begin to disengage from dependency relationships of indebtedness and indentured employment,
- that their political strength and sense of solidarity is enhanced,
- that small farmers gain better access to water through not being tailenders,
- that this social organization of surface water and groundwater irrigation technologies can reconcile the objectives of growth and equity and thereby contribute to the transformation of the rural class structure in Bangladesh, and
- that this transformation can be achieved by raising the productivity of land and the creation, through opportunities for income and employment, of a higher level of rural effective demand for the increased output of foodgrain.

Research Methodology

This section seeks to provide an explanation and description of the research design in terms of the agenda of issues outlined above. It also describes the particular organizational conditions under which the research was conducted. Our aim in covering these topics is twofold and is as follows:

- to clarify for the reader the basis of the material presented in the following chapters, and
- to assist other organizations who are considering similar projects and who may find themselves facing similar problems.

Proshika is experimenting continually to combine new and old forms of technology with innovative forms of social organization. Both the groups and the staff at different levels of Proshika therefore monitor and evaluate any new initiatives. While projects are designed between the groups and the field staff with as much forethought as possible, new forms of social action obviously generate unforeseen processes and problems, which have to be studied by those involved *as part of the social action itself.*

With such objectives, dilemmas arise in devising the organizational form within which the research and development functions can be performed. It is tempting to create a specialist research and monitoring unit, staffed by professionals who are removed from the responsibilities for group mobilization and coordination of programs. The danger in this option, for such an organization as Proshika, is the emergence of an elitist cadre, producing analysis and evaluations that constitute judgments of other people's performance without sharing the responsibility themselves. One of the organizational principles here is to avoid a separation between the action and the research function, as this tends to produce a stagnation of both.

At the same time, in actual practice it is difficult to sustain the principle of interweaving research and action, especially throughout all levels of the group-Proshika association. Divisions of labor have occurred—the writing of this book is perfect evidence of this. Proshika has therefore resisted setting up a permanently staffed Research and Development Unit. Instead, different field staff and coordinators have moved between research and action functions. The current expansion and complexity of the income-generating programs among the groups, however, is demanding more systematic monitoring as well as special coordination and extension functions. Some specialties are evolving and perhaps cannot be avoided. The expansion of Proshika's Revolving Loan Fund (RLF) requires separate management at the center; and the acquisition of computers, while assisting these management and monitoring functions, also entails the appointment of specialist staff who are less integrated into the wider program.

A further difficulty in trying to retain a participatory action research approach is the different levels of operation, both within Proshika as a facilitating organization and between Proshika and the groups. With the zonal/area structure, area-level field staff as well as group members have the primary need to translate learning from action into immediate diagnosis and remedy. Yet to gain an overall picture of a program across the different areas of Proshika, to gain comparative experience and to transfer that experience between the groups concerned, a more centralized research and monitoring effort is required, with standardized items of information. Under such conditions group members become the respondents to questions, and the field staff become the delegated conveyors of those questions—that is, research assistants who, alongside their program work, send information flowing toward a central point where it ends up in the computer before it can be translated into an analysis for practical action. A number of principles are in danger of being lost in such a process but the alternatives are not clear. Compensatory procedures include regular area, zonal, central and sector meetings that will review progress and identify problems. The comparative experience gained at these meetings is shared in regular group feedback sessions.

These organizational constraints have determined, to some extent, the structure and scale of the research design. It was defined within the limitations of the field staff's time, in the way group members recorded and presented their activities, and it was consistent with the field staff's other duties and responsibilities. The strategy tried to balance the load on the field staff between gathering data and their other work. It also recognized the limited research capacity of Proshika and the limited time of area and program coordinators in supervising data gathering, keeping records and briefing field staff. Research should not become an organizational distraction. The research and monitoring of the landless irrigation service was therefore underresourced in relation to the questions Proshika wished to ask about it.

These constraints have been responsible for weaknesses in the data. Despite attempts to keep the range of questions as simple as possible, many variables were pursued. And, despite extended briefings of field staff and area coordinators by the research initiators in Proshika's headquarters, the rationale for some of the data was not absorbed or retained under competing pressures. This reduced the incentive to maintain records and fill in pro formas as accurately and consistently as required, certainly for any overall statistical analysis. Group members were often in a similar position, with field staff lacking the time or the ability to explain the thinking behind the questions. The research initiators at the center (the authors) should have been more aware of the working situation of the field staff and group members. Furthermore, some turnover of the central staff that was responsible for both the research and ongoing monitoring of performance and financial flows interrupted continuity and the supervision of data gathering. Most of the data instruments were initially conceived in English from proposals devised by Geoffrey D. Wood in association with Proshika staff, which led to some ambiguity, especially on some landholding and tenancy questions, when questionnaires were translated into Bangla. Questionnaires were also devised before the decision to acquire computers and were based, therefore, on of manual tabulation principles similar to the 1981–82 analysis. The arrival of computers substantially increased the prospects for analysis; and Richard Palmer-Jones was invited to join the team and offer his irrigation/agricultural economic and computer/statistical skills to the work. This meant that data were left in raw form until they could be entered into a program devised for the purpose. For Proshika's long-term program, this was the most efficient course of action—but the midstream changes involved some delays in the cross-checking of data returns. Inconsistencies and missing data were sharply revealed when the data were finally entered and their status checked. With these constraints such data is difficult to retrieve.

The following reasons for weaknesses in the database also existed:

1. After the 1981–82 season analysis, it was decided within Proshika to collect the same database for the 1982–83 season and for the 1983–84 season, before conducting a further analysis. Immediate further analysis would have been time-consuming without revealing issues essentially different from those identified in the 1981–82 season. This meant that data was collected in a routine way, without the incentive of its immediate use, either at the group, Area Development Center (ADC) or central level. As a result, gaps in the data were not apparent until it was too late to retrieve the missing information.

2. The floods at the end of the 1983–84 season caused problems not only for the groups but also for Proshika, whose field staff were involved full time in a major relief effort, so that much of their routine work had to be suspended.

3. The data sources are most problematic for groups that discontinued their irrigation scheme—in many cases, those most heavily affected by the floods. Records simply were not completed under such conditions. This was inconvenient for us but understandable in the circumstances.

4. The recordkeeping and accounts procedure of the Bangladesh Krishi Bank (BKB) was an essential part of the financial database and was also a cross-check on the loan income and outgoings reported by the groups through the field staff. The records provided by BKB branches, however, were neither timely nor in a form that would enable separate group performance and area performance monitoring.

5. The under-resourcing also meant that, for some of the detailed studies appearing in the following chapters (employment, access for small farmers and technical aspects of water delivery), the samples are small and are restricted by the desire to have controls with groups outside the irrigation service as well as with other non-group irrigation schemes.

Thus our data has weaknesses (of the kind shared by other institutions conducting similar research). The weaknesses stem from a combination of design mistakes, competing demands on staff, failure to use data immediately, communication problems in explaining the utility of data, difficulties of pursuing genuine participatory action research, movement of key supervisory staff and environmental crises. But, these gaps in the data have been identified quite precisely. They are not all retrievable, but some are—especially the financial data as part of the settling of accounts in the withdrawal from the arrangement with the BKB. On other issues, field staff have been asked to plug gaps where the data is stable or obtainable from records. So the data has been cleaned up but not massaged in the sense of substituting assumptions for facts. Other modifications to samples (both individuals and groups as respondents) were made during the course of the research to cope with changing circumstances, especially those arising from the floods. As a result, the phasing of the research has been altered along with the write-up.

At the same time, the virtue of our action research efforts should also be noted. This is a detailed examination of Proshika's experience with a program that has far wider implications not only for the groups associated with Proshika but for policy and the rural poor in Bangladesh and elsewhere. The program may have revealed the inherent difficulties of action research and as such represents a case study to set against the largely untested rhetoric. But both quantitative and qualitative methods have produced substantial information on the issues listed earlier in this chapter. There may also be secondary benefits. For example, the study of employment changes among group members under different irrigation conditions involved weekly debriefing with each respondent to avoid the inaccuracies of extended recall on which most rural studies are based. This now constitutes some of the most reliable employment data on the rural poor in Bangladesh and will of course be available for time-series analysis in the future. This exercise of systematically monitoring the irrigation program in this detail has educated a large number of group members and field staff both in the necessity for certain kinds of recordkeeping and in the kind of analysis required to promote success and avoid failure.

Research Agenda

To address the above questions, the research agenda consisted of six interrelated studies in addition to the ongoing financial and performance analysis, as modified from the 1981–82 study.

The raw data for that ongoing analysis are:

- cost and return accounts taken from the exercise books in which the groups kept their records and recorded on financial sheets for each group per year; the information from these sheets is now included in a combined pro forma, along with information from group passbooks, in which disaggregated BKB or Revolving Loan Fund (RLF) financial flows are also recorded including the cumulative balance to 1984–85,

- characteristics of command areas (including soil type, area, landholding and tenancy status of farmers, fee arrangements, cultivation and irrigation practices) recorded on pro forma 2 (incorporating an earlier pro forma 1, which contained less information; pro forma 2 itself has been supported by a supplementary questionnaire for the 1984–85 season onward), and
- details of machine operation (hours of pumping, rates of diesel consumption) recorded in a log manual regularly checked along with the exercise books by the field staff.

In some cases, these instruments contained overlapping data that enabled cross-checking. The instruments are applied to all operating groups, although when groups discontinue, the application of these instruments for the remainder of the season tends to break down. Consistency tests on similar information from different instruments have also been conducted on reported command area size and the number of farmers (group/non-group, tenancy status, plot size and overall landholding in and out of command area). The simple correlation coefficients should in each case be equal to 1.00. The variable distance of different categories from 1.00 indicates particular inconsistency in land tenure information (probably arising from conceptual ambiguity in allocating status). With these well-identified qualifications to the data from the ongoing monitoring sources, analysis, with suitable caveats, is conducted in chapter 6 on financial performance and in chapter 7 on overall technical and economic performance.

The six interrelated additional studies were carried out in association with the departments of Agricultural Economics (Dr. M. A. S. Mandal) and Irrigation and Water Management (Dr. S. C. Dutta) at the Bangladesh Agricultural University in Mymensingh. Table 2.3 shows the division of research duties.

This exercise was as much diagnostic as evaluative. We are guided mainly by a desire to make the strategy work whereby the poor acquire productive assets of central rather than peripheral significance in the rural economy. It is accepted among us that, in the dynamic context of agrarian change in Bangladesh, with rising landlessness alongside the rapid capitalization of agriculture, an approach that connects employment and income-generating strategies among the poor directly to developments in agriculture and food processing is the only option. The expansion of agricultural capital (albeit stimulated by foreign aid and the penetration of multinational companies supported by the state) and the consequent proliferation of actors in the agricultural sector represents an expansion of opportunities for those currently without assets, especially in the context of social forces advocating a shift from a command to a facilitating role for the state on behalf of a privatized system of production and exchange transactions. Therefore, the principal purpose of this research is to discover the problems (technical, social and economic) of pursuing such a strategy, in order to seek remedies for them and thus make the strategy work. We will be discussing groups that have failed. No doubt this will be a source of glee to our critics in Bangladesh, and we may hand them a weapon to wage the familiar war of gossip and exaggerated misconceptions. We will run that risk, because there is no value to us or to those who broadly agree with the approach to agrarian reform outlined above to disguise the problems which have emerged. We and the group members have to learn from them.

One of our purposes in writing this book was to bring together our experience as part of the internal monitoring of performance. This has involved an assessment of the capacity within the program to maintain regular accounts and records upon which such monitoring has to be based, and which has been responsible for the weaknesses in our data noted above. The monitoring system is being revised on the basis of this experience. But of course the monitoring function also occurs in the regular group, area and central sectoral meetings that review the program, and that are designed to identify bottlenecks, regular patterns in the problems that emerged and the principal variables that accounted for success and failure. This represents the diagnostic part of the exercise, which is of immediate relevance to group and Proshika decisions.

Second, Proshika is obviously aware of its limited capacity to extend the principles behind this approach more widely in Bangladesh. It therefore presents its experience to a wider audience of government, NGOs, political parties and donors in Bangladesh in order to stimulate the widest possible debate on this area of policy. We recognize that opinion has shifted substantially toward the position advocated in 1980 by Proshika in a much more hostile policy context. At that time, both the government and its major supporters among the donors had a conception of expanding rural employment through a trickle-down philosophy. Since then, some bilateral agencies and the World Bank have developed a more specific rural employment focus—examples are the Scandinavian-funded Intensive Rural Works Program, which has now been expanded conceptually into a Rural Employment Sector Program, and the World Bank's own "Issues in Rural Employment" report issued in 1983. A group within the Bank has been pushing for more recognition of the models developed by some of the non-governmental organizations (NGOs), and even for the involvement of NGOs in training the staff of the Rural Poor Program of the Bangladesh Rural Development Board, which was started in 1984, funded by the Canadian International Development Agency (CIDA). We have this kind of audience in Bangladesh in mind, including other concerned ministries (especially Agriculture and Rural Development) and their research institutions, such as the Academies of Rural Development in Comilla and Bogra, who have an interest in similar experimentation.

Thirdly, we think there is an international audience interested in a case study of this kind of approach to rural development in which the poor are not hived off into subsidiary, small-scale employment activity, but are integrated through ownership into the mainstream of agricultural production. That audience includes not only other national equivalents of the institutions noted above but also the large number of applied research institutions and university departments specializing in these issues. We should also remember the growing awareness of the problems of world poverty among social activists in the rich countries, through development education groups, subcommittees of trade unions and political parties and, of course, the development assistance foundations.

Table 2.1   Summary of Landless Groups Deploying STW by Region, 1981–82

ADC/District	No. of Groups per STW	Group Members	Command Area Size Avg. (ac.)	No. of Cultivators per STW	Area Irrigated Avg. (ac.)	With Depreciation		Without Depreciation		Mode of Water Payment
						Net Gain	Net Loss	Net Gain	Net Loss	
Mirzapur/ Tangail	5	15	11.45	157	0.36	3	2	3	2	Cash
Chatalpar/ Brahmanbaria	1	9	6.00	24	0.25	0	1	0	1	Cash
Bhairab/ Kishorganj	14	17	13.07	421	0.43	4	10	10	4	50–25% share 36% share 14% kind
Saturia/ Manikganj	4	21	13.25	149	0.36	3	1	3	1	33% share
Ghior/ Manikganj	3	26	13.25	80	0.50	3	0	3	0	33% share
Shibgonj/ Bogra	11	27	16.08	402	0.44	8	3	10	1	Cash
Nagarpur/ Tangail	8	29	12.27	202	0.49	5	3	5	3	33% share
Madaripur/ Madaripur	5	17	13.60	167	0.41	2	3	4	1	33% share
Total/Average	51	21	13.40	1,602	0.44	28	23	38	13	

Table 2.2 Summary of Landless Groups Deploying LLP by Region, 1981–82

ADC/District	No. of Groups per LLP	Group Members	Command Area Size Avg. (ac.)	No. of Cultivators per LLP	Area Irrigated Avg. (ac.)	With Depreciation Net Gain	With Depreciation Net Loss	Without Depreciation Net Gain	Without Depreciation Net Loss	Mode of Water Payment
Ulania/ Barisal	7	16	16.50	31[1]	0.52[2]	1	6	3	4	Cash
Chatalpar/ Brahmanbaria:	—	—	—	—	—					
Rented	8	55	53.43	86[3]	0.62	6	2	6	2	7 Kind
Purchased	2	13	50.00	118	0.42	1	1	2	0	1 Cash
Total	10	47	47.00	52	0.57	7	3	8	2	Cash
Khaliajuri/ Netrakona	12	19	37.90	40	0.95	12	0	12	0	7 Kind, 3 Cash
Kalkini/ Madaripur	3	15	17.66	28	0.64	2	1	2	11	1 Kind, 1 50% share, 1 Cash[4]
Total/Average	32	27	35.93	52	0.69	22	10	25	7	1

1 One command area had missing data.
2 Calculated excluding 19 ac. of one command area where cultivators' details missing.
3 In two schemes two LLP machines used; in one case 120 ac. with 200 cultivators, 156 from groups.
4 One command area of 15 ac. on *khas* land cultivated by fifty-one group members.

Table 2.3   Allocation of Research Topics

Research Topic	Chapter No.	Conducted by
Relations with other classes	3 and 4	Proshika
Small farmers' access to irrigation	5	Mandal (BAU)
Employment (farmers as respondents)	8	Mandal (BAU)
Employment (group members as respondents)	8	Proshika
Technical aspects of irrigation management	App. 1	Dutta and Mandal (BAU)
Use of income by groups	App. 2	Proshika

CHAPTER THREE

Social Relations

THIS CHAPTER IDENTIFIES the variables that assist water selling by the landless. These include group solidarity and the fragmentation of farm plots, as well as the variables that potentially undermine the service, such as the indebtedness of group members, a high proportion of petty traders as group members motivated by individual, in contrast to collective, accumulation and conflicting loyalties among group members. In doing so, the chapter deals with a wide range of social issues.

Chiefly, it examines whether any connection exists between the involvement of landless and marginal peasant groups in the ownership and provision of water and their relationships to dominant classes in the locality. This is not only an issue of the groups' own perceptions of their enhanced status (which many of them report even in the absence of significant net profit from water selling). It is also a question of whether such a sense of status can be converted into other, tangible gains. The groups may gain greater respect from the richer farmers, landlords and moneylenders by demonstrating an ability to deal with the Bangladesh Krishi Bank (BKB), the Bangladesh Agricultural Development Corporation (BADC), the machine and fuel dealers and the management of the command area itself, along with the water delivery system. But does such respect offer leverage in other arenas? Those to be considered are employment, wages, rights to work, lower interest rates for informal credit and fewer conditions attached to loans, greater tenancy security and fairer rents, land disputes including the occupation of *khas* land, grazing rights (for example, when groups are also involved in livestock rearing, fishing rights (leasing ponds, *bheels* and canals), access to homestead land and so on. In addition to these material possibilities, other dimensions of political and social status exist in the locality and are difficult to measure but nevertheless important. For example, do group members acquire a more significant presence in the village *shalish* (informal court), either in their ability to bring cases to it or to have their views and interests represented in it? Are group members and the women and children in their families better respected and subject to less humiliation and harassment than before? Has the group's irrigation activity brought them into a wider association with other groups and institutions in the wider locality?

The study that provided the material for this (and the following) chapter was carried out on the basis of extensive group-based interviews requiring qualitative, descriptive responses. An individual-respondent study was initially proposed, but it was later decided that such individual responses were likely to be similar. A wider sample of twenty-four groups with irrigation assets was therefore chosen for these discussions, drawn from six Area Development Centers (ADCs). These discussions were personally carried out by Yunus Khan, then a senior staff member in Proshika working in a research and development capacity. Each session could last about four hours, with group members having the opportunity to initiate areas of discussion. The interview schedule was piloted by Geoffrey D. Wood and Yunus Khan in Ghior. This schedule (which also included a section on the collective use of group income, the basis of the data in appendix C) focused on the theme of negotiation and bargaining both in the context of the irrigation service itself and in the broader context of employment, tenancy and debt relations.

The Social Framework of Rural Exchange

Important social and political objectives involved landless and marginal peasants in the irrigation service. These peasants, with their new, rural solidarities, are inevitably required to negotiate with the patron or landholding classes over the provision of the service.

Negotiation refers to the purposive dimension of relationships between transacting parties and implies a quest for advantage.[1] The analysis of such interaction within closed communities was often based on assumptions of static resources in the context of unchanging, low-level technology.[2] It should be noted, however, that much of this analysis originated in the context of a more slowly changing technological environment and an apparently inviolate structure of rural hierarchy and authority, where the more abstract notions of class and class struggle could not apparently capture the personalized and socially intimate character of those structures. There has been a debate involving Wood and other expatriate anthropologists, such as Peter Bertocci, on the use of class in the study of rural Bangladesh. Bertocci regarded the notion of class as a blunt instrument of analysis that fails to express the complexity of rural social relations, but Wood wanted to describe social relationships that might be characterized either by hierarchy and domination and/or by struggle and opposition.[3]

By retaining class, we can ask to what extent vertical solidarities of the patron-client type are the form of class relations under conditions of agrarian underdevelopment in Bangladesh, and under what conditions these forms of class relations change into new forms of solidarity, thereby altering the framework of negotiations and bargaining. On its own, such a question may be too economistic or even, in the context of mechanized minor irrigation in Bangladesh, too technologically deterministic. It is important, therefore, to acknowledge deliberate attempts (such as those of Proshika) to restructure rural solidarities as the basis for securing control by poor, erstwhile client classes over new means of production that have arisen in the economy as a result of the interests of other international, national and rural patron classes. Such control not only implies new forms of negotiation and bargaining relationships between rural classes hitherto organized on a hierarchical, patron-client basis; it also entails a redistribution of income and opportunities for improved access to other goods and services (public and private), enhanced respect and status within the local community and extended participation in local affairs.

Negotiations between Groups and Users

The irrigation groups have to negotiate continually with the farmers in the command areas, some of whom come from the dominant classes in the locality, as well as with various outside agencies. Distributed as they are over twenty-three Bangladesh areas, the groups operate under different ecological and socio-economic conditions. Many variations in the practices affect agreements with cultivators, forms of payment, the value of the water fee as a proportion of the crop, size of command areas and their cropping characteristics outside the winter rice season, irrigation practices, rates of pumping, the owner-tenant composition of the farmers in the command area, numbers of group members themselves cultivating small amounts of land in the command area, prices of paddy, sources of finance and so on.

Several arenas of negotiation and several variables clearly affect the outcomes of those negotiations. The level of solidarity among group members critically determines the capacity of the group to participate successfully in these arenas.

The organizational originality of this program, compared with other small-scale income-generating programs for the poor, is the high level of interaction required between the group members and other classes in the locality upon whom they are traditionally dependent. The provision of an irrigation service obliges the groups to enter into a range of complex negotiations with landowners in order to establish, in the first place, a command area of adjacent plots, followed by the making of formal agreements in which fee income, rates of water delivery, cultivation practices and length of contract are specified. These exchanges with other classes then continue during the irrigation period and beyond into early *aman* (that is, until June) until the payments are made, to be resumed again perhaps as soon as late *aman* (late October) if the rains fade early and supplementary irrigation can be provided. In practice, then, the relationship between landless groups and cultivators around the provision of an irrigation service is more or less continual.

In addition, the groups have to develop successful working relationships with other institutions—especially the local branches of the BKB, for credit, and the BADC in the Ministry of Agriculture which, in the initial stages of the program, was the sole supplier of equipment and spare parts and also provided the certificates of feasibility required by the BKB to release loans. In some areas, the BADC also provided mechanical services. The BADC's role is now weaker, with competition from private dealers, but it has been significant. There are obviously many points of access difficulty between the groups and these institutions, with local officials likely to discriminate in favor of the richer rural classes competing in the same service, supply and credit markets. In these circumstances, the groups themselves require qualities of internal solidarity and mutual trust in addition to those needed for more self-contained, cooperative activity.

In view of the patron-client forms of class relations in rural Bangladesh, these attributes of internal solidarity can only be established slowly through dependence upon the fellowship of the poor for small victories that accumulate into wider, more reliable trust. In this process, the role of Proshika as a mobilizing force has been critical. Its presence is a source of strength for the groups, underpinning their confidence in the various arenas of negotiation: to argue for a water price, to insist upon a routine but equitable distribution system for water, to resist individual claims from farmers for special or free irrigation service, to offset inflated debt obligations from individual group members, to ensure that farmers employ local labor (and group labor where available) and to ensure that farmers implement the full cultivation practices in order to maximize yields when the payment is a proportion of the crop rather than a fixed payment in cash.

A continued reliance upon Proshika, however, might give rise to a new form of dependency—an institutional patron with group clients. To avoid this, the groups included within the irrigation program were selected, from a larger number of groups wishing to participate, on the basis of some proven solidarity. All of the irrigation groups have been in existence for some time—they were not formed just for inclusion in this program. The average time between a group's formation and its entry into the irrigation program is 1.34 years (for groups started before 1985), with 43 percent starting after one year and 29 percent after two years. The criterion for a group's selection is essentially political—the proven capacity of group members to support each other in adversity and to sustain small income-generating projects (for example, goat rearing or petty trading) against attack. This proof may appear trivial to an outside observer, but Proshika and other groups not yet included in the program often regard it as significant. For example, a group member occupied some highly valued homestead land from which his neighbor wished to remove him in order to settle families of his own expanding lineage. The rich neighbor's method was harassment, allowing his small herd of cattle to defecate in the poor member's compound and eat any available foliage. The group protested on the individual group member's behalf and, when ignored, the group rounded up the herd, took it to the rich neighbor's front door and remained with the herd until it had defecated all around the front door. This tactic was a success and the group members proved to themselves the value of mutual support as an alternative to subordinated loyalty to a class of local patrons. This was the basis for this group's entry into the program, and it required continual negotiations with the local rich farmers and landlords.

Alongside the issue of group solidarity, a second general resource for the groups is the extreme fragmentation of farms in Bangladesh. With increasing pressure on the land and the system of multiple inheritance persisting through lack of alternative employment opportunities, plots are divided to reflect a balance of soil types between inheriting sons. As a result, individual farmers with sufficient land in any single command area to exercise a monopsony influence over the price for water or to dominate its distribution are rare. The average number of farmers per STW command area/year has been twenty-nine, and for two cubic-foot-per-second (cu.sec) LLP command area/year, forty-five. We had expected that, in some cases, farmers connected by kin relations might act as a pressure group, but the groups did not encounter such organized opposition from larger farmers in the command areas. In some cases, oligarchical monopsony has occurred with farmers, perhaps connected to each other by kin relations, acting in unison on price and delivery issues. Although we have pursued this question in the second phase of research, however, there has been no significant evidence of systematic, jointly organized manipulation by large farmers in command areas or of serious conflicts betwen farmers and the groups.

On the contrary, farmers with fragmented landholdings (Glaser, from her fieldwork in Singra, 1988, reports farmers' plots being distributed among up to eighteen command areas) can positively welcome someone else taking on the management of irrigation, as it saves them from having to cooperate with neighboring farmers or function as water entrepreneurs themselves in order to secure water for their own plots. This advantage seems to outweigh the disadvantages of:

- conforming to the externally imposed arrangements for serial water distribution (although flexibility usually exists for plot preparation and transplanting), and
- accepting, as a precondition for receiving water under share-payment conditions, the full set of high-yield variety (HYV) cultivation practices that include at least the application of chemical fertilizers and regular weeding.

The fragmentation of their land also means that farmers find it difficult to negotiate individual fee arrangements and price levels (even though they may have debt leverage with group member clients), as all the farmers in a command area have a collective interest in a standard arrangement as a second-best optimum to their individual maximizing positions. Such arrangements are often established independently of the irrigation group as well, on the basis of local custom where water selling by richer landholder contractors has been prevalent.

The social composition of the farmers who hold land in the command areas is closely related to this issue. Many variations are possible. According to our monitoring data, the average number of farmers per STW command area/year per development center has ranged from fourteen to forty-five; for LLP command areas the number ranges from twenty to sixty-three. These farmers also own land outside the group's command area, and some of them are tenants as well as owners, or just tenants. The total holdings of these owners and tenants vary, and these variations in total holding size/status affect the overall position of these farmers in the local negotiating structure. A survey of twenty-four group command areas showed 854 cultivators, 81 percent of whom were owner-cultivators and 19 percent involved in tenancy cultivation, either as owners-cum-tenants or as pure tenants.[4] Across the six development centers examined, the respective variations ranged from 70 percent to 80 percent and from 14 percent to 31 percent (all percentages rounded—see table 3.1).

The distribution of owner-cultivators (695 from the twenty-four command areas) by landholding size was:

less than 1 acre	45.0 percent
1–2 acres	27.0 percent
2–5 acres	17.5 percent
5–10 acres	8.0 percent
10 + acres	2.50 percent

(See table 3.2 for detail of the regional variations in this distribution). From this data, it is clear that the twenty-four command areas are numerically dominated by marginal and small farmers. The bargaining position of the groups over the irrigation service is influenced by the relative dominance of different classes of farmers cultivating in the command area.

Groups with command areas consisting primarily of small and marginal farmers, many of whom are tenants, are less subject to exploitative pressure from patron classes. Productivity constraints under such conditions do exist, however, that negatively affect the group's income when share payments apply. Small and marginal farmers have lower levels of capital, tighter margins on high-yield variety (HYV) production and more caution when taking risks. Often they cannot engage in the full set of practices to maximize yields because they can afford neither inputs nor hired labor without loan support from private moneylenders (which represents a high cost on their production) due to their limited access to appropriate and timely institutional sources of production credit. In some cases, groups have extended loans to small farmers for irrigated cultivation or have stood as guarantor for small farmers to obtain fertilizer and insecticide on short-term loans from private dealers. Small farmers also have the disadvantage of employing less non-family labor than larger farmers, so that the opportunities for the employment of the landless are not maximized.

As a corollary, if a command area consists of a higher proportion of larger farmers, more capital is available for investment in HYV production, which includes more employment for non-family, landless labor. Under certain conditions, this situation can push up the wage-rates for irrigated winter rice in the locality. This in turn reduces the need for that employed labor to outmigrate and/or take advances from the local rich patrons, which has previously undermined their bargaining position during the normal peak employment periods of the main rain-fed *aman* rice season (in the non-single-cropped areas).

The group cannot precisely exercise a preference over the location of a command area site and therefore over the social composition of the farmers holding land within it. But there is a complex trade-off between greater political equality with small-farmer water customers and the direct economic opportunities larger farmer customers can offer to the groups.

A further aspect of the social composition of the command areas concerns the number of group members themselves cultivating land in the command area. The groups with which Proshika works are not purely landless. Target groups in Bangladesh cannot be easily defined (Wood 1985), and the determining principle of membership is the use of one's own physical labor. In the dynamics of landlessness in rural Bangladesh, many marginal and submarginal landholders rely on the sale of their labor for most of their income, but they may cling to small plots of land at any one point in time. The membership of those groups working with Proshika cannot realistically be restricted to the pure landless, especially when a degree of self-definition is encouraged to strengthen solidarity. The distinction between pure landless and *prantik* (a marginal peasant) is more significant to agrarian statisticians than to the peasants themselves. According to our monitoring data, 22 percent of the farmers who have cultivated land in the command areas were group members, owning 26 percent of the land. This can also be expressed as 6.7 percent of the group members having cultivated land in group command areas. From the survey of twenty-four command areas examined for this chapter, group members represented 20.5 percent of total farmers cultivating land in the command areas (see table 3.3).[5] The presence of these group member cultivators should have a positive impact upon the non-group cultivators in the command areas because, if they are similar marginal or small farmers, they are in a position to set the standards for customer behavior, provided the command area is not dominated by a few large landowners. Group cultivators are expected to have greater loyalty to the group irrigation service, especially as they are also entitled to any dividends distributed among group members at the end of the season.

A command area's geographical location can also affect bargaining relations between water sellers and users. In particular, the patterns of exchange can be affected by whether the command area is located near the homesteads of richer landowners, who are the direct employers and/or landlords of group members, or outside the immediate spheres of localized patronage between the sellers and the users. In one example (Rajnagar Gorib Unnayan Samity in Saturia), the command area is two miles from where the group members live, and all the farmer water-users are from outside the group's village. At the same time, however, the management problems are greater, because the pump operator and lineman have to be on duty for the season (approximately four months), the equipment has to be maintained and guarded, fuel has to be stored and guarded or delivered from the group's village frequently, the water distribution system has to be continuously supervised and disputes with farmers sorted out, the farmers' cultivation practices have to be monitored (because the form of payment is cropshare) and the cropshare fees (five-sixteenths of the standing crop) have to be collected and carried to the group members' homesteads for threshing.

The balance of power in the bargaining between group sellers and farmer-consumers can also be affected by the cropping pattern of a command area. Rotations in Bangladesh are sensitive to minor differences in elevation interacting with flooding, drainage patterns and soil types. But the main relevant distinction here is between single- and multiple-cropped areas. The attraction of much dry-season irrigation to farmers is the unpredictability of the other seasons and the precarious yields that accompany them. Low-lying land is the familiar problem, and in some areas (such as Ghior) the flooding is so extensive that the land is a single-crop area relying traditionally upon residual moisture and *dhone* irrigation. Thus, where other seasons are nonexistent or at best precarious, the introduction of mechanized irrigation with a greater potential area coverage is especially significant. Farmers have fewer options outside the irrigation period, so that while the competition for water rights may become intensified under these conditions, once the control of water has been achieved the groups are in a stronger position to negotiate the water price, insist on full cultivation practices and ensure the employment by farmers of group labor and other non-group local labor. This bargaining advantage is reinforced in single-crop areas because farmers have an incentive to maximize their yields through investment and careful husbandry.

In areas where the main rain-fed rice crop, *aman*, is secure, owners of the larger farms regard irrigated cultivation in the context of double or even triple cropping as a bonus rather than a necessity. Under such conditions, the farmer has less incentive to invest properly in fertilizer, weeding and other inputs, or to transplant winter rice rather than, for example, wheat (which has a lower value as income to the group if cropshares are being paid). In these circumstances, the group has a harder task in counteracting these tendencies and fewer employment opportunities are available to them as individuals. At the same time, wheat demands less water, so there is an offsetting possibility of extending the command area if adjacent competitors do not exist. Multiple-cropped areas of this kind are more of a problem for water sellers in negotiations with farmers if the prevailing fee arrangements are cropshares rather than fixed-cash payments. The level of cash payments, however, can be expected to reflect the respective strengths of the buyers and sellers of water in the marketplace.

Group Solidarity

The significance of internal solidarity among group members has been identified as a crucial dimension of successful negotiations by the groups. It has also been the hope that engaging in the irrigation service would enhance the solidarity and political position of the groups in the villages. There are, however, forms of economic and social differentiation among group members, and sometimes the negative implications for group solidarity can become exacerbated precisely as a consequence of a group's involvement in the program.

Variations in levels of indebtedness among group members and the obligations implied by debt can undermine the prospects for mutual trust and threaten group solidarity. If individual members are dependent on patrons with whom the group is negotiating over the irrigation service, the group is likely to be less united in its resolve, because the consequences of taking a strong stance could be disastrous for those individual members—loss of employment, foreclosing on loans where the recipient has a small amount of land as collateral or losing rights to sharecrop. All but four of the groups examined for this chapter experienced varying degrees of indebtedness among their members.[6]

There were no reported cases of farmers in these command areas trying overtly to impose or negotiate special favors on prices, delivery patterns or delays in payment by exploiting the vulnerability of group members personally in debt to them.[7] Where the level of indebtedness is high, however, group members are likely to moderate their demands when making agreements and to insist less upon the terms of such agreements being fulfilled. Their behavior anticipates the power some of the farmers have over the members, and their capacity for independent action is undermined.

The presence of petty traders within the group is also potentially divisive. Because agriculture in many circumstances cannot provide full employment for group members throughout the year, a significant proportion of group members is involved in petty trading activities, operating with small amounts of capital (often borrowed). This is a common way for rural poor males in Bangladesh to gain modest income, and consists mainly of hawking agricultural commodities such as rice and vegetables from one village to another or between local villages and bazaars. In addition to this peripatetic trading, some group members even have small shops in local bazaars and earn the bulk of their income in this way. Such income is small, but small and petty traders tend to be better off than other group members who are solely dependent on wage labor. Furthermore, engaging in such activity promotes different attitudes, especially in the context of wage struggles. Where traders are significantly represented within groups, internal cohesion is weakened by diversified work patterns and individual entrepreneurial attitudes toward the distribution of benefits from the irrigation service. Two case examples from among the twenty-four groups studied will illustrate the significance of this issue.

First, the case of Attigram Gorib Unnayan Samity in Saturia. There are twenty members in the group, and more than half of them are small traders. The leadership of the group is concentrated in a few hands. The irrigation service began in the 1981–82 season. This irrigation group has been successful, paying off its entire capital loan in the first year of operation. Thus, from the second year there was the prospect of large net profits accruing to the group that could have been deployed collectively to finance other collective activities and capture other productive assets. But instead, the small traders within the group have insisted that all of the profits be divided annually among them to add to their working capital as individual businessmen. They even declined to build up an operating cost fund out of these profits, so that operating loans are required each year. Our monitoring data indicates that the group has outstanding loans of Tk5,000 to the Bangladesh Krishi Bank (BKB) and Tk17,000 to Proshika's Revolving Loan Fund (RLF). This example reveals how individual profit taking may even undermine a successful collective enterprise, and how more structurally significant opportunities for reducing dependency upon institutional credit or engaging in other activities that would reinforce group solidarity have been sacrificed. The position of the non-traders in the group is not developed in this process. Few of the members are engaged in agricultural work in the command area, so there is little identity between the group and the scheme, which is, in effect, run by two or three members with business acumen on behalf of sleeping partners.

The second case concerns the Ragunathpur Bhumihin Samity in Ghior, which is also dominated by small traders. The group entered the program in the 1982–83 season. By the end of its third season (1984–85), it was defaulting to the BKB for failing to pay a remaining portion of the 1983–84 capital installment and the entire 1984–85 capital installment alongside the 1983–84 operating-cost loan (no operating-cost loan for 1984–85 was provided by BKB due to the default). Certainly the group shared with many other groups the problems arising out of the early floods in 1984, which seriously damaged crops, especially in Ghior, and drastically reduced the income to those groups due to receive payment through cropshares. In the event, the group cashier received Tk11,000 from sales of paddy. Instead of using this money to contribute to outstanding bank loans, the cashier and three other members of the group invested the cash in their private trading activities. When discovered by the majority of the group members, these four agreed to pay back the money before the start of the following season so that it could be used as operating capital. Although the money was refunded, this *coterie* of four obtained the support of some of the other small traders in the group and captured the day-to-day management of the scheme by ousting the previous pump driver and appointing one of their own faction as driver. This driver was expected to run up false expenses that could be distributed among the faction. But the new driver's incompetence caused repeated problems with the machine, interrupted water delivery and dissatisfied farmers. The driver resigned in midseason and the other members organized, expelled the four members from the group and attempted to complete the irrigation service for the year. At the end of the 1984–85 season, the group was left with outstanding capital installments and operating-cost loans. The STW has subsequently been moved to another site in response to competition from a neighboring DTW, but the group is persevering with the scheme.

These two examples illustrate the problems that can arise for a group when a high proportion of members oriented toward individual economic behavior, but internal economic and social differentiation of this type will not always lead to these problems. Group members do have to be convinced of the value of collective economic ventures and, where the prospects for long-term collective profits are risky, early profit taking may make sense to individual members even if it puts the collective enterprise at greater risk. Such anticipatory behavior is more likely to occur when the scheme is in difficulty from other causes, and in the context of an undisciplined financial environment in which individuals can reasonably calculate that collective defaults on institutional credit will be written off even if such defaults can be clearly attributed to individual action. We must also accept that the distribution of valid dividends to individuals may in some ways be as structurally significant in the alteration of class relations as retaining such profits for further collective projects involving the capture of other assets. Consumption or the repayment of personal debt can be enormously significant for poor people in reducing personal, patron-client ties of dependency. The weakening of such ties does not merely alter stratified patterns of income distribution but contributes toward greater personal autonomy of action among the poor. It thereby encourages group solidarity, if the group organization of economic and political behavior is perceived by such people as the necessary means for their advancement.

In the previous section, the impact of group members cultivating land within the command areas was considered. It was argued that group member cultivators would positively influence the behavior of the other cultivators toward the scheme, especially over payment of fees. While accepting that this relationship generally works, two examples where the solidarity of the group has been threatened by non-cooperation between group member cultivators and the remainder of the group managing the scheme and worth noting. The two examples are Chakmallah Prantik Chashi Samity in Gabtoli ADC (irrigation started 1982–83) and Biha Chunata Bhumihin Samity in Shibganj ADC (irrigation started 1983–84), both from Bogra District. In both cases, there have been repeated delays in the payment of water fees, with a considerable number of cultivators in default to the groups. The form of payment is fixed-cash, to be paid in two equal installments—half in advance and half at the time of harvest. The first installment, however, been paid in subinstallments, with many delays and defaults at this stage involving group cultivators as well as non-group cultivators. With the final payment, the pattern is similar. These groups were examined in November 1985 after the harvest in June 1985, but the default for the first scheme was Tk10,000 and in the second Tk5,000. In both cases, more than half of these outstanding amounts remained with group member cultivators. Thus the group member cultivators were setting a bad example to the other cultivators in the command area and undermining the groups' capacity to insist on full and timely payments from the non-group cultivators.

These examples illustrate the conflicting loyalties that can exist among group members, where the pressures are strong to serve immediate, short-term family interests at the expense of the unity of one's potential class allies among the poor. These pressures are at their strongest when the prospect of long-term collective activity is precarious. Also, group and non-group cultivators cannot simply be regarded as separate social groupings with distinctive sets of loyalties and commitments. Where group members are cultivating small amounts of their own land within the command area, they are cultivating plots adjacent to those of non-group cultivators. Adjacent plots in systems of multiple inheritance imply that their holders are related. This is less true only if there is a pronounced market in land. As cultivators of irrigated crops, group and non-group cultivators are therefore likely to share the same constraints and objectives and have some loyalty or at least appreciation of each others' interests. This will also be reinforced if non-group cultivating kin are marginally better off (which is likely if they have not joined the group) and are a source of credit, draft power or other assistance. If the group cultivators are sharecroppers, then they are cultivating under severe constraints anyway with primary obligations to the landowner for payment of cropshares. Even in command areas without group members cultivating, we must recognize that in many cases the group will be negotiating with farmers who are either kinsmen or who are patrons for credit, employment, and so on. Extracting the irrigation service from this web of customary patron-client ties cannot therefore be

automatically assumed. Although the strategy is based upon market principles of service/price exchanges between freely contracting parties, such
principles cannot simply be imposed idealistically upon preexisting relations of production with the expectation that those principles will then be
acted out in practice. Group solidarity, based *inter alia* upon explanations
of these countervailing pressures and conflicting loyalties, therefore
becomes an instrument of such change. At the same time, it is threatened
by income-generating programs that involve exchanges between patrons
and their erstwhile and sometimes continuing clients.

Status and Confidence in the Village

Some impression was gained of the effect of providing the irrigation service on the group members' political position and participation in village
institutions. The data is qualitative, rather than quantitative, and causation
is difficult for the observer to attribute. Establishing a causal link to irrigation is further complicated by the principle of allowing only groups with
some prior history of solidarity to enter the program. To some extent, we
have to rely on the group members' own assessment of the link between
the two phenomena. Some qualitative indicators exist for this discussion,
however. The groups were asked not for their general impressions but for
specific examples and illustrations, such as incidents in the *shalish,* protection from assault, access to the *madrasa* and so on.

Representation in the *shalish* seems to have improved. For example, in
Chakmalla Prantik Chashi Samity in Gabtoli, one of the group members
offered his small landholding of 0.25 acre to a middle/rich farmer for
sharecropping. This farmer is a kinsman of the village *matbar.* After the
harvest, the farmer tried to cheat the group member by underreporting
his yield and refusing to provide half of the straw as verbally agreed. The
farmer ignored the group member's pleas, so the group member informed
the group, which brought the incident to the *shalish,* attended by the village *matbar* and others. In this forum, the farmer was forced to concede to
the arguments made by the group members, and the land was returned to
the group member.

The same group, which together with two other groups constituted the
village landless coordination committee, was approached by the other villagers to assist in resolving a long-standing problem about mismanagement and misappropriation of the mosque funds. The secretary had
refused repeated requests to produce accounts. After meeting with various
sardars and the village *matbar,* the groups called a meeting of all the
households in the village in which the mosque secretary was compelled to
produce accounts and Tk4,000 was recovered from him. In the same meeting, the management committee for the mosque was reorganized and the
post of secretary awarded to an elderly group member—legitimation
indeed! The groups are now more prominently and regularly involved in

the resolution of village disputes and other decisions.

A group in Ghior (Parmastul Bhumihin and Prantik Krishak Samity) was asked to assist a man in the village unconnected to the groups. He had loaned Tk200 to someone to be repaid in three months. Despite repeated efforts over the following two years, the money was not returned. He had approached the *matbar* but the latter was linked in some way to the debtor and therefore did not use his influence to resolve the dispute. The group then raised the issue in the *shalish,* and the debtor was compelled to repay in the following week.

Protection from physical assault and intimidation by landlords, employers and moneylenders is a preoccupation with the landless. In Mirzapur, a group member from a non-irrigating group was beaten by the son of a richer landholder for allowing his cow to damage the landholder's standing crop. The irrigation group (Purba Pouli Bhumihin Samity) brought the other groups together in the village and asked for a meeting of the *shalish,* in which the son admitted and apologized for his behavior. This group was also consulted by the Union *parishad* Member about a road construction project and about the registration of destitute mothers in the village to receive *upazila* relief.

The Danga-Shimulia Bhumihin Krishak Samity in Saturia led a move in their part of the village to collect subscriptions from other groups and donations from individual villagers to build a mosque in their *para*. The local Union *parishad* Chairman then responded to this effort by procuring two bundles of corrugated iron sheets for the roof. In seven out of the twenty-four groups examined, group members were being selected as members of mosque managing committees by other people in the village. Most groups reported that their access to the mosque had improved. (They could not be formally excluded anyway, so the issue is more about the welcome offered by the other villagers attending.)

Sixteen of the twenty-four groups reported their enhanced access to drinking water either from public tubewells in the neighborhood or in some cases from the private installations of neighbors. Five of the groups had obtained drinking water tubewells from the United Nations Children's Fund (UNICEF). The Ganasingjuri Samaj Kallayan Samity in Ghior had repaired a drinking water tubewell and open well by contributing Tk800 from its own funds.

We must accept that, throughout these illustrations of improvement in political strength, participation (a slippery concept) in the *shalish* and the management of mosque affairs, a causal link to the groups' involvement in the irrigation service cannot be unambiguously established. At best, the link is indirect. The problem of analysis is similar to other studies of rural change in South Asia where observers attempt to translate a rise in economic fortunes into enhanced respectability in other status frameworks. The term "Sanskritization" is often used to summarize this process. If these issues were to be pursued in the context of these irrigation groups, the analysis would have to move beyond reporting the stories offered by the group members and their perceptions of why other classes in the village have permitted or have been compelled to accept their entry into these institutions. It would also have to explore the meaning of participation in terms of real influence not only on formal decisions[8] but also on the structure of social relations, which reproduces or determines the distribution of opportunities in the village. For example, is there evidence of groups extending the agenda of issues discussed in these forums (*shalish* and mosque) to include wage and tenancy contracts, rates of interest on local moneylending and rights to drinking water and homestead land? The preservation of patron-client structures in the management of labor and tenants seems to rely partly on excluding such issues from public debate and negotiation, in order to retain the personalized features of class relations. If the agendas don't change, participation in these forums could remain hollow and on the terms dictated by others. Institutionalized arenas of conflict resolution at the village level have always reproduced the social order rather than changed it. It does seem that there is an agenda for an anthropologist here, relying on observation rather than just interviews.

Notes

1. The analysis of this has frequently been located within the framework of zero-sum games played at the microlevel with rigid parameters.

2. This prompted a generation of literature on nonideological fractional struggle, vertical cleavages, competing patron-client dyads and normative and pragmatic rules of conflict. A variation of these assumptions applied to the study of the purposive interaction between closed communities and outsiders involving notions of cultural discontinuities and encapsulation and the methodological equipment of symbolic interactionism.

3. Following an earlier exchange between Wood and Bertocci on the validity of the "cyclical kulakism" hypothesis when applied to the minifundist Comilla region of Bangladesh (Bertocci 1972, Wood 1976), Bertocci in 1977 argued that class failed to express the structural fragmentation of rural social relations and therefore is a bad guide to the formation of consciousness that ought to be implicit in the notion of class. But this understanding of structural fragmentation involves a Weberian distinction between class and status, a distinction apparently reinforced in Bangladesh and elsewhere on the subcontinent by the failure "to correlate economic indicators of class with non-economic, culturally significant markers of relative prestige or social rank" (Bertocci 1977, p. 15). Thus this notion of structural fragmentation is similar to an earlier notion of a system of status frameworks (Bailey 1963), which allows for the possibility of individual households occupying asymmetrical positions in different hierarchies—economic, lineage, ritual, educational and so on. In this notion, fluctuating economic fortunes of the individual peasant family through multiple inheritance and the domestic cycle need not therefore affect the family's ability to reproduce and maintain its lineage, status or other indicators of social rank. Thus class, expressed in terms of economic indicators, is not regarded as a determining principle of rank and is not therefore the basis of consciousness or solidarity. Indeed the patron-client relation is identified as the main form of social solidarity at the village level, emphasizing the strength of verti-

cal ties and undermining the potential for social solidarities on horizontal class lines. These forms of solidarity, which allegedly compete with class, are supposedly further reinforced by the religious ideologies of the Bengali Muslim—involving notions of brotherhood. In this way, Bertocci could argue that "a variety of complexities in the normal political economy . . . hinder the transformation of 'peasant classes' thus far identified in the local power structure and stratification research from 'classes in themselves' to 'classes for themselves.'" This problematic distinction employs a notion of class independent of the primary concern with characterizing the exploitative, contradictory and therefore dynamic aspects of the social relations of production and exchange in which both rural economic activity and forms of rural culture and political relations are located (Wood 1981). The Marxist concept of class is distinctive from the Weberian in that it cannot be defined by reference to internal attributes. It is a relational concept. A class exists only in relation to another class either through struggle and opposition or through domination and bondage with it. Collective action involving a collective consciousness is only one advanced form of such struggle and opposition. Marx never insisted that collective action or consciousness was a necessary part of the definition of class—only that such collective consciousness of common exploitation was a distinguishing feature of the proletariat under conditions of advanced, factory capitalism. Once consciousness is therefore accepted as a contingent rather than necessary expression of class in this relational sense, it becomes a concept for explaining structural fragmentation rather than perceived as an alternative social force.

4. See Wood and Palmer-Jones, *Social Entrepreneurialism in Rural Bangladesh,* (Dhaka: Proshika 1988) chapter 10, table 10.1.

5. Also see Wood and Palmer-Jones, *ibid,* chapter 10, table 10.3. The highest proportions of group-member cultivators were in Ghior and Gabtoli (29 percent) and the lowest in Saturia (11.5 per cent).

6. 73 per cent in Mirzapur; 69 per cent in Shibganj; 24 per cent in Gabtoli; 15 per cent in Ghior; and 14 percent in Saturia. See also Wood and Palmer-Jones, *ibid,* chapter 10, tables 10.5 and 10.6.

7. We must acknowledge the validity of Lukes' distinction between different dimensions of power (Lukes 1974). Such evidence would refer only to Lukes' first dimension in which A was compelling B to behave against B's own wishes and interests as explicitly revealed. But the second (power of agenda-setting and non-decisions) and third (structural determination) dimensions are likely to apply where indebtedness is highest.

8. Lukes' first dimension of power.

Table 3.1 Distribution of Command Area (CA) Cultivators by Region and Ownership/Tenancy Category

Dev. Center	Owner-cultivator			Tenant-cultivator			Total within CA
	In Gr.	Non Gr.	Total	In Gr.	Non Gr.	Total	
Saturia	27 (11.3)	211 (88.7)	238 (85.0)	5 (11.9)	37 (88.1)	42 (15.0)	280
Ghior	34 (25.0)	97 (74.0)	131 (86.2)	10 (47.6)	11 (52.4)	21 (13.8)	152
Madaripur	12 (19.0)	51 (81.0)	63 (85.1)	3 (27.3)	8 (72.7)	11 (14.9)	74
Mirjapur	13 (13.4)	84 (86.6)	97 (78.9)	11 (42.3)	15 (57.7)	26 (21.1)	123
Shibganj	14 (16.9)	69 (83.1)	83 (79.8)	11 (52.4)	10 (47.6)	21 (20.2)	104
Gabtoli	23 (27.7)	60 (72.3)	83 (69.6)	12 (31.6)	26 (68.4)	38 (31.4)	121
Total	123 (17.7)	572 (82.3)	695 (81.4)	52 (32.7)	107 (67.3)	159 (18.6)	854

Figures within parentheses represent percentage of corresponding total. Gr. = group.

Table 3.2 Distribution of Owner-cultivators within CA by Region and Holding Size (Acres)

Dev. Center	No. CAs	<1		1–2		2–5		5–10		10 +		Total Cult
		N	%	N	%	N	%	N	%	N	%	
Saturia	7	133	55.9	58	24.4	31	13.0	14	5.9	2	0.8	238
Ghior	5	46	35.1	31	23.7	34	26.0	15	11.5	5	3.8	131
Madaripur	3	37	58.7	16	25.4	8	12.7	2	3.2	0	0.0	63
Mirjapur	3	38	39.2	22	22.7	19	19.6	12	12.4	6	6.2	97
Shibganj	3	13	15.7	36	43.4	21	25.3	8.0	9.6	5	6.0	83
Gabtali	3	45	54.2	25	30.1	8	9.6	5.0	6.0	0	0.0	83
Total	24	312	45	188	27	121	17.5	56	8.0	18	2.5	695

N = number of owner-cultivators.

Table 3.3 Distribution of CA Cultivators by Region and In-group/Non-group Category

Dev. Center	In-Group Cultivators			Non-Group Cultivators			Total Cult. in CA
	Owner	Tenant	Total	Owner	Tenant	Total	
Saturia	27	5	32 (11.5)	211	37	248 (88.5)	280
Ghior	34	10	44 (28.9)	97	11	108 (71.1)	152
Madaripur	12	3	15 (20.3)	51	8	59 (79.7)	74
Mirjapur	13	11	24 (19.5)	84	15	99 (80.5)	123
Shibganj	14	11	25 (24.0)	69	10	79 (76.0)	104
Gabtoli	23	12	35 (28.9)	60	26	86 (71.1)	121
Total	123 (70.3)	52 (29.7)	175 (20.5)	572 (84.3)	107 (15.8)	679 (79.5)	854

Figures in parentheses represent percentage of corresponding total.

CHAPTER FOUR

Market Conditions and Bargaining

MUCH MORE FLUIDITY exists in the water market than was expected at the outset of the project. This chapter studies the conditions within which the landless water sellers market their services. It continues some of the themes raised in the previous chapter and provides some case examples.

To begin with, there is in principle a large range of contractual options between the groups and the farmers over the provision of the service. It was important to record this process and also to discover how these contracts have changed in the duration of a scheme. Such negotiations clearly become a critical indicator of the group's cohesion, its solidarity and its ability to bargain successfully in other arenas. A further category of questions concerned the capacity of the groups to sustain this irrigation service independently of the support of Proshika field staff in dealings with the Bangladesh Krishi Bank (BKB), the Bangladesh Agricultural Development Corporation (BADC), private dealers and so on. Part of the strategy in this program is to develop the groups' capacity for independent action, and Proshika needs to know if this is occurring and if the irrigation program is making a contribution to this process or not.

Competition and Consumer Loyalty

The idea of a landless group providing an irrigation service has of course been as strange for farmers as for irrigation and agricultural planners. The groups, with the help of Proshika, had to persuade potential clients for irrigation of their capacity to participate in agriculture via the sale of water. This task of persuasion is affected by prevailing local conditions in the market for water—especially by the absence of neighboring competitors among larger landholders and/or water contractors and also by the cropping patterns in the locality.

In the case of one shallow tubewell (STW) group, Bangala Bhumihin Samity in Ghior Area Development Center (ADC), which started in 1983, the land is subject to perennial flooding and is virtually single-cropped, so any development in irrigation is crucially important to the landholders.

52

But landholders were initially highly skeptical of the group's proposal to provide an irrigation service. They expressed concerns not only about management competence but also about the implications of the landless controlling such a valuable potential asset under single-crop conditions with a high dependency on irrigated winter rice. Several factors, however, assisted the making of an agreement between the group and the farmers. First, a local private contractor scheme had experienced numerous problems attributed to machine breakdown and interrupted diesel supply. This heightened the farmers' general skepticism about the management competence required for mechanized irrigation but at the same time reduced farmers' loyalty to that existing private contractor scheme. Second, the farmers were reassured by the presence of some of the group members as cultivators in the potential command area. But finally, in the negotiations, the group offered to compensate the farmers if their production fell below the yields gained on neighboring private schemes. This offer of compensation was clearly a risk, but it was based in part on the mechanical skills of their pump operator member who had been trained by the BADC and had operated pumpsets elsewhere. The risk paid off. The group had two successful seasons of uninterrupted service, and landholders from neighboring schemes switched land to this scheme, raising the command area from 10.5 acres in the first year of operation to 12.3 acres in the second year. More recent reports from the ADC indicate that competition from neighbors is still strong, and indeed in the third year of operation the command area dipped to 12.0 acres.

Although further examples of opposition to the setting up of irrigation services by the groups will be discussed below, the overall picture is not characterized by opposition at this stage of a scheme. Out of the twenty-four schemes examined for this chapter, there were only four incidents of significant opposition. This confirms that our original predictions of difficulties in making agreements with farmers have not been upheld. It is important, however, to be aware of possible difficulties.

The first case is Danga-Shimulia Bhumihin Samity in Saturia ADC, started in 1982. A rich farmer owning four *bighas* inside the projected command area declined to cultivate irrigated winter rice or to sign the agreement. He had always been hostile to the formation of landless groups in the area, and this hostility carried over into the proposed landless irrigation service. Unfortunately, his plots were located in a critical position within the command area, so that the channels could not be constructed without passing through or alongside his plots. He was adamant that no channel was to be dug through his plots. The group failed to persuade him through negotiation, so a *shalish* was held with all the command area farmers, the group members and the village *matbar*. When this effort also failed, the *shalish* imposed a settlement in favor of the group by instructing that a channel be dug the following day in the presence of all the farmers and the village *matbar*.

The second case is Nepaltali Mollah Para Bhumihin Samity in Gabtoli ADC, started in 1982. When the loan from the local branch of the BKB was delayed, the installation of the STW on site was also delayed. Although the group had already made agreements with farmers in the command area, a private contractor from a neighboring village, encouraged by his father-in-law who was a middle farmer with land in the command area, seized the opportunity of this delay and uncertainty over the scheme to install a rented STW in the command area. Within a few days the group obtained its machine, installed it in the command area and asked the contractor to withdraw. The contractor refused and tried to mobilize some of the farmers behind him. The group, supported by other groups in the village, met with the farmers and justified its claim to provide irrigation to the command area by citing the agreements already made. Most of the farmers agreed to honor their commitments, and together with the group requested the contractor and his father-in-law to avoid further conflict by withdrawing the rented installation. This request was finally accepted.

The third case is Purba Pouli Bhumihin Samity in Mirzapur ADC, started in 1983–84. A private irrigation contractor, servicing a command area adjacent to an area proposed for irrigation by the group, opposed the group's scheme. The contractor was particularly concerned that farmers cultivating boundary plots in his command area would switch their plots to the group's scheme. The group, together with a local member of Proshika's field staff, assured the contractor that no such encroachment would occur, because there was scope to expand the group's command area in the opposite direction if required. The contractor persisted with his opposition, and persuaded the local branch manager of the BKB to frustrate the group's scheme by delaying the loan sanction. The manager obliged, but the group members learned of this deal. With the help of the farmers in the command area and the local Union Parishad member, the group successfully induced the bank manager to sanction the loan.

The fourth case is Mirzanagar Jubo Unnayan Samity in Saturia ADC, started in 1983–84. The scheme was originally planned for season 1982–83, and the proposed command area was located at one end of a neighboring deep tubewell (DTW) scheme. The group made agreements with farmers a considerable time in advance of the start of the season. But due to delays with the BKB, the pumping equipment could not be acquired before the second week of February 1983. By this time, it was too late for the farmers in the proposed command area to proceed with irrigated winter rice, because they faced a severe risk of losing the crop in early flooding. In the meantime, those farmers whose plots could be served by the DTW started receiving water after quick negotiations. The group therefore responded by negotiating with the farmers to commit these plots to the original STW command area in the following season. With this understanding, the group did not try to establish a competing command area in the 1982–83 season. In the following year, however, when the group installed the STW as agreed, the DTW manager and his associates opposed the move. They attempted to divide the farmers and issued threats against the group. The group, assisted by the majority of the farmers and other groups in the locality, finally sunk the boring. Having failed at this point, the DTW manager filed a false allegation with the *Upazila* Irrigation Committee against the group, stating that the group had illegally installed the machine in the DTW command area. The DTW manager relied on his superior access to the Committee to have the group thrown out of the command area. But at the official inquiry that followed, the group's claim was upheld when it presented the copy of the agreement between itself and the farmers.

These examples clearly illustrate some of the complexities of the market for irrigation in a locality, which to some extent can be analyzed in terms of Hirschman's categories of exit, voice and loyalty (Hirschman 1970). The distinction between the irrigation technologies is relevant, though the groups examined for this chapter have been using STWs. A STW can irrigate, on average, twelve to fifteen acres of winter rice, although many variables affect the actual size in a particular location. A number of these installations can therefore operate in close proximity, enabling farmers with plots scattered between them to switch their options, and even reallocate their boundary plots to the competing adjacent scheme. The farmers under such conditions can exercise an exit option. Seven farmers out of the twenty-four schemes examined for this chapter switched their plots to adjacent schemes. In three of these cases, some of the cultivators from within the group's command area established a new command area and installed their own STW, and in the remaining four cases the alternative schemes were operated by third-party private contractors. The water seller who is not effectively subsidized by low-risk defaulting on credit clearly has a strong interest in maintaining a stable clientele of water customers by making long-term agreements. The groups with Proshika make legally recognized contracts for five-year periods to cover the projected period of loan repayment on the capital asset, because the groups do not have costless default options as in the rest of the private sector. Farmers are more likely to enter these agreements if their alternatives for the plots concerned are remote. The frequency of possible alternatives is reduced if effective zoning of STW command areas occurs to prevent overcrowding, because there are fewer plots in overlapping command areas with choices of which one to enter. Such zoning is meant to be a function of the BADC. Furthermore, as we have seen from the case examples above, the efficacy of these agreements will depend not only on the solidarity and resolve of the group members (with perhaps the assistance of other groups not directly involved in providing irrigation services), but also on the credibility of the legal sanction if the agreement is broken. This credibility in turn depends on the access of the groups to legal services. In the fourth case described above, the agreement document was accepted as evidence by the *Upazila* Irrigation Committee. At the same time, it is important to acknowledge the significance of Proshika's presence as a supporting institution and therefore to recognize that the group's credibility in insisting on the terms of an agreement, or in its access to legal enforcement, remains dependent on this mediating force. If farmers are thus committed to a scheme, their voice rather than their exit is likely to characterize the exchange. But in extreme cases of farmers' voice, some groups, such as Ragunathpur Bhumihin Samity discussed above, have transferred the STW into a mobile asset by writing off the cost of the boring and irrigation drains, moving the pumpset to a new location and making an agreement with a new set of farmers. In such cases, it is the group that is exercising the exit option.

With low-lift pumps (LLPs), which are mobile within certain obvious constraints such as water sources, the exit option for the groups is easier and therefore a more credible threat to recalcitrant consumers. But consumer loyalty is likely to be quickly replaced by voice if there is evidence of competitors offering a service at more favorable rates. This had been an early problem when trying to capture command areas in Chatalpar and Aurail in Brahmanbaria that had previously been served by subsidized rental machines. At the same time, individual water users in LLP command areas have fewer options to switch their plots to other command areas, because these areas are larger, thus reducing the spatial scatter of a farmer's plots between different command areas. And where LLPs are operating in low-lying, single-crop areas, farmers also have fewer interseasonal options for exit by, for example, withdrawing from winter rice and concentrating on producing *aman*.

The groups' experience with DTWs is more recent as part of the Committee for American Relief Everywhere–Landless Operated Tubewell Users Service (CARE–LOTUS) program. Twenty DTW groups are operating as part of the Proshika program (nine in Sreepur, eight in Mirzapur, one in Serajganj and two in Dhamrai). DTWs are distinguished from the two other technologies by the immobility of the equipment once it is installed. This implies that the owners of DTWs are in stronger monopoly positions in relation to potential water users, because more difficult changes of ownership rather than displacement/replacement of the water sellers would be required to improve the irrigation service or reduce its costs. Farmers can collectively force LLP operators and even STW operators to shift sites to make way for a competitor, but a change in the ownership of the equipment is necessary along with the accompanying water rights. From the point of view of the water sellers, however, much depends on the demand intensity of the farmers in the command area. Owners of DTWs can also be trapped if farmers have a fallow or even wheat preference, which has been the case with some of the DTWs in West Sreepur, where the soils have not been appropriate for winter rice. CARE's assumptions that farmers' factional disputes were the primary cause of the defunct BADC-rented DTWs has to be tempered with an understanding of local ecological conditions in which farmers' reluctance to engage in irrigated agriculture might be quite rational. Thus the problem for the groups with this technology is that they have no credible threat of exit themselves as a response to extreme farmer voice (on fees, rates of delivery), and this is exacerbated in localities where the technical limitations to irrigation reduce any competition to take over the equipment. Where high subsidies remain, as with the CARE–LOTUS rehabilitation of the BADC rented equipment through landless group ownership (with Proshika, the Bangladesh Rural Advancement Committee (BRAC) and Grameen Bank), the full significance of this qualitative difference with DTW technologies might be disguised. But if a wider program of landless group control of new, less subsidized DTWs is envisaged, the ecological conditions for the selected sites would have to be much more favorable and farmers would either have to be much more dependent on irrigated agriculture for their own survival or the profits from such cultivation will have to be more secure. Little attention has been paid to these issues so far in the DTW programs in Bangladesh, which is one of the reasons so many of them have been a mess.

This market issue has another dimension, which is illustrated by the Mirzanagar Jubo Unnayan Samity case study above, but which applies more widely in Bangladesh. This refers to the competition between different rather than similar technologies, that is, between DTWs and STWs. The issue becomes, as it were, three-dimensional, because it refers not just to surface-area competition but also to water tables. Studies conducted by the Water Master Plan Organization (MPO) in Bangladesh show that in some, though not all, geological structures, the effect of a DTW in areas where STWs are operating is to drain the higher aquifers on which the STWs rely. Although the MPO argues that annual replenishment occurs, it points out that, with the present anarchic siting of these technologies in each other's appropriate areas, adjacent DTWs can dry out neighboring STWs in late season or make pumping more expensive and less efficient. Under such conditions, boundary plots are likely to be switched from STW command areas to DTW ones. The Mirzanagar Jubo Unnayan Samity's story may not yet be over.

Risk Sharing and Payment Options

The preferred forms of payment for irrigation differ between water sellers and users, and among localities depending on the perceptions of risk and the variables affecting those perceptions. These calculations occur in an overall context of unpredictable agriculture, replete with floods, hailstorms, droughts and pest attacks. But alongside the farmers, the non-cultivating water sellers using mechanized equipment must risk large amounts of fixed capital and recurrent operating-cost expenditure to obtain return on investment. Three systems of payment in principle exist with subvariations in practice: cropshare, fixed-cash and fixed-kind. Fixed-kind payments are very rare (4.8 percent of the total program). Cropshare accounts for 64.3 percent of the program and fixed-cash 29.3 percent. In 70 percent of the STW schemes, the payment arrangement is cropshare; in the LLP schemes 46.3 percent are fixed-cash and 24.1 percent fixed-kind. Thus the most prevalent system is cropshare, which varies from 25 percent to 33 percent of the standing crop. Sometimes the payment system preferences appear to reflect customary practices derived from traditional forms of irrigation when the logic behind the exchange calculation was different. The main explanation for the prevalence of the cropshare system seems to be the farmers' shortage of capital at the beginning of the irrigation season and their preference for deferred water fees until the end of the season, even if this may result in paying higher actual prices for water. In many instances, even richer farmers with capital to invest in irrigated agriculture prefer the cropshare system as a way of offsetting risks of crop failure. Such calculations are likely to be intensified in areas of high unpredictability, where early flooding, for example, can occur. By spreading risk in this way, farmers can also determine the intensity of their investment in high-yield variety (HYV) practices and therefore respond flexibly to a broader range of production functions with these and other plots, as well as to the opportunity costs of investing between agriculture and other sectors, and between production and family consumption behavior (that is, daughters' dowries, education expenses, medical fees and so on).

There is an important methodological issue here. Explanations of preferences for payment systems cannot necessarily be found within a command area/plot specific analysis, because farmers are always trading off against other aspects of their economic portfolios. Furthermore, if the command area is socially dominated by a small number of rich farmers, their preferences for payment arrangements are likely to prevail over others regardless of objective market conditions. Apart from water sellers' preferences for standard arrangements within their command areas to avoid conflicts and discretionary practices, the absence of significant variation between payment arrangements within command areas suggests that pressures for conformity will override plot-derived calculations based on economic and ecological criteria, unless of course that conformity genuinely reflects the collective interests of those plots anyway. It is in this sense that risk explanations of payment systems based solely on farmers' cost and return calculations for command area plots are at best partial. It should, however, be noted that in two command areas from the twenty-four studied for this chapter (Gabtoli and Mirzapur), there was a combination of fixed-cash and cropshare payment systems, with 25 percent of the farmers paying fixed-cash. These farmers were better off.

Fixed-cash payment systems have problems of interpretation. There is some evidence to support the notion that fixed-cash payments occur in areas of lower crop risk such as Shibganj, where the fixed-cash payment arrangements are concentrated. The land elevation is relatively high, and much of the land in the command areas is double- or triple-cropped. The prospect of flood damage is remote. Fixed-cash payments would appear to have the function of increasing farmers' productivity, with incentives to maximize yields beyond the known costs of the water fee. Fixed-cash payments made only at the time of the harvest have further advantages for farmers who are short of capital at the beginning of the season, while leaving the water sellers bearing all the costs of mobilizing operating funds some months prior to receiving any income. However, pure cropshare arrangements have the same disadvantages to the groups selling water. On the other hand, fixed-cash arrangements, while possibly lower in value terms compared to cropshares depending on relative strength in the original negotiations, do offer groups a predictable sum against which variable costs can be adjusted to ensure overall profitability. Fixed-cash payments introduce certainty into the equation and may reduce risk as a result. So much for theory. This assumes that fixed-cash fees are automatically paid or can easily be collected. But difficulties of collection occur even when farmers cannot cite crop damage as an excuse. So a degree of uncertainty remains in practice, and its resolution relies on the solidarity of the group members, or the support they may receive from non-irrigation groups in collecting the fee. This has been an issue in the LLP command areas where fixed-cash payments prevail mainly as a result of historical conditions under which the costs of water provision were highly subsidized through BADC rental arrangements, so that deals between farmers and water-supplying contractors were more individualized rather than incorporated into overall command area management. The groups have experienced persistent problems in collecting water fees when they have inherited these conditions.

The balance of negotiations in either of these principal payment systems had been in favor of the farmers, although poorer farmers still encountered other problems, which will be discussed below. Even after the first year of the program, Proshika could see from the pilot experience in Bhairab that these payment systems, unmodified, were exacerbating the groups' cash flow problems. The groups were meeting the full interest costs on the capital loans, as planned, but they were also meeting full annual interest on the operating-cost loans. A further sharp reminder of this financial exposure came after the 1984 floods damaged the winter rice harvest, leaving groups in affected command areas with seriously reduced gross incomes either through cropshares from a smaller harvest or because flood-damaged farmers refused to honor their fixed-cash fee obligations. This experience led Proshika to encourage the groups to negotiate risk-sharing arrangements with farmers whereby they would contribute to ongoing operating costs (mainly the cost of diesel) in exchange for a reduction in the final fee. Where the cropshare payment system applied, this usually resulted in a drop in the final cropshare proportion from 33 percent to 25 percent. In the fixed-cash payment system, a deal was commonly struck whereby the farmers paid 50 percent of the fee in advance and 50 percent at harvest time.

These arrangements are quite common in irrigation schemes with private contractors, and often involve farmers actually purchasing diesel and buying dedicated pump time on request. But this can lead to anarchic command area management and reintroduce access and tail-ender problems for the poorer farmers. But even with a less extreme advance payment system, the water sellers' control over water distribution remains threatened and equity hard to sustain. Where poorer farmers remain unable to deposit the same amounts as their richer competitors, the latter may demand preferential treatment, as in the Rajnagar Gorib Unnayan Samity in Saturia. In these circumstances, poorer farmers may need loans from the group itself in order to make advance contributions to the group's operating costs. On the other hand, a command area consisting of a few large farmers would pose an alternative threat to the group's autonomy over water distribution. The social composition of the farmers in the command area therefore becomes a relevant variable in the risk package surrounding modes of payment. Finally, though, it should be noted that groups that have enjoyed a record of success and have built up some savings, such as the Bangala Bhumihin Samity in Ghior, prefer not to receive any advance payment but instead to maximize profits through the unaltered cropshare of paddy at the end of the season. Security is being traded for profit, but this security has been achieved through collective savings rather than annual disbursements of a dividend from profits to the group members. The group is therefore displaying considerable solidarity, as witnessed by the above description of its initial negotiations with farmers.

Extension of Rights

It was always hoped that ownership of a productive asset such as mechanized minor irrigation would lead to a broader acquisition of rights by the landless. In this way, structural change among the groups and other classes in the locality would be initiated. It is clear from meetings with many of the groups involved in the program (not confined to the twenty-four studied for this chapter) that group members valued the irrigation strategy not just because of the potential financial returns but also because of the status achieved by the group members in the community. Members argue that they receive greater respect from the richer families in the village than they did before, and they attribute this to their ability to secure and install the equipment, provide the service, maintain the equipment, honor contracts through the delivery of water according to a planned system and keep records and accounts. Status is an intangible indicator. It is difficult to present quantifiable evidence in support of the proposition. The following discussion is therefore more qualitative, based on structured interviews with twenty-four groups in the program. But status can be represented by tangible gains such as greater employment, higher wages, rights to work, lower interest rates on advances and cash loans, conditions attached to loans, secure tenancy and rental rates and rights over *khas* land and ponds. These issues are part of the discussion that follows. At the same time, determining causation is a problem. Neither the groups nor Proshika claim that any gains of this kind can be attributed solely to their involvement in irrigation. Many of the groups with Proshika are making gains of this kind without participating directly in the irrigation program. It is only claimed that an involvement in the irrigation program normally assists this process.

A key indicator of structural change from the patron-client forms of class relations outlined in the introduction to this chapter is disengagement from bondage. All of the twenty-four groups interviewed reported increases in employment opportunities and wages available to them as a result of the irrigation service provided by them and by private contractors in the locality. Such claims are enormously complex to validate empirically, and we know from those studies that in some areas group members may themselves be only marginally engaged in agricultural work. Of course in areas where the introduction of winter rice represents a net addition to the cropping cycle, the demand for labor has to rise. But other variables have to be considered: deficit or surplus labor areas with/without irrigation and the availability of migrant labor. These variables are in turn affected by the elevation of land. The areas served by the landless irrigation schemes in Madaripur, Mirzapur, Ghior, parts of Saturia and Gabtoli are low-lying and had been single-cropped (broadcast *aman*) or precariously double-cropped (meager *rabi* crops followed by broadcast *aman*). Thus the employment opportunities in these areas had been especially scarce and exacerbated by the expropriation of land from the poor through indebtedness. Before the irrigation, the majority of the laborers in these localities had to outmigrate or depend on advances from richer farmers and moneylenders during the lean season. Irrigation (landless or not) has now introduced a winter rice/*T aman* rotation in many of these localities, increasing the demand for labor and reducing outmigration. This has reduced the dependence of the poorer families on annual advances and has enhanced their bargaining position for wages in both of the agricultural seasons. The income effects of this development are discussed in appendix B.

The link between providing irrigation and strengthening a group's bargaining position is illustrated by the case of Char Moheshpur Biplab Samity in Saturia. The irrigation service has been used as leverage to secure employment and increased wages for group members. When the farmers ask for water for puddling (plot preparation) and transplanting (where the response is more flexible preceding the main serial arrangements for the main, regular distribution), the group members set their own employment, including the later operations of weeding and harvesting, as a precondition for starting the water service. This exchange of water for employment is not strictly contained in the formal agreement, but constitutes a regular, informal aspect of the bargaining relationships. During the interviews, most of the groups reported that group members usually get preference when labor is hired in the command areas they serve. Often, as reported by the Rajnagar Gorib Unnayan Samity, group members providing an irrigation service have greater skills in HYV operations (especially plot preparation and transplanting) and are therefore preferred by farmers cultivating winter rice. This group has also been able to exercise an influence over non-organized labor in the morning bazaar where labor is hired and where daily bargaining over wages takes place.

There are other examples of bargaining and struggles over wages. The group members from the Purba Pouli Bhumihin Samity in Mirzapur, together with some other groups and non-organized laborers in the locality demanded wage increases at the beginning of the 1982–83 winter rice season. When the farmers resisted, this group led the other laborers in a five-day strike from transplanting. As a result, the farmers conceded the demand and increased the rate from Tk15 to Tk25 a day. In three other cases (Ganasingjuri Samaj Kallayan Samity, Poyla Prantik Chashi Samity in Ghior and Bharua Para Jubo Kallayan Samity in Madaripur), the group members had to exert strong pressure to increase the meals provided as part of the wage from two to three. The members from Poyla Prantik Chashi Samity, together with other organized and non-organized laborers, went on strike for three days during the harvest to realize this demand. All the groups interviewed reported that wages have increased during winter rice, in some cases by a factor of 2 to 2.5 for this season over other seasons.

Tenancy is a further indicator of the distribution of rights. Thirty percent of the group members from the twenty-four groups examined who were cultivating in their command areas were doing so as tenants (as was shown in table 3.2). Moreover, some of the group members also cultivate land as sharecroppers outside the command areas. Two-thirds of the groups reported that their members got preference from landowners over other potential tenants to sharecrop land in the command area. In most cases, the sharecropper provided all the inputs, but the water fee was shared equally between owner and tenant. For three groups in Gabtoli, however, landowners shared 50 percent of fertilizer and seedling costs togther with the water fee. One group in Saturia reported short-term, winter rice season tenancies (as Glaser does from her study in Singra, Rajshahi), where landowners provided 50 percent of fertilizer costs. This would seem to reflect a rationalization of landowner's supervision time during the winter rice season under conditions of plots being distributed among several command areas, with farmers attempting to reconcile cultivation cycles dictated by the variable time imperatives of command area-specific water distribution patterns. Where some of the plots of larger farmers are located in command areas served by groups from which some members wish to cultivate as tenants, the incentive to lease out these rather than other plots from the portfolio is higher because, as the tenants are part of the group irrigation service, water supply is likely to be more secure to such tenanted plots. No clear patterns have yet been established for whether irrigation reduces or increases the land available for share-cropping in Bangladesh. Conventional wisdom has always opted for the reduction position, and that is supported by the evidence of one-third of the groups interviewed for this chapter, who claim that opportunities for sharecropping in their localities have declined for winter rice while being maintained for *aman*. There does seem to be a stronger tendency for sharecropping contracts to be awarded on a seasonal rather than annual basis, but farmer rationalities for each season's leasing decisions depend on: size of farm, number of plots, command area access for plots, cropping cycles and the extent of their variability between plots depending on elevation and soil types. With such complexity, the gaining of sharecropping rights by groups as a result of providing an irrigation service cannot be determined with certainty.

Our evidence does not yet establish a significant link from the irrigation service and the acquisition of rights directly to *khas* land and indirectly to *khas* ponds. If we make the assumption that STW irrigation is most likely to occur in settled areas, then the presence of *khas* land within STW command areas is remote. But the frequency of *khas* land in LLP command areas is greater, especially in low-lying *haor* tracts where single-crop winter rice has traditionally relied more on surface water irrigation with *dhones* and buckets from river and *bheel* sources. Introducing mechanized LLPs into these areas has enabled the more interior (in the sense of distance from the water source) plots to be reached with irrigation, but these are plots that have not traditionally been cultivated with any seriousness or intensity, and many have been left fallow for nondedicated grazing. The ownership and inheritance claims to low-value land of this category have often been neglected, or left in dispute. Such land is therefore more often *khas* land. When irrigation becomes available, land value rises and the competition for it becomes more intense. But *khas* land can be effectively occupied only if the capacity to cultivate it exists.

Outside the twenty-four groups examined for this chapter, there was strong evidence for two years of groups in Khaliajuri (a *haor* tract toward the northeast of Bangladesh) using LLPs to occupy command areas, by plowing, transplanting and so on. Unfortunately, early floods destroyed the 1984 winter rice crop in these low-lying command areas. Because the crop represented the groups' only income from which to fund all the cultivation and irrigation costs, the groups were left financially exposed. Proshika compensated six of the affected groups by writing off their loans. Early floods are too frequent a hazard in Bangladesh to ignore, but their frequency (if unpredictable) does seem to be only once every five to seven years. Thus opportunities for *khas* land cultivation of this type do exist, but clearly they need to be attached to adequate compensation or insurance provision. Not all *khas* land falls into this category, and elsewhere the potential link between irrigation and occupation of *khas* land may be less direct, where the income or political strength gained by the groups from the irrigation service can be translated into the capacity to occupy such land (not necessarily in the command area, or for winter rice cultivation). Although none of the twenty-four groups reported such occupation by themselves, it should be noted that, as part of the national land reform program, many of the groups with Proshika as well as other non-governmental organizations (NGOs), independent of the irrigation service strategy, are currently occupying *khas* land.

The indirect link may apply to the occupation of *khas* ponds, which are used more for fishing than as irrigation water sources. Yet only one case of occupation was reported from the twenty-four groups, despite a national policy of giving preference on the leasing of such ponds to landless groups. The Deharapara Bhumihin Samity in Shibganj occupied a three-*bigha khas* pond with another group. Richer patron farmers were also competing for occupation and had superior access to the *Upazila* officials from whom the lease to this pond had to be obtained. But the group had gained credibility in the village and with the officials through its management of the irrigation service. It had proved that it was capable of organizing the fishing of this pond. Furthermore, its members had the cash available to purchase the lease from income deriving from the irrigation service. In this way, they could compete adequately in the lease market without undermining their bargaining position by having to seek loans for such leases from the very patrons who themselves sought to occupy the pond. It should be noted, however, that the two groups were also assisted in this claim by other groups with Proshika in the locality. This reveals the importance of solidarity between groups as well as between group members within them.

Access to Officials and Services

The negotiating strength of the groups with patron classes and farmers in the village is improved by the quality of their access to officials and services outside it. This has applied to such one-off transactions as the following:

- loan applications to BKB branch managers, where a generally negative experience has compelled Proshika to withdraw from the BKB connection and expand its own Revolving Loan Fund (RLF) functions,

- fulfilling the BADC's feasibility and zoning criteria (a technical farce but an access hurdle), and
- obtaining supplies of equipment from the BADC or private dealers.

Transactions also continue with mechanics, spare parts dealers and diesel suppliers, and a scheme's success is constrained by machine breakdowns, a shortage of spare parts and repair facilities and interrupted fuel supplies. The significance of these constraints should not be overestimated, because Proshika has assisted the relationships between the groups and these external services. Some of these constraints might even apply more strongly to the privately operated schemes, especially where the cost/income incentives to maximize the utility of the equipment are lower so that interruptions are more easily accepted. Private contractors refer to them frequently as excuses for irregular water delivery during the season.

Access to BKB and BADC has been a key problem throughout the program for most of the groups. Difficulties with the BADC were expected, because its field offices have long enjoyed a reputation of corruption and obstruction with farmers of all classes. Richer farmers have been able to manage these problems through bribery and connections, so that BADC has stimulated rural class differentiation. These practices also have the drawback of being hugely inefficient in the allocation and optimal utilization of scarce investment resources in agriculture. With such aid dependency to the agricultural sector in Bangladesh, donors (supported by the interests of frustrated domestic commercial classes) have applied a similar analysis to the evidence of state inefficiency as they have been doing in Africa, and have lobbied successfully (with significant leverage of course) for a policy of privatization in the supply of equipment and variable inputs. By abusing its monopoly so blatantly for so long, BADC officials are now obliged to compete in many of their local outlets with private competitors. The groups have undoubtedly benefited from this shift in the supply system, so that problems with the BADC have receded. The responsibility for assessing the feasibility of command areas and applying the zoning regulations that set the minimum distance between command areas remains with the BADC. But practice is variable. Approval can be purchased without even the normal cursory examination of the site. If we assume that the staff has the technical capacity to make these assessments (which is probably unrealistic), the absence of reliable technical appraisal of sites probably explains the market anarchy that currently characterizes the minor irrigation sector as a whole. Relying on a market shakedown for the optimal allocation of minor irrigation technologies could be a wasteful process indeed. Privatization is not the solution here. The groups' current choices are to accept market anarchy, with all the attendant risks of bad siting, in order to compete with private contractors (whose own economics may not require such optimal conditions) to establish command areas, or to rely on the myth of rational, technical advice with unnecessary access to it, because exit options seem to be widely available.

Relations with the BKB were expected to be better than those with the BADC. Entirely successful relations were not assumed, but one of the program's original objectives was to test the capacity of local BKB branches to reach the poor with credit, and to test the capacity of the groups to conduct financial affairs with formal institutions such as banks. Unfortunately for rural development strategies in Bangladesh, the results of this test were negative. Most of the groups reported intentional delays and occasional requests for bribes from staff before loans were sanctioned. In each group, five members signed papers issued by the bank, giving these members power of attorney to act on behalf of the group in transactions with the bank. These five members therefore had the duty of going to the branch office to submit requests for loans, supported by the necessary documentation (agreements with the farmers, feasibility statements from the BADC, invoices from equipment suppliers and so on). Appointments were made with bank staff by a group member (the chairman or the secretary), setting a date when the five members should attend to finalize the loan sanction. Even making an appointment could involve waiting in indeterminate lines, in which the group member could not easily reach the front. If he succeeded, he would have to explain the circumstances that required an appointment. Even though the branch manager and designated members of staff had been briefed both by the BKB Head Office and by Proshika locally, the group members felt they were obliged to introduce the whole program as if the listener were hearing it for the first time. Appointments were hard to get, and the staff always seemed reluctant to specify a particular time, naming a whole day instead.

For many of the groups, the trip to the bank, often located at the *Upazila* headquarters, involved some combination of walking, rickshaws, boats, buses and always time as well as fares. Usually a meal had to be bought. In short, the outing was costly if the opportunity cost of labor time was also reckoned. But many groups (not just the twenty-four interviewed for this chapter) have reported that these appointments were then frequently broken. Many of the groups report this synthesized typical story: The five members come to the bank and try to find out when they can enter to see an official. They may have to bribe an office messenger to perform this gatekeeping duty. The information that returns is usually nonspecific. The group members are left waiting, without knowing if an official has actually been approached by the messenger inside the office, or how forceful the messenger was in reminding the official that an appointment for this day existed. They try to request information from people coming out. The group members crowd round the door, try to get to the official's office and try to enter an informal line existing among the crowd in the office and the doorway. But, poorly dressed and unclear about how to address the official, they often attract hostility not only from the official but from the others in the room who question their right to be there. What business could they possibly have with a bank? Further humiliations are endured. And, on many occasions, the groups retreat empty-handed: a wasted, expensive, frustrating and humiliating day discussed bitterly as they return to the village knowing they will have to try again. For some, their first encounter with the state has revealed many truths about the replication and extension of class relations outside the village. And in many cases, these delays have had significant further effects for the scheme, by postponing the installation of the equipment and causing farmers to lose confidence, thereby declining to make preparations or switching boundary plots to neighboring command areas. In our data showing the significance of command area size in determining the profitability of a scheme, the loan access variable is critical. While the program relied on the BKB for loans, the group members had to visit the bank repeatedly to secure the initial capital loan as well as operating-cost installments. Without the intensive involvement of Proshika field staff, as well as senior coordination staff from Dhaka troubleshooting in the field, many of these transactions would never have been completed. The necessity for this intensive assistance by Proshika indicated that the attack on this dimension of agrarian social relations could not yet succeed, and failure here threatened to undermine other parts of the program that stood a better chance of altering social relations at the point of production. With this experience, Proshika withdrew from the BKB arrangements and extended its own RLF capacity to preserve the test of other dimensions of the strategy.

The experience with continual transactions has been much more positive, though the assistance of Proshika field staff has still been significant. Most of the groups made seasonal contracts with mechanics, who were then obliged to make regular visits to inspect the equipment, carry out routine maintenance and attend promptly to faulty machines and breakdowns. Rural mechanics remain scarce, however, and some mechanics were responsible for as many as fifty machines. Five out of twenty-four groups reported difficulties in obtaining required services because the mechanics were committed elsewhere. Proshika quickly introduced a program of training the engine operators (drivers) in the groups to relieve the simpler aspects of this problems. For spare parts, groups avoided purchasing them from the BADC office whenever possible, preferring to buy from private dealers with cash. Often the presence of Proshika field staff was required at these transactions to ensure the quality of the products being sold to the groups. For diesel, long-term contracts were made with fuel dealers in the local town or bazaar, where appropriate. At first, the dealers demanded cash before releasing stocks of fuel, but they are now confident enough in the groups' ability to repay that they are prepared to offer fuel on short-term credit. Most of the groups reported that dealers did not impose any special conditions on them. In view of the problems the groups were having in obtaining operating-cost loan installments from the bank, this facility from the dealers was an important contribution to relaxing cash flow problems. Not only is it an indicator of the credibility of the groups in the local marketplace, but it also reduced any fluctuations in the operation of the machine that maintains farmer loyalty and the intensity of their own investments in irrigated agriculture.

Most of the groups reported that their members were being treated with more respect by dealers over time, but it is of course difficult for an observer to interpret the value and meaning of such reports. What indicators of respect are available: forms of address in speech, body language, hospitality, trust in verbal agreements? When interviewed, group members wanted to convey a sense of improvement in their feeling about themselves and their dignity in the community, without being able to offer clear criteria. For them, a contrast existed between being marginalized in most social encounters outside their immediate kin or being deferential supplicants to patron farmers/moneylenders in the village, and a new situation in which attention was paid to them as actors in the marketplace with business to transact. They were involved in a wider set of relationships and had a purpose beyond the normal one of buying small amounts of food and other consumption items with minute calculations of how far their daily wages could be stretched. At the same time, this contrast cannot be carried too far, because some of the group members were or had recently been marginal farmers or petty traders. Two of the groups, quite independently of each other and without a leading question, were impressed when their members were offered a chair and even tea by the local BKB branch manager in one case (a welcome exception to the general rule), and the local diesel supplier in the other case. To be offered a seat in this society is highly symbolic, a recognition not so much of equality but of worth and value.

It would be wrong, however, to overestimate the independence of these access relations from the background of Proshika support. Many of the longer-term contracts with dealers and mechanics have been mediated by Proshika, and the local Proshika field staff quickly intervene if relations break down. The threat of their intervention is often sufficient to keep the relationship running smoothly, except with the BKB, where Proshika's presence appeared to be continually necessary. This reliance on Proshika is significant, therefore, in contributing to the reliability of pumpset operation and thereby to the negotiations between groups and farmers. The crucial test is still to come. When Proshika withdraws such support, can the groups sustain these bargaining relationships with outsiders and farmers? Their internal solidarity will be an important variable, but so too will be the commercial viability of the irrigation service. The important question remains—are group solidarity and commercial viability contradictory or mutually reinforcing? Much depends on whether individual group members and individual farmer/water users have exit options—the former into other employment or small business, the latter into other water services or other crops. With such micro-local variation in socio-ecological conditions in Bangladesh, a general answer on exit options is difficult. We can say that these options are reduced in single-crop winter rice areas, or (relaxing the condition slightly) where nonirrigated cropping is at best precarious. But some farmers may still choose between water suppliers under these conditions. Either the landless require monopoly control over water, or they have to offer competitive prices and services, which remains difficult when their private contractor/competitors are subsidized through default on loans.

CHAPTER FIVE

Small Farmers' Access to Irrigation Schemes

ONE OF THE BASIC contentions of the landless irrigation program is that small farmers have better access to irrigation water in landless controlled schemes than in privately managed schemes. The underlying arguments are as follows:

- Under landless irrigation schemes, the whole range of activities relating to water conveyance, distribution and fee collection is managed by the landless group members with whom small farmers and sharecroppers can interact on more equal terms (Wood 1982). This argument is reinforced where members of landless irrigation groups are also smaller owner-farmers and/or sharecroppers (there is no strict upper limit on landownership for Proshika group members, but the necessary condition for group membership is that wage labor has to be the major source of family earnings).
- Landless irrigation command areas are expected to be larger than those under privatized schemes because of more ensured and efficient water distribution in the former, so more small farmers will be served with water under landless schemes.
- Although Proshika does not strictly favor small farmers, landless controlled irrigation equipment is likely to be installed at sites more favorable for providing water to small farmers' plots, provided there is a choice.

These arguments have important policy implications for productivity and equity, and therefore require empirical verification. This chapter attempts to compare the access of small farmers to irrigation under landless and privately controlled schemes, and to explain the observed differences using empirical data. The scope of the study has been rather limited because of the very small sample size. Investigations and analyses have been further limited due to the interference of the 1984 floods with the cultivation of crops.

Methodology

The command areas for this study were the same as for the employment-farmer respondent study (see chapter 8). Respondents were selected based on the initial census of farmers taken from that study. The sample of small farmers was drawn from the bottom 50 percent of the total number of farmers in the command areas, defined in terms of total land owned. In this way a local, rather than a national, standard measure of a small farmer was obtained.

A fixed, universal definition of "small farmer" in Bangladesh is meaningless because of regional variations in soil types, elevation of land and cropping patterns. The concept of small has to reflect these regional variations. The study compared the access of small farmers to irrigation between landless and privately owned schemes. It examined the location of their plots in relation to the irrigation source, the volume of water per unit of land measured in terms of the number of hours per application and the timeliness of supply in relation to field operations. The study also asked some broader questions concerning the effects of access on landholding patterns, sharecropping rights and credit transactions. The sample is of course small, given the available research resources and the required detail. This study therefore has to be seen as offering case-study insights and perhaps a framework of issues that might be adapted for a wider statistical exercise.

Sampling

The sampling frame and the salient features of the studied schemes are presented in table 5.1. Complete lists of Proshika landless schemes and private schemes were first obtained by Proshika fieldworkers from the respective areas. To be representative, the selected schemes were those having near-average command areas estimated for the listed schemes in each area for each organizational type.

For the purposes of this study, pairs of schemes, one landless and one private in each case, were selected from Attigram in Saturia, from Singjuri in Ghior and from Dashar in Kalkini. The first two pairs used shallow tubewell (STW) and the third pair low-lift pump (LLP) irrigation methods. The selected Proshika schemes were Anantapur Bash Shilpa Samity and Gorib Unnayan Samity in Attigram, Dewbhog Bhumihin Samity in Singjuri and Udayan Bhumihin Samity in Dashar. The owners of the selected private irrigation units were Nurul Islam in Attigram, Gopal in Dewbhog and Jadunath Kar in Dashar.

Characteristics of Small Farmers

Land Ownership and Cultivated Holdings

In every location, small farmers cultivated more land than they owned. The additional land was obtained through sharecropping and mortgaging practices (table 5.2). In Saturia and Kalkini, the net amount of sharecropped and mortgaged land per farm was high and accounted for 54 percent and 49 percent of total cultivated land, respectively. There appeared to be a lower incidence of sharecropping and mortgaging in Ghior schemes, compared to the other two areas, mainly because the area is flood-prone and crop production is too risky for the poor to sharecrop under the traditional arrangements. Sharecropping under the traditional arrangement of fifty-fifty output-share with almost no cost-sharing is still the dominant form of production in Saturia and Kalkini areas.

Small Farmers' Share of Command Area

In Saturia, the proportions of farmers owning land up to 2.5 acres were more than 60 percent of all farmers in both the landless and private schemes, and they constituted the majority of small farmers included in this study. The share of the small farmers in the Saturia landless command area of 17.9 acres was 54 percent, which was higher than the small farmers' proportionate share of 47 percent in the private command area of 14.6 acres. In this respect, landless schemes had little edge over private schemes. In Ghior, the small farmers' share of the landless command area of 11.3 acres was only 19 percent, which was lower than the 39 percent share of small farmers in the private command area of 14 acres. In Kalkini, small farmers owned about 65 percent of the landless command area of 18.4 acres and 60 percent of the 13.4-acre private command area. What emerges from the above findings is that, as the command area increased, small farmers had relatively more access to irrigation in terms of their proportionate share of total command-area land. The high degree of land fragmentation provided an advantage to small farmers to have their land included in the expanded command area. In 1983–84, the landless schemes in Saturia and Kalkini had comparatively larger command areas than the private schemes, and therefore small farmers had more access to irrigation command areas in these locations.

Share of Landless Members in the Command Areas

The share of landless group members in their respective command areas can also be taken as an index of access of the small farmers, including the landless cultivator or sharecroppers, to irrigation. The survey revealed that 33 percent of all the water user farmers in the Saturia landless scheme were the group members themselves and that they, together, shared 30 percent of the irrigated command area. This gave the group members (mostly small farmers by definition) greater control over irrigation. In contrast, the landless group members had a relatively weaker position in the Ghior landless scheme, both in terms of their number and in their share of the command area. This lends support to the findings in the previous section that the small farmers in Ghior had less access to irrigation in the landless command area, compared with the private scheme.

Water Distribution Status

Location of Small Farmers' Plots

In this section, we see if the small farmers in landless schemes had any definite advantage in terms of the distance of their plots in relation to the water sources. Table 5.3 shows that the distance of the small farmers' nearest plots varied from 100 to 130 yards in Saturia and Ghior. In both areas, the reported distance was a little shorter in the landless command areas than in the private schemes, although the number of plots ahead of small farmers' plots was a little higher for the landless scheme than for the private scheme in Saturia. But the difference was not statistically significant, implying that the small farmers had no special advantage in relation to the location of plots. The average number of large farmers' plots ahead of small farmers' nearest plots was, to some extent, higher for the landless than in the private schemes in Saturia but, as the tubewell was controlled by the landless group, larger farmers might not have been able to influence water distribution.

The shorter distances of plots from water source provide some advantage to small farmers with respect to water delivery, but this does not necessarily imply that the siting of the landless equipment was deliberate to skew distribution in favor of small farmers. Siting of landless irrigation equipment may be conditioned both by technical factors and by the prospects of procuring necessary agreements with the water users for command area land. For example, the higher average distance of small farmers' plots in the landless scheme compared with the private scheme in Kalkini was coincidental. The sitings of the LLPs were conditioned by the availability of surface water; hence, the variation in distances of plots cannot be attributed to any deliberate choice.

Intensity of Irrigation

In general, the level of water delivery to small farmers' plots appeared better in the landless schemes than in the private schemes in the studied areas. The average number of water applications per plot during the 1983–84 winter rice season, the average hours per application and the total hours of delivery per plot and per acre during the season all appeared significantly higher in the landless than in the private schemes in Saturia and Kalkini (table 5.4). Given the proximity of small farmers' plots to the water source, delivering water for longer hours meant a larger volume of water given to small farmers' plots in the landless schemes than in the private scheme. In Ghior, however, the landless STW did not show any improvement in water delivery over the private STW, mainly because of frequent machine troubles and breakdowns during the 1983–84 season.

The quality of irrigation in landless schemes was superior to that in private schemes, except in Ghior. Most small farmers on the landless schemes in Saturia and Kalkini reported that water delivered to their plots was near or above average, per application, for plots of similar characteristics. But in the Saturia private scheme, 72 percent of the respondents reported that they had received water below the average for similar plots. In fact, better water distribution was one of the main factors contributing to enlarging command areas under landless schemes, although mechanical breakdowns and the landless members' limited access to land and credit caused a decline in the landless command areas in subsequent years.

A larger proportion of plots in the landless schemes in Saturia and Kalkini received water as they needed it for land preparation, compared with the private schemes in these areas (table 5.5). Even those who reported delay in getting water to their plots in the landless schemes mentioned that such delay was more or less common for all farmers in the scheme. Only a few (6 percent) of the farmers in the Saturia landless scheme reported that the delay in getting water was worse for them, as compared to a high proportion (28 percent) reporting a worse condition in the Saturia private scheme. As far as the adequacy of water application, a higher proportion of small farmers' plots in the landless schemes was fully saturated at each application, compared to the private schemes in Saturia and Kalkini. In Ghior, a larger proportion of farmers in the private scheme reported timely delivery of water compared to those in the landless scheme. The delay was reportedly due to frequent breakdown of machines, as described in appendix A.

The better water delivery to small farmers' plots in the landless schemes in Saturia and Ghior should, other things remaining the same, result in higher yields in these schemes. The absence of complete data on yields, especially in Ghior and Kalkini, where farmers had serious crop damage from the 1984 floods, precluded meaningful comparison. In Saturia, where flood damage was less severe and where almost all the farmers could complete harvesting before the onrush of floodwater, the landless scheme had about a 30 percent higher yield compared with the private scheme, conceivably as a result of better water supply.

Implications of Irrigation for
Small Farmers' Survival Strategy

Land Transfer

The limited sample indicates that farmers in both landless and private schemes have not been able to regain lost land to any noticeable extent since the introduction of irrigation. On the other hand, they continue to lose, either through outright selling or mortgaging, and the lost plots are both within and outside irrigation command areas. This implies that the processes through which small farmers lose land were still in force in these areas. One pertinent question here is whether the control of irrigation assets by landless groups can stop, revert or at least slow down small farmers' loss of land.

Sharecropping

Table 5.6 reveals that in general only a small proportion of small farmers can support their families by production from their own land. The rest are dependent on sharecropping, selling of labor or both. In Ghior, there was little sharecropping, and a significant number of small farmers in both landless and private schemes reported that they were dependent on other work, such as petty trading or rickshaw pulling.

A judgment on the implication of irrigation for small farmers' sharecropping practices would be premature. The survey revealed that three farmers in the Saturia landless scheme lost five of their previously sharecropped plots since the introduction of irrigation and, out of these five plots, four were taken back by the owner for self-cultivation, three of them within the same command area. In Kalkini, 40 percent of the small farmers in the landless command area were evicted from previously rented plots and three of these plots were rented out again to new tenants during the irrigation season.

One may wonder why landowners should bring back their previously rented-out land for self-cultivation. One possible explanation is that, in the initial years of irrigation, the high risk of production under costly irrigation was left to small farmers/sharecroppers, but as the irrigation activities were stabilized and prospects of higher income from irrigation were evident, the landowners started bringing back their land for self-cultivation.

Credit

Irrigation as a whole has important implications for small farmers' access to credit to pay for irrigation fees and costly inputs. A recent Bangladesh Agricultural University (BAU) survey in Tangail areas shows that even tubewell owners borrowed large sums of short-term credit in order to meet operating expenses for tubewells. The current study shows that a higher proportion of borrowers obtained credit from moneylenders and paid interest in both cash and kind (table 5.7). But there is no systematic variation in the extent or terms of credit transactions between the farmers of landless and private schemes.

The interest rates for this noninstitutional credit were exorbitantly high. In particular, moneylending for irrigated winter rice production, which charged very high fixed amounts of paddy as interest after the harvest of the crop, has been one of the important ways to appropriate the benefits of irrigation through exploiting small farmers' labor.

One of the possible ways to circumvent the moneylending problem is that the landless groups can extend credit directly to small farmers. They can combine this function with the supply and distribution of seeds, fertilizers and insecticides, together with the irrigation service. The implications of such an approach are that the landless groups, supplying credit and inputs, will be in a position to enforce an adequate level of input use on command-area land by the small farmers and thus raise productivity. This is also likely to minimize the dependence of small farmers on village moneylenders for production as well as consumption credit. In irrigated areas of Tangail, small farmers and landless laborers who could accumulate small savings did engage in lending short-term credit to small and large farmers against high cash or kind interest. But Proshika does not wish to encourage the landless to repeat the exploitative practices of moneylending classes with any savings that they accumulate from this or any other income-generating activity.

Conclusions

This study is limited by the small sample size. The physical and socio-economic features in each of the studied irrigation systems are so different that drawing firm conclusions about small farmers' access to these irrigation programs is difficult. The empirical evidence presented here leads to the following conclusions:

- Small farmers in landless controlled irrigation schemes do not necessarily have any special advantage except that they benefited from the fact that larger overall command areas gave them opportunities to have their plots irrigated. The trend of declining size in landless command areas in recent years seems to have reduced this opportunity to some extent.
- Small farmers and sharecroppers, some of whom are also the members of the landless groups, had greater control over water distribution in landless schemes as compared to private schemes, again as a result of their larger share of the larger command area.
- The water distribution on small farmers' plots in landless schemes appeared to be more efficient as measured in terms of above-average water supplies, increased hours of pumping per unit of land and timely applications of water.
- The plots of small farmers did not have any significant advantage with respect to distance from the landless tubewell.
- In successful landless irrigation schemes with better water supply, a substantial proportion of small farmers had been evicted from sharecropped land by the landowners, who either cultivated these plots themselves or rented them out to others.

These conclusions have mixed implications for our earlier hypotheses concerning the prospective benefits for small farmers in landless schemes. The main advantage to the small farmers is attributed to the larger command areas of the landless schemes, which offer the small farmers more chance to have their plots included. Small farmers and sharecroppers appear to have greater control over the distribution of water on landless schemes, and the distribution of water is more efficient measured in terms of above-average supplies of water, more hours of irrigation per acre and more timely irrigation. On the other hand, on the more successful of the landless STW schemes, a significant number of small farmers had lost sharecropped land that had been taken back by the landowner for cultivation or renting out to others. This might have been associated with better water supply. Finally, the plots of small farmers were not significantly closer to water sources on landless schemes as compared to the private ones.

Table 5.1 Sampling Frame Used for Selecting the Landless-
managed and Privately Managed STW and LLP Schemes

Area	Union Parishes Covered	Type of Scheme	Irrigation Device	Number of Schemes Reported in Operation	Average Command Area in 1984 (acres)	Command Area Reported for the Studied Schemes in 1984 (acres)
Saturia	Attigram	Landless	STW	8	16.61	17.50
	Krishnapur	Private	STW	56	11.93	14.82
Ghior	Balikhora	Landless	STW	5	12.86	15.60
	Singjuri	Private	STW	73	11.80	13.50
Kalkini	Dashar	Landless	LLP	9	28.20	26.48
		Private	LLP	7	7.70	16.00

Information about the number and command areas for both Proshika landless-managed and privately managed schemes were collected and reported by the Proshika field workers.

Table 5.2 Average Acres Owned and Cultivated by the Sample Small Farmers

| | | Average Acres per Farm | | | | | |
| | | Owned | Share-cropped Out | Mort-gaged Out | Share-cropped In | Mort-gaged In | Total Cultivated Land[1] |
Schemes	No. of Small Farmers	1	2	3	4	5	6
Saturia							
Landless (STW)	17	1.06	0.02	0.03	0.98	0.32	2.31
Private (STW)	14	0.99	0.03	0.10	0.86	0.21	1.93
Ghior							
Landless (STW)	15	1.71	0.09	0.07	0.38	0.02	1.95
Private (STW)	19	1.19	0.03	—	0.44	0.02	1.62
Kalkini							
Landless (LLP)	25	0.44	—	0.05	1.28	—	1.67
Private (LLP)	27	0.63	0.03	0.15	0.90	0.08	1.42

1   Column 6 = Col. 1-2-3+4+5.

Table 5.3 Location and Distance of the Nearest Plots from Water Sources

Schemes	Distance of the Nearest Plot from STW/LLP (yds.)	Average No. of Plots Ahead of the Nearest Plots	Average No. of Large Farmers Having Plots Ahead of the Nearest Plot
Saturia			
Landless (STW)	111	3.4	2.1
Private (STW)	130	2.8	1.1
Ghior			
Landless (STW)	101	2.4	1.7
Private (STW)	118	2.9	1.8
Kalkini			
Landless (LLP)	286	11.8	2.5
Private (LLP)	120	4.4	1.5

Table 5.4 Rate of Irrigation Applications on Small Farmers'
Nearest Plots during 1983–84 Winter Rice Season

Schemes	Average No. of Irrigation Applications per Plot	Average Hours of Water Delivery per Application	Total Hours of Water Delivery per Season per Plot Acres[2]		Relative Status of Water Delivery per Application[1]		
					Above Avg. (%)	Near Avg. (%)	Below Avg.(%)
Saturia							
Landless (STW)	16.8	2.4	40.3	109	6	47	47
Private (STW)	12.2	2.0	24.4	68	7	21	7
Ghior							
Landless (STW)	8.7	1.8	15.7	75	—	53	47
Private (STW)	13.4	1.4	18.8	75	16	68	16
Kalkini							
Landless (LLP)	13.4	0.9	12.1	47	20	64	16
Private (LLP)	12.6	0.6	7.6	33	15	66	19

1   Relative status of water delivery per application was estimated on the basis of respondent's opinion.
2   Per-acre estimates are obtained by dividing hours per plot by average plot size.

Table 5.5 Timeliness of Water Supply to Small Farmers'
Nearest Plots and Adequacy of Irrigation

Schemes	% Responses about Timing of Water Supply [1]			% Plots Dried Out	Plots saturated	
	In Time of Need	Delay			Fully	Partially
		Same for All	Worst for Individual			
Saturia						
Landless (STW)	82	12	6	53	76	24
Private (STW)	58	14	28	86	29	71
Ghior						
Landless (STW)	67	33	—	87	60	40
Private (STW)	79	5	16	16	89	11
Kalkini						
Landless (LLP)	92	8	—	20	76	14
Private (LLP)	81	4	15	33	59	41

1   Refers to water supply for plowing, puddling and transplanting.

Table 5.6 Extent of Dependence of Small Farmers
on Sharecropping and Selling of Labor

Schemes	No. of Small Farmers Able to Feed Family from Own Land	No. of Small Farmers Dependent on			
		Selling Labor	Sharecropping	Both	None
Saturia					
Landless	1 (6)	2 (12)	9 (53)	5 (29)	1 (6)
Private	1 (7)	—	5 (36)	5 (36)	4 (28)
Ghior					
Landless	6 (40)	3 (20)	5 (33)	7 (47)	—
Private	4 (21)	1 (5)	7 (37)	4 (21)	7 (37)
Kalkini					
Landless	3 (12)	—	6 (24)	18 (72)	1 (4)
Private	3 (11)	2 (7)	0 (37)	5 (56)	—

Figures in parentheses are percentages of sample farmers.

Table 5.7 Number of Small Farmers Borrowing and
Amount Borrowed from Different Sources during 1983–84 Irrigation Season

Schemes	Number of Borrowers and Amount per Borrower				Interest Rates for Mahajons' Credit	
	Village Mahajons	Relatives	Banks	Cooperatives	Cash	Kind
Saturia						
Landless	1	3	2		120% per annum	na
	(2,000)	(1,167)	(5,000)	—		
Private	4	1	1		120% per annum	na
	(813)	(1,000)	(100)	—		
Ghior						
Landless	5	1	3	—	na	3 maunds of paddy
	(2,500)	(500)	(3,022)		na	for Tk1,000 after winter rice harvest
Private	6	2	3	2	na	3 maunds of paddy
	(1,833)	(550)	(2,356)	(2,700)		for Tk1000 after winter rice harvest
Kalkini						
Landless	13	1	1	2	120% per annum	1.5–6 maunds paddy
	(777)	(800)	(500)	(1,125)		for Tk100.
Private	10	—	—	—	80–120% per annum	1 maund paddy for Tk100
	(410)					after winter rice harvest

Figures in parentheses are amount of credit per borrower.   na=not available.

CHAPTER SIX

Financial Performance of the Landless Irrigation Program

LOAN REPAYMENT IN the agricultural sector in Bangladesh has been very poor, even if not as poor as in other sectors.

A satisfactory financial record is neither a necessary nor sufficient condition for a project such as this to be described as successful; there are many reasons why either short- or long-term subsidies may be warranted. But the long-term accumulation of arrears of financial payments must reduce the autonomy of the debtors in relation to their bankers, and consequently would be a cause for concern. Furthermore, the financial record of individual groups indicates potential problems within the project, and should be a trigger in the monitoring or management information system for further investigations and remedial actions. In this chapter, the overall performance of the project is discussed in financial terms. In the following chapter, we move on to the technical and economic determinants of these experiences.

The original project entailed a loan from the Bangladesh Krishi Bank (BKB) to cover the bulk of groups' capital and operating costs. The groups have repaid about 77 percent of the amount of the loan from BKB that has fallen due, of which 6 percent had been rolled over with loans from Proshika's Revolving Loan Fund (RLF). The exact amount cannot be known for reasons explained below. The remainder was written off by Proshika. In fact, groups appear to have paid back considerably more than the irrigation equipment cost them, because when they got into arrears with their loan repayments, interest at penalty rates accumulated rapidly.[1] The BKB loan charged 16 percent per annum interest on capital loans and 8 percent on operating-cost loans.[2] Penalty rates of interest of 6 percent applied to overdue amounts; consequently, the accumulation of interest on overdue loans was very rapid. The RLF levies a first-year-only arrangement fee of 16 percent. The irrigation program has been financed mainly by the RLF since 1985; about 29 percent of the amount loaned from the RLF for irrigation that was due for payment at the end of July 1987 (that is, after the bulk of loans from the 1986–87 irrigation season had been recovered) was outstanding at that time. This performance should be compared with the World Bank estimate that *recovery* of official loans to the agricultural sector from 1980 was running considerably lower, at 26 percent in 1986 and 46 percent in 1987 (International Bank for Reconstruction and Development (World Bank) 1987: Table 6.3).

Proshika groups appear to have been more successful than their competitors in the private sector, who have had at least as poor a financial record—in the cases for which there is some documentation (see, for example, Bangladesh Agricultural University (BAU) 1985 and 1986). Furthermore, an undoubted advantage of the landless irrigation program is that the income that has been generated has accrued to genuinely poor people, for the most part.[3] Thus, there has almost certainly been an income distribution advantage. Nevertheless, this financial performance implies that, without significant technical and economic improvement, future irrigation loans are likely to run a deficit and therefore will be unable to maintain their real value. If Proshika were to try to offer the same conditions in the future it would have to rely on concessional funding or cross-subsidization.

Financial, Economic and Social Criteria

A financial and an economic assessment of the project differ.

- A financial assessment usually answers the question of whether the project meets its financial targets, which in this case are assumed to be the repayment of loans from project sources.
- An economic assessment is somewhat broader and tries to determine if the project was worthwhile. In the present case, this is taken to mean whether the project could have met all economic costs, including repaying its loans at the rates of interest and over the amortization period specified.[4]

In some cases, groups benefit from ownership and operation of irrigation equipment (besides other income earned with the equipment or employment related to it). These benefits are unquantifiable but their existence might be reflected in the behavior of groups who are willing to run their equipment at a financial loss (see chapter 4). No attempt is made here to produce a social evaluation using one of the methods to derive accounting prices and so on, because such economistic approaches do not generally illumine the processes at work, which are crucial to this type of project.

The distinction is important because financial decisions may be made for specific reasons, which can distort the picture of economic viability. A group that repays a large proportion of its loans in a particular year will appear to have low or negative income, despite good economic performance; likewise, a group that fails to repay its financial obligations in a given year[5] or has repaid its loans earlier and therefore has no outstanding obligations, will appear to have a net income above its real economic value. Therefore, financial assessment would bias conclusions about the economic position of the project.

Analysis of group experiences in different areas and over time requires a consistent basis for comparisons. It also implies some standards by which to evaluate those experiences. The existing normal financial and economic criteria are based on the calculus of a firm in a capitalist economy, but even here there are difficult questions of the appropriate rate of interest to use, how to amortize capital investments and so on. Many of the objectives of the landless irrigation scheme are broader than might be expected of such a firm, but the irrigation enterprise should have financial and economic objectives even if they are not all-important. Without such objectives, losses will be funded uncritically and the groups risk becoming dependent on discretion by Proshika as to whether to continue subsidizing the project. Proshika has naturally resisted these ideas, because its relationship with groups is premised on trust and solidarity with the group, and the idea of calculative neo-Hobbesian behavior on the part of either groups or Proshika workers is repugnant. Nevertheless, the evidence suggests that groups, or rather their members, often act in ways that can be understood as narrowly rational pursuit of self-interest. In particular, they try to default on their loans unless their behavior and performance is monitored. Given the lack of experience with the costs and benefits of these types of irrigation, there were few standards by which to judge the performance of groups. They have not been easy to monitor, either, because, as with most agricultural activities, the actual events occur at considerable distances and in remote and inaccessible areas. Under these circumstances, Proshika has had to build up the experience and skills to judge performance. It is still not clear, for example, for how long losses by a group should be allowed, on the grounds perhaps that losses are necessary for entry into the market; no doubt conditions vary between cases and over time. Hence some sort of financial and economic standards are required both for comparison and evaluation, even if they are not rigidly adhered to. The ability to produce meaningful, accurate quantitative data (rather than niceties of definition of criteria of viability) has been the crucial and limiting factor in interpreting the performance of irrigation groups. Details of calculation (rates of interest, economic life of the equipment and terminal values[6]) are less useful than the actual recording of incomes, expenditure and instrumental variables, such as soil type. In reality, the factual basis for deciding the life of the investment (which will vary by component) could not exist in the early years of the project, so that any procedure would be arbitrary, and even now sufficiently reliable information has not been put together.[7] Thus the exact amortization schedule and interest charges on operating-cost finance employed do not provide an absolute standard for judging performance. Since 1986–87, Proshika has adopted a longer-life, lower rate of interest and larger terminal value than we have used in this book. This partly reflects the belief that maintenance and operation are carried out better now than at the start of the project, when experience was much more limited.

The distinction between financial and economic benefits also applies to the groups' own assessment in that financial returns to groups may differ from economic returns. Groups generally borrow money to cover capital costs of engine, pump, pipes and strainers, installation and yearly operating costs—fuel, labor, spares and repairs. Interest is charged on the loans, and the equipment must be amortized, although if the loan is repaid this may be considered sufficient, because repayment presumably maintains—or establishes—the group's creditworthiness and enables it to borrow again for the same purpose. The financial repayments under the BKB loan, however, are rather more strenuous than a reasonable economic amortization schedule might be, taking into account the likely life of the equipment and its resale value.

Groups and those who assess the project's viability have many different bases for judging financial decisions. For example, a number of groups, because of their particular financial position, appear to have paid off loans more rapidly than the amortization schedule and therefore in some years have lower financial than economic returns. Such early repayment, which is at the expense of either accumulation of group funds or distribution to members, may be rational in view of the high costs of dealing with the BKB and the lack of insurance against years when the irrigation activities make a loss—bearing in mind the high interest penalty charges. Others appear not to have repaid loans according to schedule, despite having the resources to do so, in some cases. Financial returns, then, are not a simple basis for comparisons across groups, whereas economic returns as calculated are a more satisfactory basis for comparison.[8] We have therefore calculated economic returns by applying consistent amortization and operating-cost finance deductions (referred to as net margins),[9] as well as calculating financial returns from the reported figures (referred to here as net incomes). We discuss these matters extensively because of the problems caused by, and the political significance of, improved credit management for and by the poor.

Groups will of course be mainly interested in the financial returns after necessary costs have been met. Their practice has been to pay labor for some tasks involved, which superficially simplifies the problem of valuation. The pump driver and linemen who are required more or less full time have almost always been paid. The labor involved in preparing drains and harvesting the cropshare is generally done collectively by the group, unremunerated, but in a significant number of cases the laborers, whether group members or others, are paid for their work. In cases of collective or unpaid labor it should be asked whether the benefit adequately recompenses the work (see chapter 10). Because the amount of time involved is not known, this question cannot be answered. One role that goes largely unremunerated and yet requires considerable time is that of manager; someone has to organize many and diverse matters, from negotiation of loans and contracts to schedules of water, repairs, fuel supplies, collecting fees and so on. Most of these tasks cannot be delegated to the driver, who generally has mechanical rather than financial or organizational skills. The absence of a paid role for these activities raises questions about why an individual chooses to do this, and suggests that he must receive other benefits, which we have not identified.

Traditionally, economists have argued that a project can be worthwhile even if it did not repay its loans, provided it could have done so; it then becomes a matter of finding the necessary finance (and/or justifying the necessary transfers). The traditional distinction between these two types of assessment is not as clear as it might seem, because actions that follow from financial outcomes can have an important effect on economic performance. If failure to repay loans leads to loss of seasonal finance, this can cause delays—or the fear of them—at the start of irrigation or during its supply, which in turn can affect farmers' willingness to agree to irrigate and to supply their own inputs. This reduces command areas and/or yields, affecting the incomes of groups and farmers and their abilities to pay water charges and repay loans. Borrowers may invest resources to avoid loan repayment or to mitigate the effects of overdue amounts; lending agencies also have to allocate resources to loan management. There are benefits in avoiding repayment if, in the long run, loans will be written off (or if interest does not accumulate). Finally, one must bear in mind the following factors while judging the financial performance of groups:

- During the 1970s, after the traumas of independence, and the 1974 floods and their aftermath, resources from outside local society were made widely available with little or no requirement for repayment,
- Proshika-sponsored shallow tubewell (STW) groups competed with other irrigation groups that continued to be subsidized either explicitly or implicitly through loan default, and
- Proshika groups could not benefit as extensively as their landowning private competitors from the profits of irrigated cultivation.

The BKB Loan

It has not been easy to piece together the course of the loan disbursements for capital and operating costs, repayments and normal and penalty interest accumulation of the BKB loan. BKB did not initially provide separate accounts for operating and capital loans for each group; it tried to avoid providing statements for each group. Instead, it offered statements only for each BKB branch. Some branches dealt with more than one Area Development Center (ADC); some ADCs had groups with loans from more than one branch. When accounts were tendered they were often in the name of individual group members rather than in the registered group name. This was partly due to conservative procedures by BKB, which was unwilling to accept group rather than individual responsibility for the loans. It may also have been due to the recent and rapid expansion of BKB into rural areas and its lack of experience and trained staff to meet these non-traditional needs. It would have taken, perhaps, an exceptional organization, by the standards of other formal sector banks, to have coped with this new type of loan. Just how exceptional may be indicated by the case of the Grameen Bank (Hossain 1984, Rahman 1986). It is not just BKB that has had difficulty in accounting by group; Proshika has also since learned that considerable resources must be devoted to keeping track of groups and their loans in its management of its own RLF.

Many accounts that were finally produced from BKB were alleged to contain substantial errors. Thus not only were there considerable difficulties in disbursing loans and making deposits, but many of the individual group accounts were inaccurately kept. Hence it was not possible to piece together the overall position from the sum of individual accounts, and it is only since 1985–86 that we have been able to relate actual loan repayment to economic performance in any year. There was obviously a need for groups, or more likely Proshika on the groups' behalf, to keep parallel records for checking against BKB's accounts and to provide timely financial information for Proshika's own data requirements. However, the time and skills required to do this in the face of other pressing needs are debatable.

Eventually, Proshika instituted a passbook system, in which all the details of each group's loan transactions and interest accumulation were entered, with a view toward independent of monitoring of group financial performance and the overall position of the loan. Difficulties have been experienced in having the passbooks filled in on time. Each BKB branch had to be visited, often several times, to get an up-to-date account statement and, because of delays in achieving this, it was not easy to collect the passbooks in one place. Furthermore, they have been found to contain substantial arithmetic errors, in a number of cases, and the completeness of the information has been suspect. The situation has now improved and an account for the end of June 1987 for outstanding loans has been collected. No information for previous years is available, however, and it cannot be reconstructed from the passbooks, so no summation of the passbook totals has been made to obtain an aggregate picture. Instead, the agreed annual position of the BKB loan submitted by BKB and agreed to by Proshika has been used to depict its overall position. These problems, which are an important part of the training that has occurred for various actors in the project, constitute a clear set of institutional and management constraints to rural projects of this kind.

The annual statement illustrates the status of the BKB loan, shown in table 6.1 and figure 6.1. In a number of cases actual figures were available but in others they had to be estimated. Thus the target of the BKB loan had to be estimated from disbursements as if they incurred the full interest on the first year, whereas the amount incurred will in fact have been determined by the date on which the money was disbursed and repaid. These discrepancies have been kept to a minimum, consistent with the overall position.

The total outstanding on the loan exceeded the target considerably from the first years of the project. The position ceased to deteriorate in the 1983–84 season, when Proshika realized that BKB was not providing the necessary financial supervision and mounted a loan repayment drive. It is not clear whether this was because BKB had not recorded repayments, whether there were delays in reporting at BKB branches or whether groups had simply not paid. In some cases, it appears that groups were obstructed from payment in the hope of extortion on the part of BKB officials, but there is little doubt that many groups did not attempt to make the target payments. Some would have had difficulty in meeting their repayment schedules, as reported net income figures were not very high in relation to the repayments of operating and capital loans at the specified terms.[10] Figures on repayments are not available, so we cannot match repayment with availability of funds, and it is not possible to infer the element of penalty interest in the accumulated loan total. The amounts overdue fell in 1983–84 and 1984–85, despite widespread flooding in 1983–84, which destroyed irrigated crops and reduced groups' ability to repay. Nevertheless, had it not been for substantial payments Proshika made from the interest accumulated on the deposits made to cover the loan, significant overdue amounts would have accumulated in 1985 and again in 1987.

The repayment record of Proshika groups appears quite satisfactory. About 77 percent of the amount due has been repaid by groups.[11] The performance in terms of the BKB loan is not truly represented by this picture, however, because a number of the BKB loans were repaid from loans made to groups from the Proshika RLF. This was done to avoid further accumulation of interest on outstanding and overdue loans. Exactly how much of the BKB loan was paid off in this manner is impossible to identify, but at least Tk1 million of the RLF loans made in 1985–86 and 1986–87 were longer-term loans to groups that had started irrigation in or before 1984–85, that is, with BKB loans.[12] A number of these loans may have been for new capital equipment, or even to groups that started with RLF loans. The bulk, however, were undoubtedly used to pay off outstanding

BKB loans. A number of groups received short-term loans from the RLF, which they used to repay part of their BKB loans. Also, a number of groups with outstanding loans to BKB have discontinued, as have a number who had their BKB loans rolled over with loans from the RLF, despite an attempt not to take hopeless cases into the RLF. A total of Tk710,000 of the BKB loan is outstanding to groups who have discontinued. Some of this outstanding amount may be secured by the irrigation equipment retained by these discontinued groups. Subtracting Tk1.7 million (Tk1 million of RLF loans that constitute rollovers and Tk720,000 of outstanding BKB loans) from the amount repaid by groups brings the apparent default rate on the BKB loan to just over 33 percent of the amount originally loaned for capital, operating costs and interest (that is, the repayment by groups constituted 67 percent of the BKB loan). This performance must be compared with an average rate of repayment of loans to agriculture, which fell as low as 26 percent in 1986 and averaged less than 46 percent over the period (World Bank 1987). Proshika groups have evidently been able to maintain a repayment rate well above the average for the agricultural sector in a wide range of conditions. Some other non-governmental organizations (NGOs) and special projects reporting high financial success rates have either been heavily supervised and/or in geographically limited—and favorable—conditions; furthermore, we feel that few, if any, have been subject to such vigorous and searching analysis. The general economic and agricultural context of declining physical productivity and profitability (see chapter 7) relates to falling yields, increased need for fertilizers to maintain yields, rising agricultural input prices and stagnant rice prices. These factors may have contributed to the slowdown in agricultural growth and the demand for minor irrigation in particular, as cultivators and water sellers attempted to rationalize their cropping and water decisions in an increasingly unfavorable situation. The widespread flooding of May 1984 may have also severely damaged the winter rice crop, making it difficult for groups to recover sufficient income to repay their loans and making farmers reluctant to risk another winter rice season. Repayments appear to have been worst in the early 1980s, when the price of paddy relative to the price of irrigation inputs was more favorable than it was after 1983–84. Thus, the apparent improvement in financial performance was not simply due to improved economic circumstances.

RLF Irrigation Loans

The unsatisfactory nature of BKB loan disbursement resulted in widespread delays and uncertainty for cultivators[13] about the installation, the time when irrigation equipment would be available and the availability of operating capital at the start of each season. These uncertainties could introduce doubt into the minds of both groups and cultivators about when and whether loans to finance irrigation operating costs would be available, and consequently when irrigation would start—if at all. These problems led to the transfer, for the 1985–86 season, of new capital and operating loans for the irrigation program to the RLF, which had previously been financing relatively few irrigation loans, concentrating on smaller loans for cultivation expenses, trading and so on. As noted above, a number of groups obtained loans from the RLF to pay off their BKB loans.

Irrigation has been an important component of the RLF, accounting for 26 percent of all loans ever disbursed from the RLF and for 34 percent of all overdue loans.[14] Table 6.3 summarizes the disbursement and recovery statistics of the RLF irrigation loans for July 1987.

The distribution of overdue RLF irrigation loans is quite concentrated, both by loan[15] (see table 6.4) and by ADC. Of the overdue total, 53 percent is due to 10 percent of loans (forty-five total loans), and 25 percent of loans account for 83 percent of the overdue total. Most of the amounts overdue to the RLF are due from groups in Sreepur, Saturia, Gabtoli and Harirampur. The deep tubewell (DTW) groups in Sreepur alone comprise more than 36 percent of the total overdue.

Financial Problems

The financial difficulties of irrigation groups manifest themselves in a number of ways. The most obvious are those groups that have discontinued, because difficulties with repaying loans have been the major immediate cause of discontinuation (see table 6.5). Next, and usually more serious, are those cases in which Proshika has had to pay off the loan from its own resources.[16] Discontinued groups will have difficulty repaying their loans unless they can sell their irrigation equipment to cover the outstanding amount. Fifty-six groups have repaid all their loans by themselves, of which twenty-four were still operating in 1986–87,[17] and thirty-two had discontinued. The average amount owed by discontinued groups is Tk15,000. Because many owe very little, some are likely to have debts in excess of the secondhand value of their equipment. Sixty-three discontinued groups had their outstanding loans paid for them by Proshika, thirty-two of which had further outstanding loans with BKB or the RLF. Twenty-two other discontinued groups had outstanding loans to the RLF, sixteen to BKB and eight to both. Loans in the amount of Tk170,000 were outstanding to discontinued groups; of this, Tk603,000 was overdue to the RLF. A significant number of those with outstanding loans started in the early years of the project and should have paid off their loans. Evidently, a considerable number of groups have encountered financial difficulties.

Those groups with loans outstanding to BKB are also generally in difficulties, because most of them have discontinued and the rest are in arrears. Twenty-nine out of the fifty groups with outstanding BKB loans have discontinued, and they account for 67 percent of the Tk1.3 million owing to BKB. Then there are the groups with overdue RLF loans. Nearly Tk1.8 million is overdue, constituting 29 percent of the total due. In many cases, the amount overdue dates back a number of years. Of the amount overdue to the RLF, 32 percent is owed by discontined groups.

On the whole, those groups that have had financial difficulties have also had economic problems. Those with large sums outstanding to the RLF have reported lower net margins, although there are a number of cases (more than twenty-five) that have reported significant net margins but still have substantial overdue loans. Finally, the loans that have been transferred from BKB to the RLF (at least Tk1 million) appear to be groups that, although in financial difficulties, have at least some chance of meeting their operating costs and even, in some cases, repaying their capital loans.

Groups Whose Loans Were Repaid by Proshika

Many groups who started irrigation have discontinued, but just less than 50 percent (63 out of 141) of those who discontinued have had their loans partially or totally written off. The reasons for non-repayment are therefore slightly different from those of discontinuation, which are discussed in more detail below. In theory, capital loans to irrigation groups were secured by the asset purchased—the pump and engine—together with the deposit made by Proshika. The sale of the asset should have covered these loans, except where the equipment had been severely damaged (by floods, breakdowns, fires or other disasters) or, as in one case, stolen. The seasonal operating loans—to pay for fuel, oil, spares, salaries and so on—were secured only by the Proshika deposit. Because the total amounts disbursed to each group are not available, it is not possible to report what proportions of the amounts written off are due to unrepaid capital or to operating loans. In the majority of cases, net revenues generated by groups whose loans were repaid by Proshika appear lower than those of groups that either continued or have discontinued but repaid their own loans (see table 6.6). This is not surprising, because poor financial performance would be expected to follow from poor economic performance. A number of years of poor net returns leads to financial problems manifested as partial or non-repayment of loans, eventually leading to discontinuation. If net returns have been insufficient to cover the operating costs and the drop in value of the equipment, the group will be unable to repay outstanding loans from resale of the irrigation equipment. Evidence supports this interpretation, but there are a number of anomalies where reasonable net margins are associated with repayment of the loan by Proshika. This is particularly the case with the low-lift pumps (LLPs) in Khaliajuri ADC. Here there were two very successful years (1981–82 and 1982–83) at which time loan recovery was the responsibility of BKB. BKB's slackness and Proshika's failure to follow up on financial transactions meant that surpluses were distributed to group members. Floods then destroyed the crops at Khaliajuri in 1983–84 and 1984–85, when there was no revenue with which to repay loans, and the groups were in default.

Voluntary Default

The overall relationship between economic and financial performance suggests that many cases of default will have been involuntary, but some cases of voluntary default, implying financial mismanagement, did occur. An examination of the relationship between the financial difficulties of groups and the amounts of outstanding loans repaid by Proshika shows that, in general, the amounts repaid by Proshika considerably exceeded the gross margins of groups whose loans were repaid for them. But in eight of the twenty-seven cases for which enough data are available, the sum of the annual gross margins exceeded the loan repayments required, suggesting that these groups generated sufficient surplus to pay all their loans but did not do so. In the remaining cases, the sum of gross revenues were less than required to repay loans, but in only one case was the amount repaid by Proshika less than the difference between the gross margin and the estimated loan repayment requirements. If a group had used all its gross margin to repay loans due, then Proshika should only have had to pay the difference between this and loans due. In most cases, the amount repaid considerably exceeded this difference, again suggesting that these groups did not, on the whole, use the gross revenue available to them to meet their loan obligations (although a part of the difference between the amount repaid by Proshika and the excess of the loan obligations over the gross revenue can be accounted for by penalty interest on the overdue loans). These cases are for those groups for which there is enough data to calculate gross margins for *each* year of operation; this was done to avoid wrongly estimating the gross margin by including only some of the years in which the group operated. Because more data are missing for the last (and usually the least successful) year of operation, inclusion of cases in which only some data exist would have overestimated the funds available for repayment. Hence, on the basis of the data reported,[18] the cases presented are unlikely to overestimate the amounts available to repay loans. Thus these data show that, in a significant number of cases, a proportion of the default was voluntary rather than necessitated by lack of revenue. This reveals a further aspect of such projects, namely a contagious effect of general indiscipline in rural credit programs, where credit default by other groups has been tolerated by the state and its bank. This attitude was even shared by local Proshika workers who considered the resultant subsidy to the poor in the landless groups to be valid or legitimate. Default, even partial, can also be induced by competitive pressures from those for whom default has less drastic consequences.

Khaliajuri, Madaripur, Singair, Ghior and Chatalpar ADCs have the largest amounts overdue, and the bulk of these loans have now been written off. Some other ADCs have had some of their loans rolled over with new loans from the RLF (not forgetting that the amounts estimated as rolled over are not known exactly). Sixty-three groups have had all or part of their loans written off by Proshika. Most of the amounts written off have been quite large; although they range from Tk869 to Tk102,000, fifty-one of these groups had amounts between Tk23,000 and Tk76,000 written off, accounting for 77 percent of the total amount (see table 6.7).[19]

More LLP than STW groups have discontinued (even allowing for the rental LLP; the DTW program is too recent for there to be enough examples to warrant any inferences). Eighty-one percent of LLP groups have discontinued, compared to only 46 percent of STW groups. The difference in the proportions requiring loan repayment is not large or statistically significant: forty-three percent of the discontinued LLP groups had loans repaid by Proshika, while just under 50 percent of the STW groups had loans repaid for them.

RLF Loans in Difficulty

For the RLF, Sreepur ADC accounts for the bulk of the overdue loans, with 36 percent of the total. This has been caused by the poor profitability of DTWs that make up the bulk of irrigation groups in this ADC and that account for the majority of the individual loans in large arrears. Other ADCs with substantial amounts overdue to the RLF are Saturia, Gabtoli, Harirampur, Madaripur, Ghior, Mirzapur, Singair and Bhairab. Fifty groups with outstanding RLF loans have discontinued, and it is not clear whether they will be able to repay their loans from sale of the equipment. Proshika is attempting to recover these loans through sale of the irrigation equipment, its transfer to another group or other sources available to the group.

In a number of cases, groups with negative net margins have nevertheless continued—notably in Singair, Madaripur and Sreepur ADCs. These are among the ADCs with substantial overdue amounts outstanding with BKB, owing to the RLF or having loans rolled over by it, all indicating a degree of financial difficulty. Further support for the idea that financial difficulties were largely associated with poor net margins comes from the STW group data (we have noted the exception in the LLP data from Khaliajuri). In nineteen cases, substantial net margins have been reported, but the groups have large amounts overdue to the RLF. These groups are concentrated in Mirzapur and Gabtoli ADCs, and vigilance in maintaining a good repayment record will be a neccessity. It remains to be seen whether Proshika's target of a 10 percent default rate is unreasonable. It will take considerable efforts to achieve and maintain this, revealing the extent of close supervision by the intervening agency needed in projects of this kind. NGOs, operating on a small scale and and relating to the groups on a number of dimensions, may have a comparative advantage over wider-scale government programs with neither the trust nor the favorable field ratios of staff to clients. Such advantage nevertheless also limits the easy replication of such socially progressive rural production projects.

Conclusions

Before examining some of the technical factors underlying the economic performance that largely determined financial performance, the findings so far should be summarized. The following two issues are crucial:

- whether loans have been repaid, and
- to the extent that they have been, whether repayment has been from resources generated by the project.

Answering these questions is not easy. Although apparently the BKB loan has been largely repaid either by groups or by Proshika with interest gained on the deposit made as a guarantee for the loans, this repayment is misleading. Some groups have repaid their loans from other sources rather than from surpluses generated by their irrigation. This occurs either to fund entry to the market or to exercise leverage in other arenas of group struggle. Some of the remaining BKB loans at the time of writing were due to groups who have ceased irrigation. Also, some of the repayment was made by groups rolling over the BKB loan with funds from the RLF. Nevertheless, just less than 70 percent of the loans due to BKB seem to have been repaid by groups. The RLF situation is also complicated in that nearly 30 percent of the amount due is not yet paid, and a considerable amount of the total outstanding is owed by groups that have ceased irrigation. In many cases of groups who have ceased irrigation with outstanding loans, the loans may be repaid from proceeds of the sale of the irrigation equipment, but whether this will be done is not known at the present. If we assume that roughly 30 percent of the amount loaned will not be repaid, as an high estimate, this still compares favorably with loans made to the agricultural sector generally between 1980 and 1986, which, as noted, above averaged less than 50 percent of the overdue.

To the extent that groups have defaulted, there is considerable evidence (although some caution is required in its use) that the default was because they failed to generate sufficient revenue rather than because of delinquency. Groups with economic difficulties were concentrated in a few ADCs. The following chapter will argue that their financial difficulties were largely due to basic lack of economic feasibility rather than, in the majority of cases, willful default. Nevertheless, a significant number of the cases repaid by Proshika were due to laxity in loan repayment in the early years and there are still thought to be problems with underreporting of incomes by groups as a means of at least partly avoiding loan repayments. This led to improved financial monitoring by Proshika and to the employment of qualified agricultural staff who could better assess the economic feasibility and contribute to the solution of difficulties where necessary.

Notes

1. The total amount paid by the groups to BKB is an estimate, because no full statement could be compiled. Approximately 40 percent more than what would have been paid if there had been no arrears was paid to BKB in all, with groups paying roughly what they would have paid if there had been no arrears. Had loan repayment insurance been available, groups would have been able to pay the premiums and not needed arrears.

2. In the first two years of the project, the loan terms were 13 percent interest on outstanding loans plus 3 percent per annum arrangement fee.

3. See BAU 1986 for a slightly different assessment of the distributional impact in some Grameen Bank Irrigation Groups.

4. We do not address the question of Proshika's management costs. If the project is viewed as a long-term investment, aimed in part to build up Proshika's capability to facilitate this type of enterprise, the outcome so far cannot answer the question whether it was worthwhile. It is worth noting, however, that in the early years of the project one staff member was more or less full time on the project, and at each ADC managing was part of the responsibilities of one member of the field staff. Starting in 1985, eleven Irrigation Extension Workers have been appointed, each with responsibility for a number of ADCs. Proshika believes that, after a few years, the costs of the program will be covered by a charge of 6 percent of the loans made for capital and operating costs.

5. A group may decide to pay off loans early for a number of reasons, and thereby avoid the costs of arranging future transactions with BKB.

6. Different technologies in different locations and at different times, with different policies of maintenance, repairs and so on, should no doubt have different amortization arrangements. Amortization should be different for the different components of irrigation, and might be better related, at least for some pieces of equipment, to hours of operation rather than to time, because this is what determines deterioration of the equipment.

7. For example, we have not been able to show clear differences in maintenance costs among different makes and models, although there should be such differences.

8. A further factor is that because of the problems with the reporting of the BKB loan, financial returns for each year cannot be calculated. The financial position of the RLF loans are available only for July 1987, and a significant number of these loans have not yet been linked to particular groups; thus, the financial performance by group of the RLF loan cannot be derived.

9. Net incomes (NI) are the difference between reported incomes and reported outgoings; thus they are calculated as Gross Income (GI) less Operating Costs (OC) plus seasonal finance received (OCF) less loans repaid (TREP) [Gross Margin (GM) = GI -OC]. Net Margins (NM) are calculated as GM less nominal

depreciation [calculated as 0.3504 x Total Capital Costs] less nominal seasonal operating cost finance [calculated as OC x 0.08].

10. 16 percent on capital costs and 8 percent on operating costs; penalty rates of interest applied to overdue loans.

11. This is calculated from table 6.2 as: (Cum. repaid by groups)/(Cum. Sum + total overdue – repaid by Proshika).

12. Seasonal loans in these groups nominally had a duration of only one year. In order to be conservative, we have excluded the BLF loans that were due to be repaid in two years as well as those that were to be repaid in one year from the total calculated as rolled over. Of these capital loans, the bulk was made to groups starting in 1982–83, 1983–84 and 1984–85—Tk172,000, 414,000 and 258,000 respectively.

13. This would, of course, affect their willingness to prepare land and seedlings, to obtain inputs and credit for dry season cultivation and to put their land under irrigation. It can also mean that seedlings prepared on time can be overmature by the time irrigation equipment is commissioned. This is a major problem both in the year of installation, when capital and operating loans are required, and in later years, when operating loans are necessary.

14. The exact proportions of these July 1987 RLF figures vary with the date at which calculations are made, because both disbursement and repayment for most types of loans are made in different seasons for different categories.

15. It is not yet possible to calculate the distribution by group. Some groups have two loans—one for operating and one for capital. Where this is the case and any amount is overdue, it is likely to be overdue on both accounts.

16. An exception to this assumption occurs in the case of rented LLP in Chatal-par ADC, where pumps must be returned after one year and where, because of the rotation system operated by the BADC, from whom the pumps are rented, groups who have rented pumps in one year have not had them in another.

17. Most of the groups that repaid all their loans started irrigation in the early years of the project, but eighteen apparently started in 1985–86 or 1986–87. Some of these provided their own finance, but a number may have had loans from the RLF that have not yet been attributed to them. The distribution of groups by loan status is shown below (this table excludes the thirty-nine RLF loans that have not been attributed):

| | *Year Group Started Irrigation* | | | | | | | |
	80–81	*81–82*	*82–83*	*83–84*	*84–85*	*85–86*	*86–87*	*Total*
No outstanding loans		12	9	11	6	9	9	56
Paid off in part by Proshika	24	2	7	9				63
Loans outstanding:								
with RLF	2	11	9	13	18	48	41	142
with BKB			10	1	5	2	1	19
with both			1	1	4	10	8	24
Total	26	58	30	48	34	57	51	304

* Excludes seven groups who had loans repaid and also still have outstanding loans with BKB.

18. One area of doubt concerns the returns to groups in Khaliajuri, which constitute three of the eight cases with positive gross margins, but are not large enough to repay all loans. The incomes of these groups may have been overestimated if estimated income rather than income actually received was reported.

19. These data exclude the groups involved in a final write-off of Tk1.48 million. in 1988, affecting the overdue loans of forty more groups. Most of the remaining write-offs were in Saturia, Ulania, Singair, Harirampur and Ghior. These were in the main groups that had made some repayments to BKB, but had fallen behind. Because of continuing failure to improve their position, they were unlikely to catch up.

Table 6.1 BKB Loan Schedule (Tk 000)

Loan Category	80–81	81–82	82–83	83–84	84–85	85–86	86–87	87–88
Target BKB loan[1]	1,052	1,311	1,359	2,139	2,559	1,793	1,071	370
Total outstanding[2]	0	2,071	1,910	3,828	3,929	3,364	3,104	275
Estimated overdue,		760	551	1,689	1,369	1,571	2030	2,380
Repaid by Proshika						1,064	931	2,564
Loan rolled over								
by RLF (approx[3])						94	786	221

Source: BKB annual statement of irrigation loans to Proshika groups.

1 The target loan is calculated from the capital disbursed per year amortized over five years at 16 percent per annum. Operating loans should have been repaid at the end of the irrigation season and therefore should not appear in the loan schedule (that is, all overdue sums should repaid before the start of the next financial year).

2 The amount repaid by Proshika should be deducted from the total outstanding to arrive at the net amount outstanding in that year.

3 This is the sum of loans from the RLF, to be repaid after three or more years, made in 1985–86, with six or seven to groups starting before or in 1984–85. Most such loans seem to have been used to repay outstanding BKB capital and operating loans.

Table 6.2 Composition of BKB Loan (Tk 000)

Loan Category	80–81	81–82	82–83	83–84	84–85	85–86	86–87	87–88
New capital[1]	1,231	546	446	1,453	1,405			
Old capital[1]		1,386	1,486	2,783	2,875	2,683	2,384	1,665
New operating[1]	530	839	1,565	1,227	1,275			
Old operating[1]		685	424	1,045	1,053	681	720	308
Repaid by Proshika						1,064	931	2,564
Total outstanding[2]	0	2,071	1,910	3,828	3,929	3,364	3,104	2,750
Overdue capital[1,3]						731	862	1,143
Overdue operating[1,3]						585	585	907
Total overdue		760	551	1,689	1,369	1,571	2,033	2,380
Estimated repayments	157	2,307	973	3,965	4,492	1,151	1,237	3,258
Cum. sum	157	2,464	3,437	7,401	11,894	11,930	12,285	12,980
Cum repaid by Proshika						1,064	1,995	4,559
Cum repaid by groups	157	2,464	3,437	7,401	11,894	11,980	12,285	12,980
of which repaid from RLF						94	880	1,100

1 BKB annual statements.
2 Estimated up to 1985–86.
3 Not given for 1980–81 to 1984–85.

Table 6.3 Proshika RLF Irrigation Loans by Year, July 1987 (Tk 000)

All Irrigation Loans	80–81	81–82	82–83	83–84	84–85	85–86	86–87	87–88
Number of loans	1	13	32	36	36	155	178	452
Disbursed	21	33	179	186	349	3,886	3,389	8,054
Total overdue	19	5	52	56	106	979	29	1,187
Percent overdue[1]	88	4	19	30	26	37	3	20

1 The proportion overdue is the amount overdue divided by the amount of loan plus service charge due according to the loan agreement.

Table 6.4 Distribution of Overdue RLF Irrigation Loans by Size, July 1987

Amount Overdue per Loan			Number of Cases	Total Sum Overdue in Category (Tk 000)	Mean Overdue per Loan (Tk 000)
	<=	-9,750	4	-77	-19
-9,750	<=	-2,080	18	-86	-5
> -2,080	<=	-100	22	-20	-.9
> -100	<=	0	14	-.7	-.05
> 0	<=	875	167	28	.2
> 875	<=	5,700	113	309	3
> 5,700	<=	13,907	68	603	9
> 13,970	<=	21,244	23	384	17
> 21,244	<=	30,464	18	461	26
> 30,464			4	194	48

Negative overdue amounts correspond partly to groups that have paid off their loans in advance of the schedules agreed in the loan agreement, and partly to clerical errors where a group has more than one loan from the RLF and repayments have been recorded against the wrong loan. The distribution of overdue amounts by group (rather than loan) is discussed below.

Table 6.5 Loan Status of Proshika Irrigation Groups, July 1987[1]

Loans Outstanding	Total	Continuing			Discontinued		
		Number	Amount (Tk 000) RLF	BKB	Number	Amount (Tk 000) RLF	BKB
None	56	24	-7		32	-.2	
to RLF	142	122	3,676[2]		22	861	
			(1,061)			(455)	
to BKB	19	3	-2	118	16		471
to RLF and BKB	24	16	179	494	8	76	231
			(97)			(41)	
Written off			31				
Written off and overdue					32	99	42
						(59)	(99)
Not known[3]	6	6	42				
			(34)				
Total		171	3,889	588	140	967	745
			(1,192)	(536)		(603)	

1 Figures in parentheses are amounts overdue to the RLF. Amounts overdue to BKB are not known.
2 Number of ADCs with loans not attributed to groups, hence whether discontinued not known.
3 Of which the DTW in Sreepur contributed Tk 640,000.

Table 6.6 Mean Net Margins by Technology and Financial Performance[1]

Technology	Continuing		Discontinued		Rolled Over	
	Mean	*Number*	*Mean*	*Number*	*Mean*	*Number*
DTW	-5,965	20	-50,770	3		
STW	3,191	107	-6,313	44	-8,216	32
LLP[2]	9,676	32	2,873	9	-3,387	13
Mean	3,348	159	-7,002	56	-6,661	45

Write-off/Rollover Status

	Not Written Off		Written Off		Not Rolled Over		Rolled Over	
	Mean	*Number*	*Mean*	*Number*	*Mean*	*Number*	*Mean*	*Number*
STW	-2,530	102	-8,216	33	-3,171	106	-5,332	29
LLP[2]	5,566	30	-1,366	17	3,312	44	-4,893	3

Default Status

	Not Defaulted		Defaulted	
	Mean	*Number*	*Mean*	*Number*
STW	-1,369	73	-6,667	62
LLP[2]	6,371	27	-1,737	20

1 Tk per group.
2 LLP figures exclude Khaliajuri, and in the case of discontinued groups also exclude rented LLP at Chatalpar.

Table 6.7 Distribution of Loans Written Off

ADC	Amounts Repaid by Proshika per Group (Tk 000)							
	>0 ≤ 16	>16 ≤ 23	>23 ≤ 27	>27 ≤ 36	>36 ≤ 46	>46 ≤ 75	>76 ≤ 85	>85
Bhairab	1	1	5	5	1			
Singair				1	1			
Ghior			1	1	1	1		
Ulania			2	2	1			
Khaliajuri					2	5	2	3
Kalkini	1			2	6			
Madaripur			1	3	1	1		
Atpara						1	1	
Chatalpar	1	2	1			1		
Total	3	3	10	16	16	9	3	3

Table 6.8 Distribution of Financial Problems by Technology

Technology		Groups Started before 1986–87		Total
	Continuing	Discontinued	Repaid by Proshika	
DTW	8	3		11
STW	89	44	33	166
LLP	14	30[1]	29	73

1 Includes rental LLP in Chatalpar ADC

Figure 6.1   BKB Target and Actual Loan

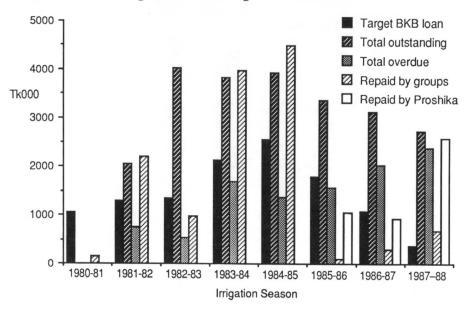

Figure 6.2   Composition of BKB Loan

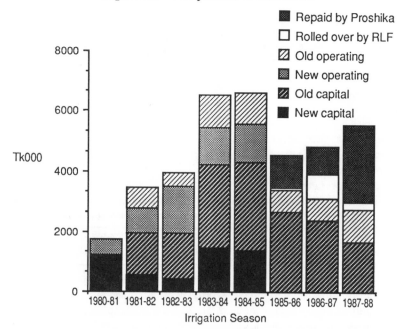

CHAPTER SEVEN

Economic and Technical Performance

THE FACTORS UNDERLYING the performance of minor irrigation equipment can be divided into five categories: hydro-geological, agro-ecological, economic, managerial or organizational and socio-political. The hydro-geological and agro-economic factors define the technical aspects of water availablity and crop-soil-water relationships that determine the production function for irrigation. Prices of inputs and outputs to water supply and paddy production are crucial determinants of the demand for and profitability of water selling. This chapter emphasizes the technical and economic factors that underly the performance of minor irrigation, rather than the socio-political factors, which receive ample treatment in the rest of this book.

Main Determinants of Tubewell Performance

In chapter 6, we showed that financial performance in terms of the proportion of the loans due that were repaid was strongly related to the economic performance as measured by net margins, even though there were a number of cases, especially during the early years of the project, in which this association broke down because of the failure of the Bangladesh Krishi Bank (BKB) and Proshika to monitor loan repayments. In this chapter, we investigate the factors associated with economic performance. We are largely restricted to analysis of the monitoring data collected by Proshika, the *ex post facto* reports of Proshika staff on discontinued groups sometimes made several years after the group discontinued, discussions with Proshika staff about issues arising from the analysis and occasional field visits during 1986–87. Analyzing past performance has generally been secondary to building up Proshika's capability to undertake its own monitoring. These constraints have been quite severe, especially because the quality of the monitoring data deteriorated considerably between 1981–82 and 1984–85. Some details of these problems are given in appendix B.

Command area and yield, together with weather, soil type and the quantity and timing of water applied, are the main components of physical productivity; command areas and yield may be inversely related beyond a certain area if extra command area entails a less satisfactory supply of water and consequent lower yield. Generally speaking, there should be some optimum combination of yield and command area. Irrigation capacity is likely to restrict command area during land preparation, and may restrict yield during the periods in April and May when the water demand of rice is greatest. In this latter period water needs can be met by rainfall, which reduces pumping costs, but this is unpredictable and if there is a drought at this time a large command area will require continual pumping to minimize yield reductions. Floods and hail are also likely to damage the winter rice crop from March through to harvest. The likelihood of mechanical breakdowns and consequent water scarcity must be taken into account; greater command areas imply longer working hours and consequent greater likelihood of breakdown. Temperatures and other environmental factors such as pests, diseases, hail and so on can also affect yields. Thus the outcome will be uncertain, and water suppliers and users must gamble on whether the extra area is worthwhile, taking one year with another.

The best combination of command area and yield will of course depend on economic factors, and in particular on paddy prices, the water pricing system and the costs of inputs (fuel, spares, repairs and salaries). Command areas and intensity of irrigation cannot be decided independently by water sellers, however; they also depend on the attractiveness of irrigation to cultivators. Prices of inputs to cultivators are relevant, because the of cultivators' choices whether to irrigate and how much fertilizer, labor, and so on to use will affect the return to water sellers, although the exact nature of the connection will depend on how water is contracted for. Furthermore, command area and irrigation intensity are determined by considerations of short-term returns to water sellers. If profits are greater than normal profits, water sellers can expect competitors to enter the market, intruding on their command areas and putting pressure on them to improve the quality of their service or reduce their charges.

Economic Background

Table 7.1 shows the growth in numbers of irrigation units in Bangladesh. The numbers of low-lift pumps (LLPs) under the rental system grew rapidly up to 1973, after which the growth slowed considerably; following the introduction of the privatization policy in 1980, the rental LLPs were sold off to the private sector. Many of these machines either went to other uses or were old and no longer serviceable, so in 1986 a census of minor irrigation equipment found only 30,500 2 cubic-feet-per-second (cu.sec) LLPs in operation out of the 50,000 that had been sold. Installation of deep tubewells (DTWs) started in the mid 1960s and between 1,000 and 1,500 per year have been installed since the mid 1970s. The numbers of shallow tubewells (STWs) sold per year increased steadily during the 1970s and rose dramatically in 1980–81 and 1982–83. Sales by the Bangladesh Agricultural Development Corporation (BADC) fell sharply in 1983–84, as a result of investigations into allegations of corruption after the assassination of General Zia, and as the Ministry of Agriculture (MoA) imposed controls on sales of STWs in some *Upazila* because of estimates that numbers had reached the safe extraction limit. BADC was left with large unsold stocks, especially of the less-desired 2,200 revolutions per minute (rpm) models. Restricted sales by BADC were allowed but were limited by lack of demand for the 2,200 rpm models. Sales in the private sector and by BKB remained buoyant in 1983–84 and 1984–85 (they were unaffected by bureaucratic restrictions), and there were limited sales through Bangladesh Rural Development Board (BRDB) under the World Bank's Rural Development 2 (RD2) project. Sales started to pick up again in 1986–87, but these were mainly of stocks of the less-desired 2,200 rpm models held by BADC, which were sold at knockdown prices as pumping sets (that is, an engine coupled to pump only, without tubewell pipe, strainer and so on). A new feature gave rise to imports and sales of much cheaper Chinese diesel engines for STWs entirely in the private sector (not linked to any aid project); the numbers of these engines used for STWs have had to be estimated, but comparison of the estimated numbers distributed with those found in the censuses conducted by the Agricultural Sector Team (AST) in 1987 and 1989 (see table 7.1) are approximately consistent given that considerable numbers of STW engines are known to have been diverted to other uses, at least seasonally. There has been considerable controversy over the causes of the slowdown in agricultural production in the mid 1980s and the linked fall in STW sales (Agricultural Sector Review 1989). The World Bank attributes these trends to bureaucratic impediments to STW imports and distribution. Leftist paternalists suggest the slowdown was due to the contradiction of private-sector market-oriented strategies promoted by the World Bank and the United States Agency for International Development (USAID) (for example, Osmani and Quassem 1985). Below, we show that the slowdown, which was also experienced by the Proshika irrigation groups, was associated with unfavorable import-to-export price trends, which reduced the profitability of winter rice cultivation and also the profitability of Proshika irrigation groups. This economic explanation has significant policy implications.

Another expected major source of agricultural growth was increased numbers and improved capacity utilization of DTWs; however, although reliable figures are hard to come by, there appears to have been little improvement in the poor capacity utilization of DTWs reported earlier (see Bottrall 1983) for a summary of the evidence on the 1970s; BADC gives an average command area of just over 47 acres in the winter rice season of 1985–86, and the International Development Association (IDA) DTW-2 project monitoring reported an average of about 40 acres for fifteen hundred DTWs within that project in 1985–86, increasing to 57 acres in 1988–89[1]). Furthermore, the rate of installation of DTWs slowed because of lack of demand, even at the subsidized prices at which they are made available. Here again, sales improved toward the end of the 1980s, partly, no doubt, for the same reasons STW sales improved.

The rapid rise in STW irrigation in the early 1980s largely accounted for the impressive rate of growth in agricultural production, estimated to have been between 2.0 and 3.5 percent per year since independence in 1971 (as the growth in LLP irrigation had in the early 1970s (Boyce 1987). Since 1983–84, following the decline in the sale rate of STWs, agricultural growth has apparently slowed to below the rate of population growth, although the fall in production growth rate was not as dramatic as the fall in rate of sales of STWs. This is causes considerable concern, because continued growth of STW irrigation was expected to be a major source of growth of agricultural production during the Third Five-Year Plan (3FYP)[2]. Growth of winter rice output picked up strongly in 1986–87, but total production has been stagnant because the monsoon flooding damage in 1987 and 1988 offset the dramatic rises in winter rice in those years.

These recent trends have been explained in different ways. The downturn in demand for tubewells and agricultural production is variously attributed to the following:

- the policies of privatization and the removal of subsidies, pursued since 1980, that have resulted in higher input and irrigation equipment prices and the failure of rice prices to rise to offset these cost increases[3],
- the technical and institutional factors that caused poor capacity utilization of irrigation equipment, following a period of rapid growth of sales in the early 1980s to meet unsatisfied demand at existing levels of capacity utilization (these problems have been largely attributed to irrigation management deficiencies), and
- institutional constraints, particularly the restrictions on imports, spacing and credit.

The determinants of tubewell demand are complex (see, for example, Gill 1983). Not only do numerous factors affect the costs and returns to the main irrigated crop, but irrigated cropping entails shifts in the cropping pattern in other seasons. The main demand for tubewells has been to irrigate the winter rice crop that has generally in recent years been planted in January or February and harvested in May or June. Formerly, winter rice was planted and harvested earlier, but this resulted in lower yields and higher pumping costs, compared with later plantings. The later the planting, the more likely it was that the period of peak water demand would coincide with early rains, in April and May, which herald the main monsoon. This, however, also increased the likelihood of early flood damage, as occurred in May and June of 1984, and hail damage. Also, in some cases it was difficult to arrange early planting if there were delays in harvesting the *aman* rice crop. Later planting has meant that it was usually impossible to grow *aus*, mixed *aus/aman* or jute on winter rice land. Earlier plantings also prevented the growth of *rabi* crops, whereas later plantings allow a short season of *rabi* crops such as mustard or potatoes. In other areas, especially in North Bengal, irrigation has extended and supplemented existing rainfed seasons, enabling earlier transplanted *aus* and more water for *aman* at the end of the monsoon. In parts of western Bangladesh (Kushtia and Jessore), tobacco crops have needed some irrigation.

The main economic influences on the demand for tubewells (with appropriate allowance for risks) will be their capital and operating costs, the costs and returns to winter rice and the opportunity costs of alternative crops, especially *aus* and jute. The appropriate prices in recent years for these variables are not easy to determine for the following reasons:

- The nominal prices of STWs, which are almost universally sold with credit, have increased rapidly, but the real cost to buyers depends on the level of credit repayments which, as noted in chapter 6, have fallen well behind,
- Rental payments for irrigation equipment are often not made, and nonrepayment of credit applies to operating as well as capital costs,
- In the imperfect factor, product, and credit markets of rural Bangladesh the seasonal expectations of prices of crops and of agricultural inputs that affect cultivation and irrigation investment decisions also defy simple definition, and it is not clear how accurate and meaningful official statistics are on these variables, and
- Marked regional and local variations in hydro-geological, agro-ecological and economic conditions affect the economics of winter rice production.

Tables 7.2 and 7.3 set out price and quantity series from official sources for some of the main variables.

Under the policy of privatization, the nominal unit cost of all types of irrigation equipment rose sharply in the early and mid 1980s (table 7.2); however, from 1979–80 to 1982–83 the sales of STWs and LLPs rose rapidly, presumably because of increased availability, liberal credit and bureaucratic efforts by government agencies. The price of fertilizers relative to the price of rice (table 7.3) also rose sharply between 1980–81 and 1982–83, and while fertilizer use stagnated until 1981–82, it rose rapidly between 1981–82 and 1984–85, notwithstanding the continued high relative prices. Most fertilizer (about 50 percent) is used on winter rice and *rabi*, mainly wheat, crops.[4] The price of diesel fuel, which accounts for 50 to 60 percent of irrigation operating costs, rose sharply until 1981–82 but remained constant thereafter. Rural wages increased from 1979–80, especially after 1983–84, when they seem to have risen in real terms; because labor costs are a more important component of winter rice production

costs than fertilizers[5] this probably had more of an effect on the profitability of winter rice production than did the earlier rise in fertilizer prices.[6] As
noted above, irrigation equipment was purchased mainly with formal sector credit, whose repayment rates were very low. The rate of disbursals
rose rapidly until 1984 and fell sharply in 1986; in 1987 there was a sharp
increase in repayments, following pressure from international aid agencies, giving rise to a credit squeeze. The price of rice fell sharply at the harvest of the 1984–85 winter rice crop, but has risen steadily from 1986
through 1987, although there have still been sharp falls in the price at the
time of the winter rice harvest. Nevertheless, the main input-output price
ratios for irrigated winter rice production, which deteriorated significantly
from the early 1980s, and especially after 1984, improved from 1987 as the
paddy price continued to rise, while fertilizer prices and wage rates actually fell slightly. This made irrigation considerably more profitable (see
below).

The area of wheat rose rapidly in 1979–80 and 1980–81, and winter rice
acreage rose steadily up to 1984–85 (with the exception of 1983–84). These
increases appear to have come partly at the expense of the areas under
aus and jute, which declined steadily from 1977–88. The decline in the
combined jute and *aus* acreage has been partly due to the rise of winter
rice, but the decline in jute has been the more precipitate due to its relative
price fall, at least until 1985–86, when there was a sharp increase in jute at
the expense of *aus* following the sharp jute price rise in 1984.

Thus, taking a naive view of these trends, it seems that there was a
sharp rise in irrigation at a time when prices of inputs, particularly irrigation equipment, fertilizers and diesel, were rising sharply in relation to the
price of rice; the price of the competing jute and *rabi* crops had been
falling in the early 1980s when winter rice acreage was rising. Costs of
spares and maintenance of irrigation may have increased in part because
of the aging of irrigation equipment, although this would have affected
new sales only if it had altered expectations of profitability. The rise in the
acreage of jute in 1985 seems not to have greatly reduced the winter rice
acreage (reported in 1984–85), and therefore probably came mainly at the
expense of *aus*. The downturn in STW sales has occurred while these
input-to-rice price ratios have risen less sharply, been roughly constant, or
declined; the exceptions are that the real wage rate-to-fertilizer price ratio
rose sharply from 1983 and the availability of credit declined as it became
evident that repayment of loans was very poor for irrigation equipment, as
for most formal sector credit. Easy opportunities for irrigation may have
been taken up first and remaining sites may be more marginal, or the first-
comers, having sunk costs, may be able to remain in business until they
have to replace their equipment, while potential competitors cannot enter
the market. Alternatively, early expectations were perhaps overoptimistic;
or there may have been supply constraints other than through the credit
supply. Falloff in demand, however, remains the most likely explanation for

the decline in the agricultural growth rate and irrigation equipment sales in the mid 1980s, due to lower levels and expectations of profits from winter rice cultivation and water selling.

Some statistical support for these arguments can be provided; thus when the rate of growth of winter rice production from year to year is regressed on input-output price ratios, the regression coefficients are of the expected sign and are statistically significant. Using data from 1979 to 1989, we estimated the following:

$$BGr_t = 0.017 + .0025 \ \frac{BP_{t-1}}{W_{t-1}} + 0.032 \ \frac{BP_t}{U_t} - 0.334 \ D_{1984}$$

$r^2 = 0.75$ (2.66)   (2.29)   (3.66)

where BGr = growth in winter rice production
$BP_{t-1,t}$ = winter rice harvest price in last and current year
W_{t-1} = agricultural wages last year (annual average)
U_t = urea price in present year
D_{1984} = a dummy variable to represent the effects of the floods in 1984[7]

figures in parentheses are "t" values

A regression of the growth in area of winter rice with the same variables does not give such satisfactory results, although all the coefficients are of the same sign. But an alternative specification, regressing growth rates of winter rice production and winter rice acreage on the ratios of growth in the winter rice price to the growth in wage rates (both lagged by one year) gave expected and statistically significant results.[8] The results of this type of exercise are not expected to be very precise because structural changes in the production system are taking place (hence the restriction of the data series to the period 1981–89, because prior to 1981 supplies of STW and other minor irrigation equipment were bureaucratically controlled rather than responsive to market demand) and the system must be far from equilibrium. Prices and government policy are changing rapidly (for example, rice and input prices, also short-term and medium-term agricultural credit policies), making it hard for farmers to adjust in the short run. There are also major shifts in production functions and major fluctuations due to weather, floods, prices and so on.

Many of the trends up to 1982–83 might be explained in terms of unsatisfied potential demand in the early 1980s. This period has been followed by a process of rationalization from 1983–84 as the most favorable sites were used up, the unfavorable trends in price incentives that had followed privatization were not reversed and credit was less freely available (for similar views see Osmani and Quasem 1985; and Hossain 1984). Agronomic problems arising from the increase in cropping intensity may have also limited response to fertilizer and high-yield varieties (HYV) (Hossain and Salim, in BAU 1986). Renewed growth in demand was evident in 1986–87 and numbers of STW sales increased sharply in 1987.

The bureaucratic restrictions imposed by the MoA have been blamed for the collapse in STW sales, which was partly mirrored in the fall in sales of DTWs, although here there were added problems of conflict between BADC and the BRDB. Several years passed before this fall was expressed in installations of DTWs. Here it will be argued that the restrictions on siting and imports, while undoubtedly potentially significant, were only part of the problem. More significant was the fall in demand that came about because of (a) a rise in the agricultural wage rate relative to the harvest price of winter rice and (b) a fall in the winter rice price relative to the price of fertilizer. Both these factors resulted in a decline in the profitability of winter rice cultivation for farmers and hence a fall in the derived demand for STWs. This decline in profitability was reflected in declining economic and financial performance of landless water sellers. As an account of developments in minor irrigation, this argument has considerable significance in redirecting the attention of policymakers and their advisors, away from its almost exclusive focus on institutional obstacles to agricultural growth, toward the macroeconomic factors affecting agricultural input and output prices.

Demand was tailing off in 1984–85 as a result (as shown above) of declining incentives for winter rice production. This, following the damaging floods in May 1984, caused many water sellers and winter rice cultivators to suffer heavy losses. Demand for STWs collapsed in 1985–86 as a result of the dramatic fall in the winter rice price in May 1985. Several thousand STWs, imported by the private sector in 1983–85 for the RD2 project of BRDB, remained largely unsold because of bureaucratic red tape and other difficulties with sales to KSS through the project. These could have been sold outside the project but, by the time this was realized (about mid 1985), demand had collapsed. Most were eventually sold in 1988 (following the rise in demand rather than the deregulation of STW siting). Thus the collapse of STW sales in 1985–86 had little to do with the import ban on STW engines that had been imposed by the Ministry of Agriculture in 1985, because there were ample STWs in private-sector hands to be sold if there was a demand. The restrictions on imports may have temporarily prevented the import of the much cheaper Chinese STW engines. Informal barriers to importing were already imposed by the need for importers to obtain a letter from the Secretary for Agriculture certifying that the use of the equipment would be for agriculture so that preferential (zero) tariff rate could be obtained. These restrictions were the result of a panic about groundwater drawdown externalities started by some problems with a seasonal drawdown of the pumping water level in some areas of Rajshahi in 1983; members of the Bangladesh bureaucracy also objected to the policies of privatization based on the belief that this would lead to increased inequality and impoverishment of the poorer classes. These leftist nationalists and neopopulists were widely supported by academic and consultancy reports, which generally supported bureaucratic restrictions on siting of irrigation equipment, control of DTWs by cooperatives and the promotion of appropriate labor-intensive irrigation technologies (see Hossain and Jones 1983; Howes 1985; Osmani and Quassem 1985; Boyce 1987; Biggs and Griffith 1987; and others). The seasonal drawdown seems to have been the result of unusual conditions; the rains were less than normal at the end of the monsoon in 1982, and there was a very rapid rise in the numbers of STWs installed in 1981–82 and 1982–83. Fears about groundwater externalities were widely repeated (see Boyce 1987) and controls on STW siting almost universally supported until 1988, when all controls were temporarily lifted. The ban on imports was lifted in 1986 but the informal restrictions remained until 1988 when all imports of diesel engines of less than 20 hp were allowed in duty free. Demand increased somewhat in 1986–87, following the good winter rice harvest price in May and June 1986, but sales of STWs did not pick up significantly. Perhaps this was partly because demand was still limited, especially for the higher priced machines available, and partly because of caution after two years of poor returns to winter rice cultivation (due to floods in 1984 and unfavorable input/ouput price movements). BADC, however, was able to start selling off its huge stocks of the less desired 2,200 rpm models at nearly 60 percent discount (these stocks may well have contributed to the reluctance of the private sector to import more STWs for fear that BADC might spoil their market by dumping its stocks, as in fact happened). In 1986, some Chinese engines suitable for STWs were imported for the first time, and it appears that these imports have increased every year since. BADC had sold off most of its stocks by 1989 and was able to sell newly imported models again in 1989.

Since 1986, winter rice prices have become steadily more attractive relative to wage rates and fertilizer prices. The effect would have been even more pronounced had the government been willing to implement a procurement policy to support its announced prices. Instead, in each of the last three years, as in 1985, the paddy price collapsed immediately after the winter rice harvest, so that those relying on the sale of paddy to pay debts incurred for water supply and winter rice cultivation costs suffered unnecessary declines in returns. Government has been unable to procure more because of the orientation of food procurement and stock policy to meeting urban food demand rather than farmers' needs for incentive prices. More surprising, perhaps, is the failure of institutions such as the World Bank (which recently has placed so much emphasis on getting prices right) to notice or give sufficient emphasis to its importance in this case. For example, it argues that "there is little evidence to suggest that inadequate incentives are a cause of the recent slowdown in foodgrain production" (World Bank 1989:39).[9] It bases this argument on comparisons of average farm budgets, input-output price ratios and nominal protection coefficients with neighboring countries that (apart from the major problems with all such comparisons) completely fail to take account of the differing risks, ability to take risks, income and asset levels of producers in these different countries. However, as we have shown, given the effects of fertilizer price rises in the early 1980s, wage rises in the mid 1980s and harvest paddy price rises toward the end of the 1980s, about 75 percent of the variation in growth rates of winter rice acreage and production can be accounted for. This, we believe, also broadly accounts for the overall pattern of demand for irrigation equipment. The techniques of the landless program have to be assessed within this context.

Changes in Performance over Time

In view of the fairly optimistic assessment of the groups' performance in 1981–82, the changes in performance over time are worth examining. The Proshika program grew fairly rapidly until 1983–84 (see Tables 7.4 and 7.5).[10] Following the loan repayment drive and the floods of that year, a number of groups discontinued, and the number of new groups was significantly lower in 1984–85. The number of new groups picked up again in 1985–86 but in 1986–87, despite a considerable number of new starts, the termination of a considerable number meant that the overall number of groups irrigating increased only slightly. It is worth noting that, although it falls outside the period discussed in this work, there were no discontinuations in 1987–88, and approximately eighty groups took up irrigation for the first time. We can see from these trends that the Proshika irrigation program was expanding at a time when many other irrigation supply units were coming into the market, and seemed to have encountered a slump similar to that experienced more generally, just one year later in 1983–84. Growth of new schemes under the Proshika scheme seems to have picked up one year earlier than the apparent increase in demand more generally in 1987–88. It is against this background, together with their different credit repayment record, that the Proshika irrigation groups' performance should be judged.

The basic statistics on command areas, operating costs, gross incomes and computed net margins (NM) of the Proshika groups over time are given in tables 7.6 and 7.7.[11] There are no suitable data from the private irrigation sector in Bangladesh to compare with these figures, which come from a quite wide range of locations but are comparable with estimates from other studies. As noted elsewhere, there is some bias in the missing cases, because they are concentrated among groups that discontinued. The crude mean figures disguise considerable variation.

Although reliable figures for STW command areas are not readily available, the average of 12.42 acres (5.03 ha) is high compared to figures recorded in other studies in Bangladesh. For example (see BAU 1986), the

AST survey conducted for the Ministry of Agriculture reports an average of 11.1 acres for STW in sixteen *Upazila*, although the sampling frame used is highly unrepresentative of the bulk of STW areas.[12]

The economic performance of the STW schemes is shown by the net margins, calculated as gross margin less notional interest on working capital (8 percent) and depreciation (16 percent interest on outstanding capital amortized by constant annual sum to zero terminal value in five years; this corresponds to the financial terms of the BKB loan). Net margins declined in 1982–83 and 1983–84 compared to 1981–82, when the fairly optimistic review of the performance of the schemes was made (Wood 1982, 1984). The figures indicate that LLP schemes had a very successful year in 1982–83 while STWs performed poorly on average, but 1983–84 was, as for STWs, not a good year for LLP groups. Thereafter, economic performance of both LLP and STW groups improved steadily. Performance varied considerably between groups, and after 1983–84 many of the poorly performing groups discontinued. This has contributed to the improvement in performance, but the general economic circumstances have also played a significant part.

The decline in performance in 1982–83 was due to a sharp rise in fuel and oil (table 7.3) and repair costs and consequently in operating costs (table 7.8 and 7.9). The price of diesel and oil increased by 50 percent, and unit spare part prices likely also increased, although some of the rise in expenditure on spare parts may have been due to increased repair requirements as machines aged. Operating costs did not rise greatly in 1983–84 but gross income showed a sharp fall, due to the fall in yields (see table 7.10)[13] following the heavy flooding in many areas in May 1984. The price of paddy received by groups from the sale of their share of the output rose but not sufficiently to cover the fall in yield (tables 7.10 and 7.11). Interestingly, the fall in income to STW groups occurred both for groups with share payment and those receiving fixed-cash payments (table 7.12; for LLP groups the numbers of valid cases are too small to be reliable).

The improvement in performance since 1983–84 has been due to a rise in income while costs have been controlled; yields increased in 1984–85 (table 7.10)[14] and paddy prices improved significantly in 1985–86 and again in 1986–87 (table 7.11), when yields were also slightly higher. For STWs the sharp increase in incomes in 1986–87 was partly due to a rise in command areas (table 7.6). The poor performance of LLPs in 1985–86 appears to have been due to a sharp increase in operating costs, mainly fuel and oil, the reasons for which are not known.

Statistical Analysis

These findings can be summarized with greater precision by regression analysis. One would expect that economic performance would be positively related to command area, yield and the price of paddy, and negatively related to the number of pumping hours (after controlling for command area), the cost of diesel fuel and fertilizers. The effects of prices of fertilizers and paddy on the economic performance of groups will be both in the current season and with a lag; the effects on schemes with share payments may be reflected more directly than for those that are paid fixed-cash amounts. On share-payment schemes, yield directly affects income, so that variables that affect yields in the present season more directly affect performance. Yield expectations will also affect water seller incomes in schemes with cash-payment systems, because payments are generally made in installments, with the final one near or after harvest, and the final payments are affected to some extent by the quality of the harvest. Natural hazards also affect returns. The returns on irrigated agriculture to the cultivator will also affect performance on fixed-payment schemes in the next year after cultivators have adjusted their decisions to the changed economic circumstances, affecting both their expectations and the resources available to them. For these and other reasons,[15] estimation of the effects of economic variables on the performance of minor irrigation schemes is complicated and difficult. It is further limited because we have access only to those variables available through the Proshika monitoring system. More data are available about groups that discontinued irrigation, because these were of specific interest to Proshika.

Discussion of Regression Analysis

All three regression equations show a positive relation between command area and economic performance and a negative relation between pumping hours and performance. These relationships are statistically significant in the cases of STW groups under share payment for water, and LLPs. In all three cases, the paddy price shows a strong and statistically significant positive relation to performance. The price of fertilizer is negatively related to performance for STW under fixed-cash payment. Yield of paddy is, not surprisingly, positively related to performance for share-payment STWs. For LLPs, dummy variables (which capture the effects of floods for the years 1983–84 and 1984–85) are also significant. All these results are in accordance with our expectations and demonstrate the significance of economic factors, in particular fertilizer and paddy prices (and floods) in determining the economic performance of minor irrigation.

Regional Variation in Performance

These effects can be further explored through the examination of case studies. There are some strong regional variations in the performance of Proshika irrigation groups; this is most striking in the concentration of financial problems and of discontinuations in some Area Development Centers (ADCs), although nearly all have experienced some of these problems. We discuss these variations in terms of the four sets of factors outlined in the introduction to this chapter; the hydro-geological, agro-ecological, economic and socio-political.

Hydro-geological Factors

The case of Madaripur best illustrates the hydro-geological factors. Madaripur was one of the first ADCs to start irrigation; two groups started in 1980–81 and four, three and four in the following three years, respectively. None of the original groups are still irrigating and only one of those starting before 1982–83 has continued. Of the four groups starting in 1983–84, however, only one has discontinued and all four of those starting in the next two years are still in business. The financial performance of the early groups was poor: Tk88,000 was written off in 1985 for four groups and a further Tk212,000 had to be written off in 1987 for six of the early groups.

The most frequently given reasons for discontinuation were water supply problems. Eight of the ten groups that discontinued gave this as a reason; breakdowns, agronomic problems, and floods were other frequently given reasons. The water problem was mainly that initially the discharge from a sinking was good, but after some time it would decrease as the filter became blocked with sand. This problem, though related to the layers of sand in the aquifer, was also, apparently, due to the techniques used for sinking. Performance could be improved, at some expense, by adding a blank pipe below the filter and packing stone chips around the pipe after sinking. This would prolong the economic life of a boring, for an extra cost of Tk1,500-2,000, and was the recommended technique. In fact, it was specified in the Proshika rules for irrigation groups. In this district, however, the cost of sinking was high because there was little competition among sinkers of wells. The local sinking technology used was considerably cheaper, and because the additional sinking costs of the proposed technique were sunk, this would reduce the potential for the group to move the STW in the face of strategic bargaining by cultivators in the command area.

The relatively small command area, mentioned as a problem in only one case, was associated with the low discharge, rather than with unsuitable soils or competition from other water suppliers, which was not apparent in the area. Because the layer problem could affect a well in the middle of an irrigation season, discharge often fell after a larger command area was planted than could be irrigated, giving rise to dissatisfaction among cultivators. This meant that some groups had to resink wells in the middle of seasons and between seasons in the same command area, and that they also had to move command areas as they or the cultivators became disillusioned. Not only was the aquifer unreliable in that discharge could fall suddenly, but in a number of cases groups failed to find water at all, even after three sinkings, and gave up.

The low returns that resulted, in part from the water supply and also from the agronomic problems (hail being the most frequently mentioned), meant that groups could not repay loans, and were unwilling to maintain their engines to the required standard. This contributed to the relatively high incidence of engine breakdowns, although the scarcity of experienced mechanics also contributed to this. In part, the lack of competition and of satisfactory machine servicing was the result of the less intense development of mechanically powered tubewell irrigation in this area, compared to others.

The relatively low level of competition, together with the high costs generally experienced by STWs in this area, is reflected in the maintenance of the one-third cropshare payment for water. There is pressure to reduce the share, not so much because of increased competition, but because the high share reduces the attractiveness of winter rice irrigation to cultivators. The more recently started LLP schemes are able to charge only a one-fourth share. The sinking techniques were inadequate for the type of aquifer encountered, which caused discharge to fall after a few years, often in the middle of a season, with adverse effects on returns. Floods also affected some groups in 1981–82 and 1982–83; these do not seem to have caused much of a problem in these years but contributed to losses in 1983–84. The initial occurrence of the sand blocking the pipes was the main cause of losses in 1982–83. Mechanical breakdowns were also a feature of the difficulties of a number of groups from the start; this problem must in part be attributed to inadequate training and supervision by Proshika.

Flooding is another hydro-geological factor that has an important effect on performance of minor irrigation, particularly LLPs whose command areas are vulnerable to early flash floods in May and June. Severe flooding was the most frequently given reason for problems leading to discontinuation of irrigation groups in Khaliajuri ADC. The monitoring records imply that there were two highly successful seasons; in the following two, severe floods destroyed the crops. Verbal reports imply that flooding was a problem even in the early years.[16] Outstanding overdue loans with BKB of more than Tk486,000 were written off by Proshika in 1986 for six of the twelve groups that had discontinued. The loans should have been dealt with earlier to minimize the interest payments but disputes between the groups and the ADC, and between the ADC and Proshika headquarters, about whether at least part of the loans could be recovered from the groups on the grounds that they had had two very successful years, delayed settling the accounts. This could be a successful LLP area, as there are a number of private rental LLPs operating there; what was perhaps lacking was adequate allowance for insurance or credit support and backup from Proshika to carry the groups over one, or at most a few, years of losses caused by flooding. Excellent trust must exist between the principals (Proshika) and agents (the groups) for such arrangements to work.

In Kalkini, also, flooding was the most common explanation for discontinuation. In a number of cases, however, machine breakdowns (in one case due to poor maintenance) and the low return to irrigation caused by the low price that cultivators were willing to pay for water (less than Tk900 per acre in 1984–85), were also given as reasons. This low price was said to be the result of the ability of private LLP water sellers to accept that price, because they rented machines from BADC at rental rates well below the amortization schedule required by the BKB loan for Proshika groups. Also, cultivators could cultivate *aus/aman* and *rabi* crops instead of winter rice. In this ADC, considerable sums were written off in 1986. None of the groups had been able to repay all their loans and Tk337,000 was paid for the ten groups. The apparent profitability of at least some private LLPs in the area was something of a mystery to the ADC Coordinator, although he felt it might be because they irrigated their own land. This could be a matter for future investigation, but it cannot be taken for granted that this was the origin of the comparative advantage of some private LLPs.

DTWs in some cases also experience hydro-geological factors that lead to poor performance. In the first instance, DTWs should be sited where the water table lies below the suction limit of STWs and hence will have to pump from greater depths than STWs. Also, in Bangladesh greater depth of groundwater is associated with lower transmissivity of the aquifer, leading to greater specific drawdown. Although DTWs have some advantages of scale and greater efficiency of force mode pumps, these will in general be offset by the greater total pumping height. Some DTWs, however, are sited in areas where STWs work and consequently do not pump from these greater depths. Most of the Proshika DTWs are in proper DTW areas (where STWs will not work). Because of the greater depth of the water table and greater operating heights to obtain the same discharge or to irrigate the same area, fuel costs will be greater and DTW engines and pumps will be under greater mechanical strain than in lowland areas, resulting in more breakdowns and higher maintenance costs. If repairs are not particularly prompt there will be longer periods without water and crop damage will be higher. Because many of the upland areas are relatively isolated and undeveloped, with poor communications, access to maintenance has been poor, with the types of results described above. This problem has been partly responsible for the poor reputation of DTWs in these areas.

In the lowland areas, the water table is higher and STWs can operate. DTWs have been put into these areas and they generally have considerably lower pumping costs than do upland DTWs. These areas are suitable for STWs. As the intensity of use of groundwater rises, however, the water table falls in the periods of peak irrigation (April–May). Then, depending on the intensity of use, the level of recharge during the previous monsoon and the amount of water stored in the aquifer, the water table may fall so low that the discharge from a surface-mounted STW greatly diminishes or even stops. In much of Bangladesh it seems that, by deep setting the STW (lowering it into a pit of some 10–20 feet), the discharge can be restored to an economic level. In other areas, DTWs become the appropriate technology. The choice is in some cases technological (the water table falls so far that deep-set STWs (DSSTWs) could not operate) but in the main it will be based on economic criteria. At some point, the extra costs of installing, pumping from and managing DSSTWs, combined with the loss of yield in some years when discharge declines because of exceptional falls in the water table, will make DTWs the more appropriate technology. So far, deep setting is unusual and the costs involved are not known. Moreover, the differential rate of subsidy (DTWs are much more highly subsidized than STWs) makes the private choice different from the social. It is cheaper to have the Government install and operate a DTW at present rates of subsidy. All the Proshika DTWs in Sreepur and Mirzapur are in upland areas in the Mudhupur Tract; those in Dhamrai and Serajganj are in the lowlands. These differences show up in the operating costs per acre for DTWs between ADCs and average operating costs per acre between DTWs and STWs; costs are higher in the upland.

To summarize this section, hydro-geological factors determine the aquifer characteristics. The effects of these factors on performance are illustrated by the higher pumping costs of DTWs in Sreepur, and in Madaripur, where gas was encountered fairly frequently instead of water during drilling to install STWs, and where the tubewell discharge fell and pumping costs rose as sand clogged the filters. The amount of water stored in the aquifer, together with the amount of extraction, also determines the amount of drawdown as groundwater is increasingly exploited. In Madaripur, variable aquifer conditions for many of the sites chosen mean that the filter at the foot of the tubewell pipe can become blocked with sand. This causes reduced discharge and higher pumping costs per unit of water delivered, necessitating longer pumping hours and imposing greater strain on the engine and pump, which increases the likelihood of breakdowns. These conditions also occur in a number of ADCs and have been associated with poor performance there without always leading to discontinuation. Examples are Saturia, Harirampur, Ghior and Singair. In a number of ADCs that were visited it appeared that privately owned wells in the same area, which had sometimes attempted to use the same command area as the landless group, had not been successful, and there were no continuing private STWs in areas with similar ecology.

Floods also had considerable effects, especially on the LLP areas. Preventing floods completely is not technically viable for much of Bangaldesh, but this problem will either have to be treated as a risk (by providing insurance perhaps) or, alternatively, if the floods could be delayed so that crops could be harvested, the risks of irrigated cultivation could be considerably reduced in these areas.

Agro-ecological Factors

Agro-ecological factors include soil, crop, temperature, rainfall and humidity, crop pest, crop disease and crop husbandry practices. The more sandy soils require more frequent irrigation for a given crop because drainage is more rapid and water storage may be less than in more silt or clay soils. The poor performance of the first batches of STWs in Nagarpur and, to some extent, at Madaripur and Bhairab, encountered this problem. The high pumping hours and diesel use at Nagarpur and Madaripur reflect this. At Bhairab, pumping seems to have been contained but, no doubt as a result, low yields gave rise to low income, despite the share-payment system. Other agro-ecological factors reported to have affected performance are hail and pests. The apparently low average yields, which we can estimate for share-payment schemes by dividing the harvest share by the share and the command area, are greater than the national average but nonetheless much lower than recorded in other countries. The average for STWs is 1.44 tons per hactare (t per ha). The national average is approximately 1.3 t per ha; other south Asian countries average over 2 t per ha. Yields are especially low in the case of DTWs. Data from other studies do not allow a clear comparison, because they are collected by other methods from other samples, none of which can be relied upon (see, for example, Mendoza, 1989). There is some suggestion that these are underestimates of yields (which, as noted, can be only calculated for schemes which charge a cropshare for water by using the paddy receipts, which may be underreported[17]), and it is possible that yields are higher on schemes that pay fixed-cash costs (see below), but these low yields suggest considerable room for improvement by increased inputs and better management.

High availability of groundwater may not translate into successful irrigation if soil conditions are not suitable. Many of the most promising areas for groundwater appear to be in the recent floodplains of the Brahmaputra as in Saturia, Ghior, Singair and Harirampur, or in those parts of northwest Bangladesh in either the Brahmaputra or Teesta floodplains (Debiganj and Domar). But while groundwater seems abundant, the soils tend to consist of a mosaic of types with extensive sandy patches that will have high irrigation costs because of their low water-holding capacity. Some schemes may be located on better soils, but others even immediately adjacent may face higher irrigation costs and lower returns. Some of the schemes in Shibganj and Gabtoli may have similar characteristics because, as noted previously, they cover floodplain areas of mixed soils including the lower Teesta and the Brahmaputra floodplains.

For DTWs, as seen above, pumping costs are greater because of the greater height to which water must be lifted.[18] In some areas the soils are heavier, allowing rice to be grown with less water (this seems to be the case in the Barind Tract), but in others the soil is sandy or the heavier soils are in patches surrounded by higher and less suitable land for rice (as in the *chala* and *baid* soils typical of much of the Mudhupur Tract). In these cases, more water must be pumped to grow rice, either because of the unsuitability of the soils or because of high conveyance losses, and in some cases wheat is grown instead.

In Bhairab, the high level of discontinuations was undoubtedly related to the sandy soils. Predominantly sandy soils cause water demand for paddy to be particularly high, so that the command area that can be irrigated with a given discharge from the pump will be smaller and costs will be higher in relation to returns, compared with irrigation units that are sited on heavier soils and have more favorable aquifer conditions.

In Ulania, where Proshika groups supplied water from LLPs, the soils do not appear suitable for irrigation, having low water-holding capacity and giving poor yields; furthermore, even these slightly suitable soils are quite widely distributed among unsuitable and elevated land. This meant high water losses from canals. This, together with the high water demand by the sandy soils, meant that command areas were relatively small (twenty acres on average was reported for the thirteen valid out of twenty-five potential cases). There are relatively few private LLPs in these areas now, which supports this interpretation.

Economic Factors

Prices are the main economic variables determining performance. These include both the prices of inputs and outputs to water suppliers (such as the price of irrigation equipment, fuel, spares, labor for water management and water), and also the prices of agricultural inputs and outputs that determine the demand for water (such as fertilizer, pesticides, tillage, paddy and so on). The pricing system is also thought to play a role through its effects on the structure of incentives, and the report the Proshika program report of 1981–82 suggested that the share-payment system was optimal for the groups if they obtained a 33 percent share. But the relationships are likely to be complicated both by the recent uneven development and rapid change in economic conditions, which would mean that equilibrium in the relevant markets has not been reached and, even in STW areas where there can be considerable competition among water suppliers, there may be monopoly at least for a time. The better results from the share-payment system in 1981–82 have not been generally repeated, as shown in tables 7.12, 7.13 and 7.14. The lack of a large and significant difference in results between the two payment systems is perhaps not surprising if more or less competitive conditions in the water market prevail; the adoption of a payment system probably reflects local characteristics (as the outcome of economic and bargaining processes). One of the reasons given for adoption of a share-payment system is that it transfers much of the risk of water selling onto the sellers; hence, one would expect the share-payment system to have higher variability with greater returns in good years and the opposite in poor years. The similarity of returns for STWs in 1983–84, when large floods damaged crops in many areas under both systems, however, seems inconsistent with this hypothesis (LLP groups with share-payments actually did better in this year). Both systems impose considerable costs on groups for harvesting, hand-threshing or collecting the fees, respectively. In fact the fixed-cash payment system does not relieve groups of all risks of water supply, because payments are usually made by installments, and in the event of crop failure further instalments are stopped. Thus, under the fixed-payment system, part of the risk, by comparison with the share-payment system, is borne by culti-vators, but part is borne by the water sellers who collect these charges by installment. Earlier installments do not generally cover operating and over-head costs, and the last installment may not be completely collected, espe-cially in the event of partial or complete crop failure. For both LLP and STW groups, the share system resulted in lower average returns in 1985–86 and higher average returns in 1986–87. As the data quality improve a more consistent picture may emerge.

Shibgonj and Gabtoli provide an interesting contrast in performance that hinges largely on economic factors. Although these two ADCs are quite close geographically, ecological and economic circumstances are dif-ferent and have resulted in a considerably different outcome. Average net margins in Shibgonj have been just negative and many groups have dis-continued. Operating costs, fuel use and so on have been low yet incomes have been low, largely because of small command areas. Yields are not known because of the fixed-cash payment system, but reported incomes per acre have not fallen far short of those in Gabtoli. The difference has largely hinged on the failure to secure command areas as high as in Gabtoli. Machine breakdowns were frequently reported in Shibgonj but it is not known if this was due to machine type, poor cost control or inade-quate expenditure on, and poor quality of, maintenance. Machine troubles may be the result of poor quality machines (almost exclusively Yanmar 70s, which have a reputation for being unreliable[19]), or poor or inadequate maintenance practices, which may reflect in part the low net incomes resulting from inadequate command areas. Of course, once a group's water supplies become inadequate or unreliable for whatever reason, culti-vators often move to other suppliers or cease irrigation, thereby reducing incomes and further aggravating financial problems, possibly causing the group to skimp on maintenance. A number of other problems were report-ed in individual cases in Shibgonj, such as poor soils, poor aquifer and so on; but the main factor seems to have been the greater competition to sup-ply water, both by other STWs and by DTWs being promoted in the region under a government program. The cases of poor or distant command areas are also partly the result of competition. Groups in Shibgonj do not have the same organization as those in Gabtoli; the jobs of tubewell manager and driver are done by a single individual in the group, who is remunerated, whereas in Gabtoli these jobs are rotated among group members. These organizational differences may account in part for a lack of bargaining power in obtaining command areas and, perhaps, the somewhat higher operating costs and apparently less satisfactory machine performance.

Competition from private STWs and BRDB DTWs, rather than the prevalence of sandy soils, seems to have meant that some Proshika groups in Shibgonj could obtain only small command areas. In a few cases, groups could obtain command areas only on less suitable soils and at some distance from their homes. The small command areas and relatively low water charge (compared with other STW areas with fixed-cash payment per unit area water charges[20]), which resulted from competition, put financial pressure on groups. In some cases this led to insufficient maintenance, which could then cause poor water supplies. Farmers went to competing suppliers or lost interest in irrigation altogether. Sometimes the group lost interest or took to alternative activities. Cultivators sought to arrange alternative water supplies, while groups, trying to keep cultivators satisfied, increased the number of pumping hours per acre, thereby increasing operating costs. Hence an initial problem could become a ratchet, preventing recovery by precipitating a vicious circle of problems.

A number of other problems increased the groups' vulnerability to competition, particularly machine breakdowns due in part to poor maintenance. In a number of cases the machine problem was the result of poor financial returns, which led to economizing on maintenance. The poor financial returns were themselves due in part to competition, giving rise to small command areas, but in some cases the machine problem seemed to be entirely technical.[21] Failure to maintain the machine properly, or bad luck with the original machine, could trigger loss of command area, worsening financial performance. This is attested to by the opposite situation, namely the relationship between successful maintenance of the machine and the ability to maintain or increase command areas. In the two continuing groups out of the original eleven, success was attributed in large part to a good mechanic, whose skills had been increased by training organized by Proshika.

Some of the competition came from DTWs being installed under government programs but this was not the case universally. In a number of ongoing projects there was evidently considerable competition from private STWs, restricting the groups' command areas. The increasing competition in Shibgonj can be seen in the way average command areas declined there between 1981–82 and 1984–85, from around fifteen acres to just under ten. Unlike Bhairab, this trend was not the result of the realization that pump capacity was insufficient to irrigate relatively sandy soils with sufficient intensity; it was the result of increasing numbers of STWs and increased competition. Total incomes declined over this period despite a rise in the water price.

Socio-political Factors

At the outset of this research, the main obstacle to economic improvement by the poor was assumed to be their socio-political oppression and lack of access to economic resources. Hence, once the poor were given access to resources (in particular credit and irrigation equipment) and organizational and political support from Proshika, they would be able to earn greater incomes and improve their economic and social status. This, however, was not always the case. Frequently groups experienced poor or negative economic returns despite access and support. In many cases this was due to environmental or economic factors of the types described above. There were other cases, however, where group cohesion or support from Proshika fell short of the standards required; these groups failed only partly because of the technical reasons outlined above (see also chapter 9). Nagarpur provides an example where poor socio-political factors (as well as relatively unsuitable soils) contributed to poor economic returns, leading eventually to discontinuation.

Nine groups started irrigation in Nagarpur in 1981–82, two more in 1982–83 and one in 1983–84. Five discontinued before the floods of 1983–84, two after the floods and the remaining four after the 1984–85 season. Tk160,000 was written off in 1985 for four groups, and a further Tk27,000 in 1986 for one more. Group management, group conflict, mechanical breakdowns and floods were the reasons most frequently given for discontinuation. What were described as group problems, however, turned out to be partly a problem with the support and supervision that Proshika offered to the groups, especially when they got into difficulties. One of the Proshika field staff also caused problems. In a number of cases, the scheme was basically viable, but the groups gave up after one setback, such as flood damage. In their place a private STW scheme has been established. Competition did not contribute to discontinuation, although there has been a tendency for the share paid for water to decline from one-third toward one-quarter. There is other evidence of unsatisfactory support from Proshika in the relatively high incidence of mechanical breakdowns and poor maintenance of equipment. In another case, the STW is still operating with a group that used to be with Proshika but now operates without it (although there are outstanding loans on the equipment and operating cost).

In some cases, the conflict between the groups and the field staff arose over the fact that the groups consumed the surplus rather than repaying capital and operating loans. It is not known what effect the discontinuation has had on the groups and group members concerned, although, after a period of inactivity some of the discontinued groups appear to be active again.

The high rate of discontinuation in Nagarpur has been attributed mainly to these group problems, but breakdowns, floods and poor (sandy) soils were also mentioned as factors. Discontinuation may not have been necessary if Proshika's follow-up had been more satisfactory. Financial results in the first year seem to have been good.

In contrast, socio-political factors have contributed to the success of groups in Gabtoli and Mirzapur, although in both cases environmental conditions are relatively favorable. In Gabtoli, absentee landlordism is common; these landlords apparently do not object to landless groups providing irrigation and are not interested in installing and operating STWs themselves. Organization by the landless groups was also exceptional; thus there has been considerable mutual support among the landless irrigation groups, with successful groups training others. The irrigation groups have formed a district organization to formalize the dissemination of experience and to coordinate help in cases of need. In Mirzapur, the groups have organized themselves into a structure that provides mutual support and a means for the transmission of experience.

Discontinued Groups

A total of 309 Proshika groups have at one time or another taken up irrigation, but only 159 of these were in operation in the 1987–88 winter rice season; 150 have discontinued.[22] Proshika irrigation groups are not, in this respect, unlike those managed under other institutions, including the private sector. In the last decade many irrigation units have been installed in Bangladesh. Agricultural development programs give considerable prominence to the number that have started, but far less is known about those that have discontinued (Biswas et al. 1986). Not much publicity has been given to the very high rate of disappearance of irrigation groups; nevertheless, it seems likely the Proshika experience is far from exceptional. Thus Mandal (1986) reports that out of 99 irrigation units that were studied in 1984–85, nearly 30 percent were not in operation in the same command area in 1986–87.[23] Some of these units were transferred to another site and a number were operating under different management, but the bulk had ceased operation as irrigation units, either because they were permanently broken down, or had been transferred to other uses.[24]

This phenomenon has not been widely studied. There are no satisfactory longitudinal studies of irrigation in an area that could be used for this purpose. Discontinuation is particularly likely in STWs and LLPs, compared to DTWs, because of their mobility. This may explain in part why so little attention has been paid to the phenomenon, because most detailed studies have been of DTWs, which do not have ready alternative uses. Many DTWs are out of use and have been so for a number of years. The significant number of experimental programs aimed at improving DTW performance are premised on this fact.

The true number of DTWs that are out of use is not known, but a recent complete enumeration of BADC-owned DTWs normally rented out found that 20 percent of the 1,150-odd DTW schemes in Tangail District were actually not operating, and many more were years in arrears with rental payments. In many other areas significant numbers of DTWs are out of use. In Rangpur District in the north of Bangladesh, out of 952 commissioned DTWs owned by BADC, 121 needed minor repairs. Of these, 13 were completely unrepairable and 68 were out of use, requiring major repairs. Similar situations existed in many other areas.

Why Groups Discontinue

Irrigation groups discontinue for different reasons, which are often related in a complex manner. The main immediate causes of discontinuation are generally financial, although, as we have suggested, these financial problems are largely due to economic factors. Behind these, in some cases, lie political and social factors; however, it would be easy to exaggerate the importance of these and thereby pay less attention to the economic factors, which have become more important as a result of the privatization and commercialization of irrigation and other agricultural factor and product markets since the adoption of more market-oriented strategies in 1979. Once a group gets into economic difficulties, these are often increased in a vicious downward spiral of cause and effect. To understand the way this happens it is important to bear in mind that there are two crucial determinants of the performance of tubewell and LLP irrigation—the ability to obtain large command areas and the ability to obtain high yields. When yields are high, cultivators are satisfied by the high returns from their efforts, and when command areas are high, water sellers receive large incomes. In most cases such success leads to an easy relationship with cultivators who continue to be satisfied with the group as water suppliers, although it may also encourage other potential water sellers to enter the market to compete with the group.

High yields and large command areas are partially conflicting goals, however, because both increase the demand for water and in periods of peak water demand this can create shortages, which lead to conflicts. By pumping for longer hours and at greater engine speeds (an option available only for diesel, not for electric-powered installations) these shortages can be minimized, but this strains the motor, leading to breakdowns during the peak periods. The breakdowns in turn have had disastrous effects on crop yields, cultivator satisfaction, and the groups' returns, not only in the present season but also, in many cases, in future seasons. Dissatisfied cultivators may respond to this longer-term effect in any of the following ways:

- reducing their inputs on their irrigated land,
- reducing yields,
- stopping irrigation,
- changing their water source to a neighboring supplier,

- seeking collectively to replace the existing supplier with another, and
- investing in an irrigation unit to supply themselves.

The new supplier eventually has to obtain a sufficiently large command area to be financially viable; but if he is also a cultivator or has privileged access to credit, he may be viable where the landless group is not. The continual adjustment of plots within and among command areas in response to economic and social factors is characteristic of some competition in the water market (Mandal and Palmer-Jones 1987). Further evidence of competition is the response of STW sales to the economic forces outlined earlier and the tendency for profits from water selling to be competed away by the adjustment of the terms and the conditions of water sales, namely, the trend of the cropshare from one-third to one-quarter or less. These patterns are as common among non-landless owned tubewells as they are among the landless.

The next section discusses the distribution of discontinuations. Most ADCs experienced some discontinuations, but a number experienced considerably more and a higher proportion than others. The reasons given for discontinuation are discussed by technology and ADC, because these categories have common factors that help to explain the distribution observed. These reasons were partly given in writing by the responsible Proshika workers, and partly derived by interviews in ADCs with the relevant field workers and area coordinators. In a few cases, these explanations were backed up by discussions with the relevant groups. This last approach, though desirable, was limited, in part because discontinuation was often a fairly traumatic event for the groups concerned. First there was failure, disappointment and loss of potential income involved. Also, evidently, discontinuation was sometimes associated with conflict within the group, between the group and local landowners and/or competing water sellers and with Proshika. Furthermore, in the characteristic period of decline, during the downward vicious spiral described earlier and after irrigation had actually ceased, Proshika workers had to try to motivate discouraged groups and to induce them to repay loans from minimal and even negative returns. This could strain relationships considerably.

The Number and Age of Discontinued Groups

Nearly 50 percent of the Proshika irrigation groups have been discontinued within five years of starting. Figure 7.1 shows that nearly 90 percent of the irrigation groups that started in 1980–81 and 1981–82 had discontinued by the start of the 1986–87 season; more than 60 percent of all those more than three years old have discontinued. The proportion of groups that discontinue at a given age has not declined. It would be desirable for the proportion discontinuing after three or four years in existence to decline over time, because this would imply that Proshika had learned enough about the water selling business to obtain an improved performance for the groups it supports, and to support only groups in more favorable circumstances, by carrying out better feasibility studies.

For those groups that started in 1983–84, more than 60 percent had discontinued by the end of their third year, which is similar to the proportion discontinued by the end of their third year for those starting in 1982–83 and 1981–82. The proportion discontinuing after two years has decreased steadily since 1981–82; also, no groups discontinued in 1987–88.

Figure 7.2 shows that discontinuations have been concentrated in two years, in 1984–85 (that is, their last operating year was 1983–84) and in 1986–87. A considerable number also discontinued in 1983–84 and 1985–86. These findings are not greatly altered by the removal of rented LLPs from the number of discontinued groups. Of course the results look much more favorable if the new groups starting in 1986–87 are added into the continuing groups, but these do not fall within the project that is being evaluated.

Distribution of Discontinued Groups by Development Centre

Discontinuations have not been evenly distributed across all Development Centers, although nearly all ADCs have had some discontinuations (table 7.15). The discontinuation pattern gives some insight into the causes.

The ADCs with a large proportion of discontinuations fall into two groups according to whether the groups used LLPs or STWs; in ADCs that used LLPs there was a high rate of discontinuation. Table 7.16 shows that 46 percent of STWs have discontinued compared to 80 percent of LLPs (this proportion falls to 51 percent of LLPs discontinued if rented LLPs are excluded). Table 7.17 shows the concentration of discontinued groups in a number of the ADCs; some have had a large number of discontinuations. All the irrigation groups started in Nagarpur, Ulania, Khaliajuri and Kalkini discontinued, and there were also high proportions of discontinuations among irrigation groups in Shibgonj, Chatalpar, Bhairab, Madaripur, Singair, Ghior and Harirampur.[25]

Discontinued STWs

At most of the ADCs where groups have taken up STWs in any numbers, there has been at least one discontinuation, but the majority of STW discontinuations have been concentrated in Bhairab (13), Shibgonj (13), and Madaripur (9). Nagarpur (9), with Ghior (6), Singair (6), Saturia (5) and Harirampur (4) contributed slightly fewer, and a number of others had one or two each. The reasons for the discontinuation of these STWs varies both between and within ADCs. For most discontinued STWs, a number of reasons, generally interrelated, have been given. These reasons are unlikely to be complete and in some cases they may be misleading because they are the often delayed reports and possibly misleading interpretations of the Proshika staff.

Mechanical breakdowns were the most common reasons for discontinuation of STWs (table 7.18). This parallels the finding from field research that in recent years there has been a high and possibly increasing incidence of mechanical problems in mechanical minor irrigation equipment. Small command areas, soil and water table problems, group management problems, low returns, floods, agronomic problems and competition were reasons given quite frequently. Despite the preponderance of mechanical problems (thirty-two out of seventy-seven discontinued STW groups gave them as one of the reasons for discontinuation) this cannot be taken for granted as the ultimate reason for the high rate of discontinuation. In some cases discontinuation may have been due to other causes, which led to poor maintenance, resulting in large numbers and excessive costs of breakdowns. These vicious circles of deteriorating performance have been discussed earlier in this chapter.

Discontinued LLPs

LLPs were expected to perform better than STWs, partly because their greater mobility provided groups with greater bargaining power. In the event STWs have proved highly mobile, and although the reported average net margin for LLPs is slightly greater than for STWs, the prevalence of missing information and questions about the validity of some of the information raise doubts about the significance of this figure. Furthermore, the expansion of LLPs depends on the availability of suitable sites with good soils and available surface water that will last through the irrigation season. Much of the potential for LLPs in Bangladesh, without some form of surface water augmentation, have already been exploited, which will limit future potential. Also, LLP irrigation schemes are more varied than STW because of the greater dependence of command area and soil type on the local circumstances. Both water supply and the availability of suitable soils are apparently more varied than in the case of STWs. LLP irrigation may also be more risky, more vulnerable to flooding and to the disappearance of the water supply, than STW irrigation. These characteristics will increase the variance of statistics, making interpretation more difficult. Estimation of the risks, to assess whether the return in good years would be one sufficient to provide insurance for the failures in the bad years, is not possible. For example, the monitoring information revealed Khaliajuri groups as highly successful for two years, but there is no information, even on operating costs, for later years, when floods caused extensive damage. Inclusion of cases from Khaliajuri would consequently give a misleading picture of the performance of LLP as a whole.

The discontinuations among LLPs[26] have been predominantly in Kalkini, Ulania and Kaliajuri, which account for thirty-four of the discontinued LLPs. The main reason given was crop damage due to floods, which caused loss of crops by cultivators (see table 7.18), which caused loss of revenue by the groups and consequent decisions to discontinue these projects. Out of sixty LLP groups that have discontinued altogether, twenty-three gave floods as a reason, but mot the only reason. Even in those cases affected by floods, low returns, mechanical problems and small command areas were other frequently given reasons, and slightly less frequently given reasons were poor support and mismanagement by Proshika, group management problems and loss of water source. This last reason reflects the instability of watercourses in many areas; rivers shift their course and sources of surface water disappear so that irrigation is no longer possible at a previously viable site. At other times or places, presumably, suitable water sources arrive and create new opportunities for irrigation schemes. This implies high risks, and the need for flexibility and adaptability.

DTWs

Proshika has only recently started facilitating irrigation with DTWs. The program was started in 1985–86 with eleven units, nine in Sreepur and one each in Mirzapur and Dhamrai. Most of the projects were part of the Committee for American Relief Everywhere–Landless Operated Tubewell Users Service (CARE–LOTUS) project,[27] under which old DTWs (installed in the 1970s and formerly rented out by BADC but subsequently fallen out of use) are purchased by the groups provided the groups are involved in the LOTUS project.

The program got off to a late start in its first year due largely to the usual administrative and bureaucratic delays resulting in late handover of the machine and late planting. Cultivators reacted to these delays and in these cases only small command areas were cultivated. In other cases, small command areas are the result of either lack of suitable land and/or skepticism among cultivators that the landless groups will be able to overcome the problems that had resulted in previous discontinuation of the DTWs. In at least one case there was also skepticism about the involvement of CARE, which had previously been involved with the DTW and was held largely responsible for some of its previous problems. Command areas of all the DTWs of Proshika groups were small, by the standards required of DTWs, and operating costs were high compared with both LLPs and STWs. In a number of cases wheat was grown as well as, or instead of, winter rice because the soils are sandier and hence less suitable for winter rice. All the DTW groups had substantial financial losses in 1986–87 except in Dhamrai, although a minority had positive gross margins. The DTW in Dhamrai was rented rather than purchased and consequently had lower capital charges.[28] Three of the DTWs in Sreepur are reported to have discontinued. But because the installations remain with the groups they may come under the project again once their problems have been solved. One of the three was said to be operating in 1987–88 on a small scale using its own funds and payments from cultivators to pay for operating costs. Partly as a result of the exclusion of these three DTWs, and partly because of greater controls on disbursement of operating-cost loans to control pumping and reduce fuel expenditure, the financial results improved in 1986–87. Average command areas were greater; higher yields and paddy prices also contributed to this improvement. But there was considerable variability in the performance of different DTWs, with those in Sreepur still having quite large negative net margins, with one exception.

DTWs are located in two distinct types of ecological situations. There are upland areas, such as the Mudhupur Tract which runs through Dhaka, Tangail and Mymensingh Districts, and the high Barind Tract in Rajshahi District. There are also lowland areas such as those that cover most of the rest of the country apart from the Chittagong Hill Tracts and parts of the northeast of the country. In the upland areas the water table is between fifteen and twenty feet below ground level and readily falls below the suction limit of the STW.[29] In these areas the pumping costs are higher than in lowland areas and the soil characteristics differ. The high proportion of mechanical problems experienced with DTWs in most of the ADCs generally reflects a number of factors. (a) The machines are old, and the repairs and maintenance undertaken before handover by BADC may not have corrected all the weaknesses. (b) The greater depth to the water table means that the machinery is under greater strain, which will result in more breakdowns. (c) The mechanical problems are more difficult to solve locally, and, despite the good offices of CARE where it is involved, maintenance from BADC may be less than entirely satisfactory, causing bad repairs leading to further breakdowns. Predictably, the different agencies espouse different explanations, and again we are unable to provide objective assessments of these. There is no doubt that the monopoly of both imports of DTW spares and maintenance held by BADC has not resulted in an entirely satisfactory position. Comparison of the performance of the Proshika DTWs in the LOTUS program with those not in it suggests that there may be little benefit to the LOTUS program *per se,* apart from facilitating access to DTWs in the first place.[30]

The difficulties experienced by the Proshika-supported DTWs in the upland areas should serve as a warning to other organizations proposing to develop DTW programs. The success of the DTW in lowland areas may not carry over into the higher cost circumstances of upland sites.

Conclusions

The paddy price is positively correlated with performance of STW under both fixed-cash and share-payment systems, and the price of diesel fuel is negatively related in both systems. For the share-payment system, the interpretation seems quite simple in that higher paddy prices provide incentives for both water sellers and cultivators, and the higher fuel costs directly reduce incomes. But for those schemes with a fixed-cash system, the effect would be only through the incentive to cultivators. The paddy price, however, is not positively correlated with command area for this system of water payment, although it is correlated with pumping hours. Higher paddy prices may mean that water sellers expect be able to collect a greater proportion of the water charge and therefore supply more water, which in turn may result in higher returns to cultivators, which would then enable them to pay water charges.

The fertilizer price, using the official scheduled price, is negatively (but not significantly) related to net margins for fixed-payment systems and positively related in the share-payment schemes. There can be no simple explanation for this difference. Higher fertilizer prices would suggest lower returns to winter rice cultivation and to water selling, as found for the fixed-payment system. The positive association under share water payment may be the result of the accidental correlation of rising fertilizer prices over time and the rise in net margins in the last two seasons. Some observers suggest there was no shortage of fertilizer before the privatization of fertilizer distribution, but others believe there were shortages and misallocation. Much of this has been reduced by privatization, so that rising fertilizer prices were associated with increased availability and profitable use, and farm gate fertilizer prices have been stable or declining in recent years.

The paddy price-to-fertilizer price ratio is likely to be positively related to the profitability of irrigation and under the fixed-payment system it is positively related to net margin, command area and pumping hours, but it is quite strongly negatively related for share-payment systems, largely because of the unexpected positive relation between fertilizer price and net margins noted above.

The most likely explanation for the successes at Gabtoli have to do with the soil and aquifer conditions, but organizational characteristics also may have contributed to its success. It is the only ADC where irrigation groups circulate the water management tasks among group members rather than delegating them to paid individuals. Also, as noted above, characteristics of the social structure may have contributed. Boyce (1987, p. 244) has noted that the agrarian structure in Bogra is relatively egalitarian, and this may have accounted for the apparent better capacity utilization of irrigation there. According to Proshika workers, this did not account for the success at Gabtoli; it was rather the higher proportion of absentee landowners. Success has not been so great at neighboring Shibgonj ADC, which is also in Bogra District. There are differences in the soil classification between the *Upazilas* that give their names to these ADCs; this may have contributed to the difference in performance. Half of Shibgonj *Upazila* is covered by soils of the flat Barind, and half by lower Teesta floodplain, while Gabtoli falls mainly in the floodplain of the new Brahmaputra. The difference between the Barind soils and those of the two floodplains is likely to be significant. The two floodplains have been formed from different upstream conditions, which may affect their hydro-geological and agro-ecological characteristics in ways that lead to differences in irrigation performance. Without more information about other irrigation units and their performance and soils characteristics, however, we cannot test this. Also, without more detailed knowledge of the classification of the soils irrigated by Proshika groups, we cannot pursue this line of investigation.[31] A further difference between Gabtoli and Shibgonj was the extent of competition from other irrigation units; this was also a factor in Saturia.

Success is clearly related to command area and fuel costs (which reflect the amount of pumping), but these are only intermediate variables in the sense that they are themselves determined by other factors. We have not been successful in identifying what and how important these other factors are. Some of them will be exogenous, including such things as the soil type or the aquifer conditions; others will be determined by decisions made on the one hand by Proshika or the management of the scheme and on the other by cultivators with land in its potential command area. For example, fuel costs have been restricted on the DTWs by limiting pumping, but for STWs this is more difficult if cultivators can seek an alternative water supplier who may be expected to supply more water. In competitive circumstances, both the command area and the amount of water to supply will be partly determined by market forces. Among the economic variables we have related to performance so far are the price of paddy (positively related to performance) and the price of fertilizer and diesel fuel (negatively related). These variables would be expected to affect the determination of command area and pumping, but no simple relationships between these have been found in the data. For groups with STWs using the cash-payment system, the price of paddy and the number of hours of pumping are positively related, but no such relationship exists for those using the share-payment system. The fuel price is negatively related to pumping hours under the fixed-cash payment system, but not related under the share system. It is not at all clear why these relationships should have been found and, although it is tempting to argue that the payment system has some role in these differences, it must be remembered that the share- and fixed-payment systems occur in different areas, on the whole, and one or more of a number of differences between the areas may account for this difference in price response.

Command area and pumping are in part decided by the management of an irrigation unit, but at the same time these decisions are constrained by what the cultivators will accept. It is likely that these decisions are partly contingent on environmental factors such as soil, weather and so on, but they are also partly made on the basis of economic factors such as the price of paddy or of diesel fuel. For example, if the price of fuel falls or an electric engine replaces a diesel one, the amount of water applied would be expected to increase. Command area might also increase as it became more economic to enlarge the irrigated area.

In this chapter we have seen that economic determinants (and hence, as we have shown in chapter 6, financial performance) are strongly associated with technical and economic factors. These factors can be grouped under the following headings:

- hydro-geological: depth and quality of aquifer and well vulnerability, floods,
- agro-ecological: soils, weather, cropping systems, and so on,
- economic: input and output prices, and
- socio-political: agrarian structure, group organization, and the like.

The records of profitability of Proshika irrigation groups and the analysis of relevant agricultural input and output prices show that the economic returns to minor irrigation varied considerably over the course of this project, despite its relatively brief life. The difficulties experienced by the landless irrigation groups in the mid 1980s mirrored the more general experience of winter rice irrigation in Bangladesh. Production of winter rice grew more slowly, and sales of minor irrigation equipment declined over this period. A number of reports, including those of the World Bank and the Agricultural Sector Review, have attributed these macrophenomena largely to institutional obstacles posed by the Bangladesh Government. It is clear from the evidence presented here, however, that economic factors also played a significant role. For the World Bank to neglect the role of incentives in determining agricultural performance is perhaps surprising, given the current enthusiasm for pricism, but this can be explained by another enthusiasm—for deregulation, and in particular a largely ideological need to remove bureaucratic controls on the siting of STWs and tariffs on the import of STW equipment. There is some validity to this argument and we support appropriate deregulation of STW siting. But releasing the power of market forces will be of limited value unless incentive prices are maintained, and it will be important to maintain incentives if the private sector irrigation is to fulfill the expectations held of it. Furthermore, Proshika and other organizations must realize that macroeconomic factors affect the outcome of their projects as do organizational and technical factors, over which they have some control.

Finally, the way projects get into difficulties that then lead the groups into a vicious circle of declining performance needs to be understood so that the appropriate decisions about when, how and at what point to intervene are expeditiously identified. Cases of basic infeasibility must be separated from those of temporary or remediable difficulties. Delays in either resolving problems or halting projects can lead to declining incentives and performance and either unnecessary termination or escalating debt. In agriculture, however, performance will always vary, and it is only with experience that Proshika will be able to separate cases of infeasibility from those of temporary fluctuation in performance (or, more rarely, malfeasance). To avoid the the latter becoming the former (as, for example, when a crop failure in one year leads to arrears on loan payments, penalty interest rates, reduced machine maintenance and so on) some form of loan insurance may be desirable, so that financial obligations can be met. As with all insurance schemes, however, Proshika would have to guard against the phenomena of moral hazard and adverse selection. An example of the former is when the insured groups no longer take adequate precautions against failure of the scheme; an example of the latter is when successful groups would be unwilling to pay the premiums to cover the average losses of less successful ones. All this implies that Proshika may have to continue to provide considerable support for the irrigation groups.

Notes

1. These figures have not proved reliable; nevertheless, some increase in command areas of IDA and other DTWs from the mid 1980s is to be expected as a result of the improvements in incentives documented here.

2. 1985–89.

3. See particularly *Bangladesh Development Studies*, Vol. XIII, (3 and 4), Sept.–Dec. 1985. The course of paddy prices is strongly affected by the import and subsidy policies, which are discussed briefly below.

4. The use of official paddy prices, or even the farmers' prices given by BBS, should be treated with caution, as our data show considerable variation spatially and over time, especially the few weeks around the harvest of winter rice. The price often starts high in May, but falls rapidly and does not recover until toward the end of July. Landless groups may be particularly disadvantaged in selling their paddy as they do not often have information (or resources) to take advantages of higher prices in other areas, or slightly later in the year, nor do they have storage facilities. They also have particularly urgent needs for cash, and in many cases for food.

5. Hired labor costs were 2.3 times more per acre of winter rice production, and total labor more than 4.4 times the expenditure on all fertilizers in 1986–87, according to the official Agro-Economic Research Unit of the Ministry of Agriculture.

6. This argument applies even if family labor is excluded, because (a) hired labor is still a greater expense than fertilizers and (b) the opportunity cost of family labor will move in the same direction as wages.

7. And possibly also some slowdown due to the groundwater shortage that occurred in some parts of the northwest of Bangladesh following the drought of the autumn of 1983.

8. In this case, the dummy variable for 1984 reflects only adjustment to the drought that affected water tables in parts of the northwest in 1983.

9. This document argues not only that STW sales were obstructed by bureaucratic constraints, but also that fertilizer sales had not been adversely affected by price rises that accompanied the early years of privatization of fertilizer distribution.

10. To economize, data have been presented by year and technology only for the most part; breakdowns for each ADC were published in an earlier report (Wood and Palmer-Jones 1988). The Proshika monitoring system collects these data by group and compiles a database from which the aggregate tables are prepared. The raw data can be obtained from the authors or Proshika.

11. The raw data from which these averages hage been calculated are available from the authors or Proshika.

12. This is not untypical of the weakness of statistical practice in Bangladesh; *Upazila* were chosen on the basis of greatest and least absolute numbers of STWs, rather than numbers in relation to potential, which would have been a better approximation to areas of highly developed and underdeveloped potential.

13. Considerable caution in interpreting these figures is required because of the small numbers and bias in the reporting caused by the smaller proportion of discontinued groups reporting in general and in their last year of operation, when performance is likely to have been worse.

14. Prices of paddy are available for most groups because this was reported separately, but yields as noted above can be calculated only for groups that received a share of the crop.

15. Besides the normal problems of estimation of production and profit functions, estimation of these relationships will be affected by simultaneous equation bias (see Palmer-Jones, *Multi-user Irrigation Schemes and the Theory of Clubs*, 1988, available from the author).

16. In a number of cases the monitoring records reported estimates of acreages and crop incomes rather than those actually experienced.

17. The monitoring data of CARE are produced by an intensive system of crop-cutting, and show considerably higher yields on the DTW than those derived by estimates from the paddy income received. But detailed study of their data shows a number of faults that undermine confidence in their estimates; for example, the elimination of one plot (out of five) because no yield on it was reported in one case. Elsewhere, such plots were quite likely substituted by ones with at least some yield.

18. Both because of the lower static water level and because, in some of the aquifers, the transmissivity is low, resulting in higher specific drawdown.

19. In the case of one batch, faulty manufacture was certainly partly responsible for breakdowns.

20. For example, the fixed water charges in Mirzapur at the same time were Tk1,300 to 1,500 per acre.

21. In one case, the engine suffered a severe breakdown only days after a major overhaul; in another case, repeated attempts to solve persistent lack of power from the engine were unsuccessful.

22. Of these, twenty-three were rented LLPs, which apparently are normally given up at the end of each season.

23. The census by the MoA referred to above reports that out of 210,000 STWs imported or locally manufactured, about 167,000 were in operation in 1987.

24. Including spare parts for irrigation, rice husking, river boat power units and so on.

25. The high proportion of discontinuations recorded in Chatalpar is of groups that rented LLPs from BADC for only one year at a time.

26. Apart from those at Chatalpar, which were rented.

27. CARE initiated the LOTUS project following its Deep Tubewell Irrigation Cooperative Project (DTICP) project. CARE does a feasibility study and suggests repair and maintenance work to be done prior to acceptance. It provides agronomic advice and a link with BADC to facilitate mechanical repairs, for which BADC is responsible three years after handing over the facilities.

28. The annual rent for a DTW was Tk5,000, as compared to amortization of about Tk10,000 to 30,000, depending on the price paid for the DTW.

29. In some parts of the upland areas, there are valleys and lower lying areas where STWs can function at least until the groundwater resources become heavily utilized. It is also possible that there are areas where deep-set STWs (DSSTWs) can exploit all the economically worthwhile groundwater resource, although the

viability of this technology has yet to be established.

30. CARE has evaluated the LOTUS project positively, as it did for its precursor, the DTICP, which has subsquently been shown to have had serious lacunae (Biswas et al. 1986). Evaluation of the LOTUS project is not an easy task, particularly as CARE's own evaluations have substantial inadequacies, either in methodology (inappropriate or lacking with and without comparisons), or lack of or inadequate data (for example, the the yield estimates from crop-cutting; see Mendoza 1989).

31. Our information on soil characteristics used local names for soils and the proportion of each command area under them. Because local names are likely to classify them relative to other local soils, the differences between quite widely separated areas may not be captured by this method of reporting; that is, the classification of one command area as relatively sandy by comparison with its neighbors does not mean that it is relatively sandy by comparison with those of a distant scheme.

Table 7.1   Growth of Groundwater and Power
Pump Irrigation Units in Bangladesh

Year	LLP Rental	LLP Sold	DTW Census	DTW Operating	Sales-aided	Pump Sets	STW Private[1]	Cumulative Estimate	Census
1962–67	2,020								
1967–78	6,558			102					
1972–73	32,924			1,237	938			938	
1977–78	36,730			7,453	8,104			14,714	
1978–79	35,895			9,329	5,259			19,973	
1979–80	37,381			9,795	17,551			24,458	
1980–81	31,688	2,206		10,131	17,551			42,009	
1981–82	28,117	9,594		11,491	26,465			68,474	
1982–83	17,619	21,973		13,794	39,145			106,408	
1983–84	9,308	34,307		15,519	33,565			141,973	
1984–85	8,337	42,324		16,901	27,598			169,568	
1985–86	0	49,837	30,494	18,044	5,353	1,415		178,330	146,908
1986–87	2,699	54,665	32,563	18,806	2,482	13,083	2,000	190,705	160,278
1987–88	7,291	65,623	33,927	21,507	7,482	8,816	5,000	211,697	186,473
1988–89	0	72,328	40,755	22,448	13,462	1,126	10,000	236,285	235,816

1   Estimated.

Table 7.2   Current Prices of
Irrigation Equipment

Year	Procurement (Tk 000)	LLP Rent (Tk/year)	Sales (Tk 000)	Procurement (Tk 000)	DTW Rent (Tk/year)	Sales[1] (new) (Tk 000)	STW Sales[2] (Tk 000)
1975–76	17	600		140	1,200		(10-12)
1976–77	19	600		160	1,200		(10-12)
1977–78	22	600		160	1,200		(10-12)
1978–79	26	600		180	1,200		(10-12)
1979–80	27	600		220	1,200		(10-12)
1980–81	30	900	22	260	1,200	60	17
1981–82	35	1,100	22	340	1,200	60	20
1982–83	35	3,600	25	310	1,800	70	25 (32)
1983–84	41	3,600	29	407	3,000	85	28 (35)
1984–85		3,600	(29)	540	5,000	112	(28-35)
1985–86		3,600	(26-34)	600	5,000	175	(30-38)
1986–87		5,000	(26-34)	640	5,000	175	(20-42)
1987–88		5,000	(26-34)	640	5,000	175	(20-42)
1988–89		5,000	(26-34)	640	5,000	175	(20-42)

Sources: BADC and field surveys by authors
Figures from 1983–84 were derived from fieldwork rather than from official sources in many cases.
1   A few rental DTWs were sold for between Tk30,000 and Tk60,000 according to age of equipment.
2   Sales prices of STWs between 1980–81 and 1983–84 are BADC official prices for new Yanmar ts70 engines and standard accessories (pumps, pipe and strainer, excluding installation—see Gill 1983); those in parentheses are from field survey information and refer in some cases to different models and accessories.

Table 7.3   Prices of Main Agricultural Inputs and Outputs, Crop Acreages and Fertilizer Use

Year	Paddy Price (Farmers) Tk/Ton[1]	Official Fert./Paddy Price Ratio			Agric. Wages Tk/day	Wage/Paddy Price Ratio Tk/md	Diesel fuel Tk/liter	Acreages (in millions of acres)					Jute Price Tk/md
		Urea Tk/Nutr. Ton	TSP Tk/Ton	MP Tk/day				Aus	Aman	Boro	Wheat	Jute	
1974–75	—	0.90	—	—	—	—	—	7.86	13.47	2.87	.31	1.41	—
1975–76	1,955	1.59	1.19	0.68	—	—	9.05	8.45	14.24	2.84	.37	1.28	85
1976–77	1,741	2.00	1.60	1.03	—	—	9.28	7.95	14.36	2.11	.40	1.60	115
1977–78	2,192	1.59	1.27	.82	9.44	0.117	11.46	7.81	14.26	2.70	.47	1.80	159
1978–79	2,542	1.60	1.26	.79	10.88	0.117	13.79	8.00	14.35	2.62	.65	2.05	134
1979–80	3,273	1.60	1.24	1.06	12.46	0.104	22.52	7.50	14.76	2.84	1.07	1.87	110
1980–81	2,698	1.84	1.80	1.07	13.97	0.141	23.66	7.68	14.92	2.87	1.46	1.57	111
1981–82	3,440	2.08	1.77	1.06	15.48	0.123	33.67	7.77	14.85	3.22	1.32	1.41	116
1982–83	4,020	2.15	2.02	1.22	17.05	0.107	33.67	7.80	14.81	3.54	1.28	1.42	193
1983–84	4,359	1.99	1.87	1.12	19.58	0.123	33.67	7.76	14.85	3.46	1.30	1.43	203
1984–85	4,042	2.21	2.14	(1.31)	24.45	0.165	33.67	7.26	14.11	3.89	1.67	1.49	433
1985–86	4,457	2.28	2.21	1.68	29.54	0.181	33.67	7.03	14.87	3.79	1.33	2.61	185
1986–87	5,340	1.87	1.87	1.46	32.60	0.167	33.67	7.18	14.96	4.08	1.45	1.91	113
1987–88	5,520	1.78	1.86	1.12	30.28	0.150	33.67	6.89	13.82	4.80	1.48	1.27	265
1988–89	5,560[2]	1.79	1.84	1.12	(30.00)	0.147	33.67	—	—	5.88	—	—	—

Sources: Bangladesh Bureau of Statistics, Statistical Yearbook of Bangladesh, Yearbook of Agricultural Statistics of Bangladesh, Statistical Pocketbook of Bangladesh and Monthly Statistical Bulletin. Figures in parentheses are derived from fieldwork.
1 Ideally, seasonal expected prices of paddy should be used.
2 Estimated from field surveys.
Nutr. = nutrient; md. = maund.

Table 7.4   Number of Irrigation Groups Operating
by Technology, ADC and Year

Technology/ ADC	1980–81	1981–82	1982–83	1983–84	1984–85	1985–86	1986–87	Total
DTW								
Mirzapur	—	—	—	—	—	1	8	9
Sreepur	—	—	—	—	—	9	9	18
Serajganj	—	—	—	—	—	—	1	1
Dhamrai	—	—	—	—	—	1	2	3
Total	—	—	—	—	—	11	20	31
STW								
Bhairab	14	14	14	14	2	4	5	67
Saturia	—	4	6	13	20	26	23	92
Singair	—	—	1	6	10	9	4	30
Harirampur	—	—	1	5	7	7	5	25
Ghior	—	3	8	11	8	11	10	51
Nagarpur	—	—	8	8	6	4	2	28
Madaripur	2	6	9	9	9	4	4	3
Mirzapur	—	5	5	9	10	11	12	52
Shibgonj	—	11	14	14	11	12	7	69
Gabtoli	—	—	2	6	6	14	22	50
Kaliakoir	—	—	1	1	1	1	—	4
Atpara	—	—	2	2	1	—	—	5
Sreepur	—	—	—	—	1	1	1	3
Chatalpar	—	1	—	—	—	—	—	1
Domar	—	—	—	—	2	2	—	4
Kuliarchar	—	—	1	1	2	1	5	—
Serajgonj	—	—	—	—	1	3	6	10
Muksudpur	—	—	—	—	1	1	1	3
Debiganj	—	—	—	1	1	—	—	2
Bhanga	—	—	—	—	—	3	3	6
Brahmanbaria	—	—	—	—	1	1	2	—
Narail	—	—	—	—	—	1	1	2
Uzipur	—	—	—	—	—	—	2	2
Total	16	52	71	98	96	115	108	556
LLP								
Bhairab	—	—	—	—	—	1	3	4
Ulania	6	7	6	2	4	2	—	27
Khaliajuri	4	12	11	7	—	3	1	38
Kalkini	—	2	2	9	5	1	—	19
Madaripur	—	—	1	2	4	8	15	—
Mirzapur	—	—	—	—	—	2	4	6
Atpara	—	—	—	—	1	1	2	4
Sreepur	—	—	—	1	1	1	1	4
Chatalpar	—	10	—	5	—	—	2	27
Gournadi	—	—	—	—	2	3	2	7
Serajgonj	—	—	—	—	—	—	1	1
Muksudpur	—	—	—	—	1	1	2	—
Brahmanbaria	—	—	—	—	—	2	2	—
Bhola	—	—	—	—	—	1	7	8
Ulipur	—	—	—	—	—	—	1	1
Total	10	31	26	25	15	23	35	165

Table 7.5   Number of Groups Stopping in a Year by Starting Year

Date Started	Total Starting	Year Stopping (including rented)						Continuing
		1981–82	1982–83	1983–84	1984–85	1985–86	1986–87	1987–88
1980–81	26	1	0	6	16	2	—	1
1981–82	58	—	17	10	13	5	3	10
1982–83	31	—	—	10	3	5	3	10
1983–84	49	—	—	—	11	7	12	19
1984–85	33	—	—	—	—	4	6	23
1985–86	58	—	—	—	—	—	8	50
1986–87	51	—	—	—	—	—	—	51
Total	306	1	17	26	43	23	32	163
% stopping	—	0	7	10	17	9	13	—
Cumulative %	—	0	—	7	17	34	43	56
Total excl. rented	—	1	7	19	38	23	30	—

Table 7.6   Command Area Statistics

Technology/Year	Mean	Count	Valid Number	Standard Error	Median	Maximum	Minimum
DTW							
1985–86	22.40	11	9	2.93	20.00	40.00	9.40
1986–87	37.14	20	20	3.03	35.52	74.00	19.65
Total/Average	32.57	31	29	2.59	30.95	74.00	9.40
STW							
1980–81	—	16	0	—	—	—	—
1981–82	13.67	52	50	.56	13.00	26.00	6.00
1982–83	12.78	71	54	.44	13.08	19.02	6.00
1983–84	12.36	98	81	.45	11.50	23.40	4.59
1984–85	11.07	96	89	.40	10.44	27.00	4.80
1985–86	11.41	114	97	.40	11.00	24.00	5.20
1986–87	13.88	108	95	.68	12.85	25.00	5.61
Total/Average	12.41	555	466	.21	12.00	25.00	4.59
LLP							
1980–81	—	10	0	—	—	—	—
1981–82	34.95	31	31	3.78	33.50	120.00	6.00
1982–83	37.06	26	18	3.50	39.00	78.00	14.00
1983–84	27.34	24	15	2.19	25.00	45.70	15.00
1984–85	21.50	15	11	2.72	21.00	40.00	9.18
1985–86	31.44	23	16	5.80	20.62	84.00	12.00
1986–87	32.99	34	30	5.72	27.50	194.00	15.00
Total/Average	32.15	163	121	1.99	28.00	194.00	6.00

Table 7.7   Gross Income, Operating Costs Gross and
Net Margin

Technology/ Year	Mean			
	Gross Income	Operating Cost	Gross Margin	Net Margin
DTW				
1985–86	34,533	48,902	-14,369	-18,281
1986–87	60,501	47,590	12,911	2,210
Average	52,442	47,997	4,445	-4,149
STW				
1980–81	—	—	—	—
1981–82	18,817	9,703	9,626	3,049
1982–83	17,389	12,517	6,881	-612
1983–84	14,533	12,751	2,460	-6,117
1984–85	16,637	11,952	4,531	-4,215
1985–86	19,858	12,203	7,406	480
1986–87	26,275	13,514	12,697	4,335
Average	19,224	12,299	7,327	-554
LLP				
1980–81	—	—	—	—
1981–82	31,190	15,088	16,102	9,922
1982–83	43,977	22,711	25,213	19,042
1983–84	21,186	18,976	3,027	-3,687
1984–85	24,001	13,734	10,267	3,960
1985–86	29,035	21,742	7,293	2,818
1986–87	48,131	25,689	22,442	14,155
Average	35,110	20,147	15,670	9,105

Table 7.8   Income, Cost, and Margins per Acre by
Technology and Year

Technology/ Year	Mean			
	Gross Income	Operating Costs	Gross Margin	Net Margin
DTW				
1985–86	1,434	2,242	-809	-988
1986–87	1,608	1,355	254	-36
Average	1,554	1,630	-76	-332
STW				
1980–81	—	—	—	—
1981–82	1,380	746	706	181
1982–83	1,484	1,019	480	-141
1983–84	1,219	1,054	161	-569
1984–85	1,523	1,157	370	-493
1985–86	1,729	1,132	603	-60
1986–87	1,992	1,051	939	262
Average	1,595	1,054	553	-144
LLP				
1980–81	—	—	—	—
1981–82	869	463	435	181
1982–83	1,196	572	625	396
1983–84	683	591	92	-247
1984–85	1,254	666	587	293
1985–86	1,080	730	349	167
1986–87	1,489	834	655	372
Average	1,125	646	488	227

Table 7.9   Operating Costs per Scheme by Technology and Year

Technology/	Costs				
Year	Salaries	Fuel	Oil	Spare Parts	Other
DTW					
1985–86	4,389	23,523	3,045	2,789	15,073
1986–87	6,033	25,074	2,796	4,949	8,021
Average	5,211	24,298	2,920	3,869	11,547
STW					
1980–81	—	—	—	—	—
1981–82	1,644	5,983	867	592	398
1982–83	1,636	6,852	1,246	1,534	634
1983–84	1,990	6,769	1,207	1,214	912
1984–85	2,183	6,402	1,115	1,398	612
1986–87	2,128	6,722	885	1,462	1,664
Average	1,946	6,685	1,054	1,310	867
LLP					
1980–81	—	—	—	—	—
1981–82	2,543	9,524	1,368	553	611
1982–83	3,132	15,154	1,992	847	642
1983–84	3,380	9,109	2,251	1,811	1,357
1984–85	2,170	7,279	1,522	2,069	427
1985–86	2,428	13,044	2,258	1,889	2,255
1986–87	4,115	12,210	2,158	3,037	3,898
Average	3,085	11,226	1,901	1,673	1,689

Table 7.10   Yield Statistics by Technology and Year

Technology/ Year	Mean	Count	Valid Number	Standard Error	Maximum	Minimum	Median
DTW							
1985–86	21.83	11	9	5.37	41.82	2.70	29.23
1986–87	26.25	20	20	.82	47.40	2.70	26.50
Total/Avg.	24.78	31	29	2.34	44.19	2.70	27.41
STW							
1980–81	—	6	0	—	—	—	—
1981–82	—	52	0	—	—	—	—
1982–83	40.00	71	26	1.90	52.94	16.67	41.81
1983–84	28.90	98	44	1.83	55.75	3.72	29.56
1984–85	36.42	96	55	1.78	72.26	12.36	37.06
1985–86	34.09	115	83	1.41	59.52	3.71	35.67
1986–87	38.65	108	80	1.44	72.73	3.23	39.26
Total/Avg.	35.54	556	288	1.76	72.73	3.23	36.92
LLP							
1980–81	—	10	0	—	—	—	—
1981–82	—	31	0	—	—	—	—
1982–83	—	26	0	—	—	—	—
1983–84	19.45	24	2	15.75	35.20	3.70	19.45
1984–85	37.99	15	5	10.70	65.85	13.96	26.40
1985–86	25.25	22	10	6.27	58.67	6.40	16.78
1986–87	37.24	35	17	1.85	47.73	23.48	37.80
Total/Avg.	32.78	163	34	2.78	65.85	3.70	34.95

Table 7.11 Paddy, Diesel Fuel and Oil Prices

Year	Paddy Official Groups (Tk/maund)		Diesel Official Groups (Tk/liter)		Mobil Oil Groups (k/gal.)
1979–80	121	—	—	13.8	—
1980–81	100	—	—	22.5	—
1981–82	128	—	23.7	26	96
1982–83	150	130	33.7	35	122
1983–84	160	147	33.7	35	123
1984–85	160	150	33.7	34	122
1985–86	175	171	33.7	35	135
1986–87	205	197	33.7	32	128

Table 7.12 Performance of Proshika Groups by Water Contract, Technology and Year

Technology/ Year	Gross Income			Operating Costs			Net Margin		
	Fixed per Acre	Share of Crop	Other	Fixed per Acre	Share of Crop	Other	Fixed per Acre	Share of Crop	Other
DTW									
1985–86	—	27,255	60,006	—	-11,758	-23,505	—	-14,880	-30,185
1986–87	50,522	61,026	—	26,630	48,693	—	19,874	1,281	—
Average	50,522	51,934	60,006	26,630	46,087	83,511	19,874	-3,070	-30,185
STW									
1980–81	—	—	—	—	—	—	—	—	—
1981–82	—		18,817	—	—	9,703	—	—	3,049
1982–83	16,303	21,444	11,274	11,015	13,175	14,814	-1,605	620	-2,686
1983–84	12,863	16,354	9,744	10,970	13,289	14,613	-6,022	-6,141	-6,278
1984–85	16,826	17,171	11,535	11,152	12,630	8,561	-2,342	-5,015	-3,251
1985–86	18,522	20,205	—	9,624	13,054	—	3,606	-347	—
1986–87	20,950	27,766	—	11,066	14,209	—	993	5,283	—
Average	17,150	21,016	15,580	10,776	13,314	10,212	-1,036	-773	192
LLP									
1980–81	—	—	—	—	—	—	—	—	—
1981–82	—		31,190	—	—	15,088	—	—	9,922
1982–83	39,317	—	48,636	18,204	—	28,220	12,958	—	26,479
1983–84	23,910	20,382	9,916	20,048	9,953	21,033	-2,701	878	-14,661
1984–85	25,546	18,697	26,550	15,644	7,620	16,221	3,094	4,631	5,987
1985–86	21,460	23,364	47,475	10,196	18,902	36,792	4,612	32	7,739
1986–87	41,551	51,353	54,000	27,224	24,091	29,122	6,404	18,689	16,885
Average	32,080	38,069	35,952	20,009	20,078	20,313	4,741	10,763	12,004

All numbers are mean values.

Table 7.13 Net Margins by Water Contract, Technology and Year

Technology/Year	Fixed per Acre			Share of Crop			Other Contract			Total		
	Mean	Standard Error	Count	Mean	Standard Error	Count	Mean	Standard Error	Count	Mean	Standard Error	Count
DTW												
1985–86	—	—	—	-14,880	6,938	7	-30,185	5,889	4	-18,281	5,840	11
1986–87	19,874	—	1	1,281	5,740	9	—	—	2,210	5,524	20	—
Total	19,874	—	1	-3,070	4,744	26	-30,185	5,889	4	-4,149	4,529	31
STW												
1980–81	—	—	—	—	—	—	—	—	16	—	—	16
1981–82	—	—	—	—	—	—	3,049	053	52	3,049	1,053	52
1982–83	-1,605	733	23	620	1,711	27	-2,686	2,504	21	-612	945	71
1983–84	-6,022	1,283	24	-6,141	1,368	52	-6,278	4,549	22	-6,117	1,010	98
1984–85	-2,342	893	22	-5,015	765	61	-3,251	2,232	13	-4,215	595	96
1985–86	3,606	1,111	20	-347	1,051	77	—	—	18	480	867	115
1986–87	993	1,050	21	5,283	1,109	75	—	—	12	4,335	910	108
Total	-1,036	545	110	-773	573	292	1,192	939	154	-554	405	556
LLP												
1980–81	—	—	—	—	—	—	—	—	10	—	—	10
1981–82	—	—	—	—	—	—	9,922	2,161	31	9,922	2,161	31
1982–83	12,958	3,671	12	—	—	—	26,479	5,678	14	19,042	3,520	26
1983–84	-2,701	2,737	16	878	13,510	2	-14,661	5,147	6	-3,687	2,630	24
1984–85	3,094	1,823	7	4,631	5,535	3	5,987	8,621	5	3,960	1,921	15
1985–86	4,612	4,534	3	32	6,841	9	7,739	10,071	10	2,818	4,512	22
1986–87	6,404	9,577	11	18,689	3,539	17	16,885	3,752	7	14,155	3,964	35
Total	4,741	2,707	49	10,763	3,236	31	12,004	2,171	83	9,105	1,536	163

Table 7.14 Returns to Water Contracts by ADC

Technology/ ADC	Fixed per Acre			Share of Crop			Other Contract			Total Mean
	Mean	Count	Valid N	Mean	Count	Valid N	Mean	Count	Valid N	
DTW										
Mirzapur	—	—	—	8,053	9	9	—	—	—	8,053
Sreepur	—	—	—	-11,556	14	14	-30,185	4	2	-13,885
Serajganj	19,874	1	1	—	—	—	—	—	—	19,874
Dhamrai	—	—	—	3,162	3	3	—	—	—	3,162
Total/Avg.	19,874	1	1	-3,070	26	26	-30,185	4	2	-4,149
STW										
Bhairab	2,847	2	1	3,995	12	12	-946	53	12	1,577
Saturia	—	—	—	-1,878	80	80	7,756	12	5	-1,311
Singair	—	—	—	-6,198	29	29	—	1	—	-6,198
Harirampur	—	—	—	-1,581	21	21	-4,070	4	3	-1,892
Ghior	—	—	—	-1,299	43	42	7,929	8	5	-317
Nagarpur	-5,599	1	1	-5,619	10	10	528	17	11	-2,545
Madaripur	—	—	—	-4,721	28	25	-112	15	6	-3,829
Mirzapur	-1,444	19	17	4,857	22	21	-428	11	7	1,655
Shibgonj	-1,524	54	50	—	—	—	1,667	15	11	-949
Gabtoli	3,174	15	15	6,451	34	34	—	1	—	5,448
Kaliakoir	-6,606	2	2	—	—	—	964	2	1	-4,083
Atpara	-13,027	3	3	—	—	—	—	2	—	-13,027
Sreepur	—	—	—	-13,001	3	3	—	—	—	-13,001
Chatalpar	—	—	—	—	—	—	—	1	—	—
Domar	2,784	2	2	—	—	—	—	2	—	2,784
Kuliarchar	—	—	—	—	—	—	5,076	5	1	5,076
Serajgonj	146	10	10	—	—	—	—	—	—	146
Muksudpur	3,589	1	1	-3,494	1	1	-5,115	1	1	-1,673
Debigonj	-9,085	1	1	—	—	—	—	1	—	-9,085
Bhanga	—	—	—	8,045	6	6	—	—	—	8,045
Brahmanbaria	—	—	—	—	2	—	—	—	—	—
Narail	—	—	—	-3,298	1	1	—	1	1	-1,649
Ulipur	—	—	—	—	—	—	—	2	—	—
Total/Avg.	-1,036	110	103	-773	292	285	1,192	154	64	-554
LLP										
Bhairab	11,796	1	1	—	—	—	16,713	3	2	15,074
Ulania	—	2,904	5	5	—	—	-480	22	8	821
Khaliajuri	20,379	11	7	—	—	—	21,219	25	12	20,909
Kalkini	-5,533	14	14	—	—	—	-1,802	5	4	-4,704
Madaripur	—	—	—	14,723	14	14	14,608	1	1	14,715
Mirzapur	—	—	—	15,210	6	6	—	—	—	15,210
Atpara	—	—	—	11,142	2	2	—	2	—	11,142
Sreepur	-2,977	1	1	-7,784	2	2	—	1	—	-6,182
Chatalpar	9,718	4	4	—	—	—	13,418	23	23	12,870
Gournadi	4,910	3	3	-276	4	4	—	—	—	1,947
Serajgonj	—	—	—	37,407	1	1	—	—	—	37,407
Muksudpur	—	—	—	-3,373	2	2	—	—	—	-3,373
B-baria	47,362	2	2	—	—	—	—	—	—	47,362
Bhola	—	-1,982	7	7	—	—	—	1	—	-1,982
Ulipur	-9,622	1	1	—	—	—	—	—	—	-9,622
Total/Avg.	4,741	49	45	10,763	31	31	12,004	83	50	9,105

N = number

Table 7.15 Number of Irrigation Groups Starting
and Ending by ADC up to 1985–86

ADC	Number up to 1985–86		Discontinued %		Technology
	Started	Discontinued	of ADC	of All Groups	
Bhairab	18	13	72	9	STW
Saturia	28	5	18	4	STW
Singair	10	6	60	4	STW
Harirampur	9	4	44	3	STW
Ghior	16	6	38	4	STW
Nagarpur	11	11	100	8	STW
Ulania	11	11	100	8	LLP
Khaliajuri	14	13	100	9	LLP
Kalkini	10	10	100	7	LLP
Madaripur	17	10	59	7	STW
Mirzapur	15	2	13	1	STW
Shibgonj	20	14	70	10	STW
Gabtoli	15	1	7	1	STW
Sreepur	11	3	27	2	DTW
Chatalpar	26	25	96	18	LLP
Other	24	8	33	6	STW/LLP
Total	255	142	56	100	—

Table 7.16 Distribution of Discontinuations by Technology

Technology	Number	Discontinued % of			Number	Operating % of		
		Total	Row	Col.		Total	Row	Col.
DTW	3	1.2	27	2	8	3	72	7
STW 4"	79	31	46	56	90	35	53	80
STW 6"	—	—	—	—	1	0.4	100	0.9
LLP 6"	59	23	80	42	14	6	19	12
LLP 4"	1	0.4	100	0.7	—	—	—	—
Total	144	—	56	100	113	44	. 44	100
Excluding rented LLP								
LLP 6"	35	12	51	30	34	12	49	21

Table 7.17 Reasons Given for STW Discontinuation

| | | | | | | | Number of Groups Reporting Problem | | | | | | | |
ADC	Soils	Command Area	Mgmt.	Proshika	Floods	Break-downs	Water	Group	Low Return	Competition	Agronomy	Other	Total Cases
Bhairab	12	11	3			1		6	1		1		13
Saturia	1	1				1				3	3	2	5
Singair	2		1		3	2	1		1	2	2		6
Harirampur			1		2	2			4	1		1	4
Ghior		2	1		3	5		2					10
Nagarpur	1	1	6	3	4	5		5					10
Madaripur	1			1	3	5	8	1	1		4		9
Mirzapur		1				2						1	2
Shibgonj	1	6	5	1		7	2	3	5	6		4	14
Gabtoli			2			1		1	1				1
Kaliakoir			1			1	1	1					1
Atpara							3					2	3
Chatalpar		1					1						1
Domar	1						1		1		1		1
Kuliarchar							1		2	1	1		1
Debigonj			1				1		1				1
Total responses	19	24	20	5	16	32	19	18	17	13	12	10	77

Table 7.18 Reasons Given for LLP Discontinuation

| | | | | | *Number of Groups Reporting Problem* | | | | | | | | |
ADC	Soils	Command Area	Mgmt.	Proshika	Floods	Break-downs	Water	Group	Low Return	Compe-tition	Rented Cases	Agronomy	Other	Total Cases
Ulania	4	6	1	2	3	1	1	—	4	—	—	—	4	11
Khaliajuri	—	—	2	1	12	1	—	2	—	—	—	—	1	13
Kalkini	—	2	1	1	8	6	1	—	6	1	—	—	—	10
Madaripur	—	—	—	—	—	1	1	—	1	—	—	1	—	3
Chatalpar	—	—	—	—	—	—	—	—	—	—	24	—	—	24
Gournadi	—	—	—	—	—	1	—	—	—	—	—	—	—	1
Total responses	4	8	4	4	23	8	4	2	11	1	24	1	5	60

Figure 7.1 Percent of Groups Discontinuing by Start and End Year

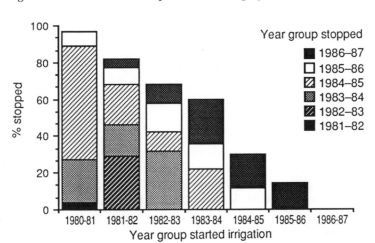

Figure 7.2 Percent of Groups Discontinuing by End and Start Year

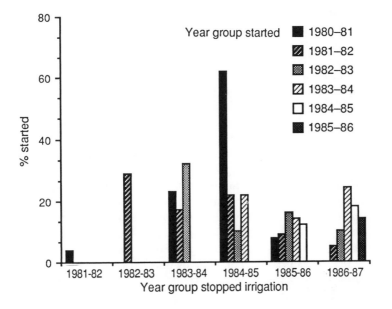

CHAPTER EIGHT

Employment

A CRUCIAL QUESTION in assessing the landless irrigation strategy is whether it significantly enhances the welfare of the poor through employment. It is a common assumption that minor irrigation, by creating a winter rice season and contributing to wheat and supplementary irrigation of *aman*, not only enhances the productivity of land but also thereby increases the opportunities for the employment of landless workers. It is surprising then, that little research has been directly focused upon the employment implications of the Second Five-Year Plan (2FYP) minor irrigation strategy. Apart from occasional references in the 1982 study by M. A. Hamid and others, "Shallow Tubewells under IDA Credit in North-West Bangladesh," no further evidence is yet available with which Proshika can compare its own experience. Obviously Proshika cannot substitute for a necessary national research effort on these issues but, for its own satisfaction, it must seek the answer to the following two questions:

- Is there any significant difference in employment generation between the different ways of socially organizing the service of water through minor irrigation technology?
- How are the opportunities for employment (and therefore the survival strategies of landless workers and marginal peasants) affected by the introduction of minor irrigation?

Bearing in mind the caveats we have entered before about drawing firm conclusions from these limited studies, our answers to these questions are that there is probably some increase in employment due to higher command areas on landless-owned irrigation schemes compared to privately owned ones, but apparently not due to more intensive cultivation. Winter rice irrigation does, however, generate significant extra employment for agricultural laborers, which eases seasonal troughs in employment and may increase agricultural wages during peak periods. Thus, so far, the main benefits to the poor appear to come from the expansion of irrigation and through any implicit rent from their ownership of irrigation assets, rather than from significantly increased productivity or employment under the landless-owned irrigation equipment (leaving aside the possibility of greater demand-based growth linkages due to higher incomes of the poor generated in this way).

There is no *a priori* reason why the opportunities for employment should be greater on landless-serviced command areas than on privatized or Krishi Samabay Samity (KSS) command areas. Under competitive conditions the coefficient of person days per unit of output should be constant. So we do not proceed from the assumption that, other things being equal, the landless irrigation service will create superior employment opportunities. Rather, we proceed from the assumption that other things are *not* equal and that other differences will affect the rate of labor utilization positively in the group schemes. We could expect employment opportunities to be indirectly and disproportionately enhanced in the group schemes only when the following conditions apply:

- if, under conditions of landless irrigation, command areas tend to be maximized (as suggested by Mandal's initial surveys to determine average command areas in the study locality—for further analysis see chapter 5, appendix A and chapter 7);
- if, on balance, the incentives for raising productivity are higher, involving fuller cultivation practices (see chapter 7 for comparison of effects of share- and cash-payment systems),
- if the landless groups become more involved in providing a wider range of services to farmers in their command areas, and
- if the land of small farmers is more equally and in a timely fashion served with water.

This is the basis for responding to the first question noted above. The second question involves a different kind of assumption in which situations are more equal. It raises the wider issue of the impact of change in cropping patterns upon the *net* increase in the opportunities for employment as the seasonal distribution of work alters. There are also the related issues of how the patterns of physical mobility of labor and the terms of labor contracts are affected.

These matters concern Proshika not just because it would like to see more employment opportunities for landless workers and marginal peasants, but because such opportunities mean less reliance upon advances and loans and more independence in wage bargaining. Furthermore, if the male adult in the household is less obliged to migrate seasonally in search for work elsewhere, the women and children in his family are less dependent on advances, less vulnerable and more likely to receive market wages in postharvest work.

To pursue this range of employment issues, a dual strategy was adopted, recognizing from the outset that this would not exhaust all the possibilities for dealing with comparisons between organized and unorganized sections of rural labor. A rigorous comparison would entail a sample of unorganized labor and the maintenance of regular contact with them (as was done with group respondents). The dual strategy involved a study by Mandal at Bangladesh Agricultural University (BAU) with farmers as respondents, and a study by Proshika, through the field staff, with group members as respondents. The first part of this chapter presents a comparative analysis of labor employment for winter rice production by farmers in landless and privately owned irrigation schemes; the second part of the chapter looks at the labor market, the relationships between patterns of employment and individual and group characteristics and the effects of the development of irrigation on the amount and seasonal distribution of labor.

Employment Generated by Landless and Privately Owned Irrigation Schemes

The major purpose of this analysis is to see whether the amount of labor employed for winter rice production in landless irrigation schemes is significantly different from that in privatized schemes. On conceptual grounds there can be two possible sources of increased employment in landless schemes—larger command areas and higher labor inputs per unit of land. A further possibility, not explored here, is that higher incomes from irrigation to the landless and poor will lead to expenditure patterns that will lead to greater local production and greater local employment opportunities than if the income from irrigation goes to the already better off.

This part of the employment study strategy was designed to measure and compare the labor use between minor irrigation schemes under different forms of social organization, with a sample of farmers with land in the command areas as respondents. The original intention was to compare the landless schemes with both KSS farmer group and private ownership schemes. It was not possible, however, to find KSS group schemes located in areas of landless group schemes where agro-climatic variables could be held constant.[1] The comparison was therefore between landless and private ownership schemes in each of the three research areas: Saturia, Ghior—shallow tubewell (STW) schemes—and Kalkini, a low-lift pump (LLP) scheme. This study was based on the 1984 winter rice season. The comparison was meant to be for the whole year, to obtain the *net* employment effects across the agricultural year, but the floods seriously disturbed the pattern of labor demand for the following *aman,* so the comparison was confined to the winter rice season. Because the study had been carried out up to the floods, the data for labor use during the winter rice season itself were still valid. So the comparison does not include postharvest processing. Because Mandal at BAU was not available to repeat the data collection and analysis in the following year, the floods forced us to accept this restricted focus. The schemes were selected on the basis of average command area size for the respective landless and private forms of organization. The survey on which this selection was based indicated that, in each region, the command areas for the landless schemes were higher than for the private schemes (see table 8.1). The required detail restricted the study to a pair of schemes in each region, with attempts to control for cropping pattern, soil type, land ownership and tenurial arrangements. Within the command areas, the farmers were selected to represent a matched variation in topography and tenancy status. Data from the sample of farmers consisted of plot/crop labor use descriptions for the year of study compared with the same plot/season labor use in the year preceding the introduction of irrigation. The overall finding from this study was that, although farmers in the landless schemes employed a greater number of labor days per unit area, especially in the preharvest operations, the main explanation of higher labor utilization in the landless command areas came from the larger command areas in such schemes.

One might expect that landless irrigation provides greater opportunities to increase the command area as well as the labor inputs per unit of land because water distribution is expected to be more efficient and water users are likely to have more confidence in the landless group water supply. The landless members should have no preference with respect to water delivery because they themselves have very little land in the command areas. Partly as a result of this, because of incentive and informational advantages due to their owning the irrigation equipment and doing the work, and for other reasons elaborated upon in the introduction, the landless could have lower transaction costs in negotiating with water users. Furthermore, the ensured water supply is likely to encourage water users to apply complementary inputs, including improved crop husbandry practices that require increased labor per unit of land (for elaborate discussion of this hypothesis, see below and Wood 1982). In contrast, private owners of irrigation equipment are likely to give preference to their own plots in allocating water, often at the expense of other farmers. This leads to distrust and non-cooperation between water users and private water suppliers, which may ultimately be manifested in a low command areas, inadequate water supply, low complementary inputs and, consequently, poor average yields or, possibly, larger command areas but with inefficient water supply and even poorer yields.

There is mixed evidence on command area performance by landless and private schemes. In the initial years of operation, Proshika landless groups appeared to have larger command areas than the private owners in the study areas (as emerged in chapter 5, table 5.1.) In recent years, however, landless command areas, especially STW command areas, in Saturia and Ghior, appeared to have declined to the extent that there is no significant difference from private tubewell command areas (Ali 1986). The average command area of these Proshika landless STWs has been estimated as 12.05 acres, which appears to be not significantly different from the average STW command area of 13.73 acres for Dhaka district or 11.48 acres for Bangladesh for the year 1981–82 and 1983–84. (For estimates of individual years, see chapters 6 and 7 above; however, as noted in chapter 7, comparison between Proshika figures of command areas and official figures are problematic, because the different methodologies involved lead us to believe the Proshika ones are the more accurate).

In the following sections, empirical results show the pattern and extent of labor use for winter rice production in the two types of scheme. Given the range of changes in the cropping patterns and cropping intensities caused by the introduction of irrigation, a comparison of employment for only the irrigated winter rice season cannot fully explain the variation in the aggregate employment of the command area farmers. Nevertheless, as winter rice is the major irrigated food crop, a comparative analysis of employment in its production may provide important insights into the nature and extent of employment created in the landless irrigation schemes when compared with the private ones.

Methodology

Sampling

The sampling frame used for the access study, as described in chapter 5, was also adopted for this survey. An initial census was conducted of all farms cultivating land in the landless and privately controlled schemes selected for study.

Selection of Farmers

Most farmers had only one plot in the studied command areas, while others had more than one plot. For farmers having more than one plot in the command areas, plots were of different topography, soil type and tenure status, and care was taken to include all of them. All farmers were included in the selected command areas for the purpose of the survey, but a number of them could not be approached because of the distant location of their residence and difficult communication from the scheme sites. Finally, plotwise labor-use data were collected from the sample farmers through a multivisit farm survey conducted from March to June 1984.

Labor Use in Winter Rice Production

Labor Use by Crop Operation

Plowing, puddling, seedbed preparation and transplanting are the important preharvest crop operations that (in addition to weeding) required the most labor in both landless and private schemes (see table 8.2). Because there was serious flood damage to the winter rice crop, with harvesting unfinished in some cases, especially in the Ghior landless scheme, labor use for preharvest operations was shown separately and used as a more logical basis for comparison. In Saturia, there was virtually no difference in per-acre preharvest labor use between landless and private schemes. But in Ghior and Kalkini, total preharvest labor use per acre appeared to be greater in the landless schemes than in the private schemes, although the difference was significant at the 1 percent level only in the case of the Kalkini LLP scheme (table 8.3).

The most important crop operation was weeding. Farmers used more labor for this in the landless than in the private schemes. Crop operations such as plowing and transplanting required more or less equal amounts of labor in both types of schemes across different locations. The variations in the use of labor for weeding are likely to have caused variations in yield but we could not verify it for the lack of complete yield data, except in Saturia, where the 1984 flood was less severe than in Ghior and Kalkini. One of the possible explanations for the higher labor use for weeding in the landless schemes was the comparatively better crop growth, which one would expect, given the adequate and timely supply of water in landless command areas. Chapter 5 discusses more efficient water distribution.

About 95 percent of the labor days used for winter rice production were provided by male labor. Female labor was mainly used for postharvest operations such as threshing, drying and cleaning of the crop (table 8.3). In Kalkini, female labor in some cases was also used for transplanting and harvesting.

Labor Use by Sources

Two major sources of labor were family and hired labor. Casual labor on a daily basis constituted the major proportion of hired labor used for winter rice production. An insignificant proportion of hired labor was provided by contract laborers, and they were paid on a piece-rate basis. Contract labor was used for crop operations such as land improvement, plowing, transplanting and harvesting of crops. Small farmers who do not have enough draft animals used contract laborers with animals for plowing land. Contract labor is usually employed for piece work, mostly unsupervised by employers, and hence the quality of work is reduced. This is one of the reasons for preferring casually hired labor to contract labor.

Table 8.4 shows the amount of family and hired labor used per acre of winter rice in the studied schemes. In Saturia and Kalkini, the proportions of hired labor were much higher than those of family labor. In Kalkini, about 70 percent of farm labor was casually hired. In Ghior, family labor constituted more than a half of the total labor used per acre. The main reason for the higher use of family labor in Ghior was that there were not enough off-farm employment opportunities. Furthermore, Ghior is virtually a flood-prone, single-cropped area with a limited number of crops to compete with the winter rice crop, so opportunities for employing family labor in other crops are also limited. In Saturia, most farmers had non-farm activities such as petty trading, which implies that non-farm wages were higher than agricultural wages. In Kalkini, farmers used a higher proportion of hired labor because a substantial proportion of family members were not available for farm work due to their greater involvement in education, salaried jobs and petty trades.

A comparison of the landless and private schemes reveals a similar pattern of family and hired labor use. In general, crop operations such as land improvement, plowing, puddling, seedbed preparation and postharvest operations required more family labor than hired labor. On the other hand, operations such as transplanting, weeding and harvesting required much more hired labor than family labor, basically because these are the most time-specific, critical operations and have to be performed within a short span of time.

Wage Rates

As wage rates are more or less equally fixed in a locality, daily wage rates did not differ significantly between landless and private schemes in the respective areas (table 8.5). Wages did vary between crop operations performed in different months. For example, the highest wages were observed for the harvesting operation. In Kalkini, harvest laborers were paid in terms of cropshare, ranging from one-ninth to one-tenth of the harvested crop. This is a traditional mode of payment and the harvest laborers are better paid this way than under a cash-payment system as practiced in Saturia and Ghior.

Labor Use by Farm Size and Teneurial Status of Land

Table 8.6 presents a comparative analysis of preharvest labor use between farmsize groups. As expected, medium farmers in general used more labor days per acre, compared to small and large farmers, except in the Ghior private scheme, but the difference was not statistically significant. There is no perceptible pattern of differences in labor use between farmsize groups in landless and private schemes.

Table 8.7 shows per acre preharvest labor use on the owned and sharecropped land of the sample farmers. The table reveals that labor days used per acre of winter rice on owned land were higher that those observed for rented land in all areas, although the difference was statistically significant only in the case of the Saturia private scheme. But the difference in labor use is more prominent in the case of private schemes as compared with landless schemes. One of the reasons for the reduction in the gaps between labor use on owned and sharecropped land may be that the sharecroppers in landless schemes, who are also predominantly small farmers, were better served with water and did not discriminate in labor use between owned and sharecropped land. An implication of this is that, although the landless schemes do not appear to have any special opportunities to create greater employment in aggregate terms, these schemes might have improved water use efficiency, thus stimulating higher labor inputs on sharecropped land. As the landless irrigation command areas stabilize and the initial mechanical problems and uncertainties of cultivating irrigated crops are reduced, however, landowners might tend to evict tenants from the sharecropped land, at least during the winter rice season —as was illustrated in chapter 5.

There is mixed evidence on the intensity of labor use for winter rice production by farmers in landless and private schemes. We have confined our comparison to only preharvest labor, but landless schemes in Ghior and Kalkini appeared to entail marginally higher employment as compared to private schemes; in Saturia, there is no difference in labor use between the two types of schemes.

Increased command area, rather than increased labor intensity per unit of land, seems to be a more important source of increased employment for landless irrigation schemes. But the comparative evidence on command area estimates is mixed. Although the Proshika landless command areas were larger than private command areas in the initial years, they appear to have declined on the average in the recent years in highly competitive situations. The overall conclusion one can draw is that, although farmers in some landless schemes had employed more labor days per unit of land, especially in the preharvest crop operations, landless schemes did not appear to have created significantly greater potential for increasing aggregate employment. Whatever the initial success with bigger command areas, the potential for enhancing employment has to some extent diminished because of the decline in the command area over the recent years. This implies that the major advantages of landless irrigation have to be sought not on productivity grounds, in the main, but on broader, equity ones. The access of the landless to irrigation equipment, greater control of small and marginal farmers over water distribution, more efficient water supply by the landless and a wider distribution of irrigation benefits through wider ownership of the irrigation equipment by the poor can substantially contribute to reducing rural poverty.

Irrigation and Employment of Landless Group Members

This section describes the results of the year-long weekly survey of a sample of members of six Proshika groups who have different access to irrigation. The aim of the survey was to see whether the development of irrigation affected the amount and seasonal distribution of labor, and whether ownership of irrigation assets by the group enhanced their access to this employment. Unfortunately, the sample and survey methods were unable to provide answers to these specific questions, and these were partly the wrong questions anyway because of the following:

- the sample was too small and unrepresentative,
- the overall increase in employment opportunities and wage rates from mid 1983 to the end of 1985 overshadows the effect of differences in access to irrigation, and
- an extensive and integrated labor market means that employment depends more on individual characteristics than on collective ownership of irrigation assets.

Hence, the main questions concern employment and income patterns according to the characteristics of individuals and to some extent the local labor market, rather than according to their relationship to irrigation assets. Although this provides good evidence of irrigation's impact on the seasonal pattern of employment and the level of cash incomes (from land control and petty entrepreneurial activities), little can be said about its impact on the total employment or labor income by comparison with areas where irrigation is less developed.

Survey Methodology

The data for this study were collected from February 1985 to January 1986, after collection had been aborted in the previous year as a result of the floods, which not only diverted the field staff but also produced an atypical year. The data consisted of a single questionnaire per respondent (household and general employment details), the completion of a weekly employment data sheet to reduce the unreliability of longer recall data and self-kept diaries. The working patterns and logistics of the field staff were therefore important factors in determining selection. After original intentions for a larger population of respondents across more categories of groups, these constraints restricted the frame to a comparison between groups with irrigation assets, groups in an area of privatized irrigation and groups in nonirrigated areas. Three such sets of group respondents (50 percent of members chosen at random) were studied in the two STW locations of Saturia and Ghior (with the LLP area of Kalkini dropping out through inadequate supervision of data collection). Obviously the steady trimming of the sample base undermined initial hopes of a large enough population for statistical comparison between systems, but the data on these six groups of respondents is comprehensive and offers some basis for quantitative inferences as well as for qualitative case study interpretation.

Group Characteristics

Saturia and Ghior Area Development Centers (ADCs) are both in Manikganj District, in old Dhaka District, some thirty miles west of Dhaka. They are densely populated and are located in the floodplain of the new Brahmaputra, which is widely subject to flooding. The development of irrigation had been rapid but, at the time of the 1983–84 Agricultural Census, not quite 16 percent and 11 percent respectively of the net cultivated area had been irrigated and there was still considerable potential for further growth of STWs in the Third Five-Year Plan (3FYP) period.[2] These are among the poorer areas of Bangladesh, but their proximity to Dhaka has provided better communications and access to employment.

One group from each ADC was chosen from the following three categories:

- groups who had invested in an STW,
- groups that resided in an area of private irrigation but did not themselves have an STW, and
- groups from an unirrigated area.

The idea was to test for the effect of these circumstances on employment and income. But other circumstances that had a strong influence on the dependent variables were not, in the event, controlled. The interpretation of the results is complicated by differences in the ownership of land and in the self-employment patterns of the groups concerned.

The two groups with irrigation are those that were chosen from these two ADCs for the other studies reported in this book (Attigram Gorib Unnayan Samity from Saturia and Ragunathpur Bhumihin and Prantic Krishak Samity in Ghior). Table 8.8 shows the numbers of households interviewed from each group. A 50 percent sample of respondents was chosen from each group, which resulted in a smaller sample size than is desirable for groups with few members. There are inevitable problems where respondents are mobile, staying away from their homes both for short periods and when they seasonally migrate for months at a time, perhaps never to return. One of the groups was lacking in cohesion. When visited in 1986 it was not merely not functioning; there seemed to be no clear recognition of group activities at all. This may have been due in part to the transfer of the Proshika worker.

Demographic Composition

The following significant differences in household composition affect the presentation and interpretation of statistics:

- in two cases, the respondent (group member) was not the "household head" (most senior effective male),
- in eleven cases, more than one adult male was present for at least part of the year (in two of these cases there were two other adult males, some of whom were reported as engaged in income earning activities),
- most respondents were reported as living in households with one

adult female (a wife), but some households had no adult female, and in others there was more than one adult female, either a second wife or a mother or some other female relative, and
- not all adult household members were present for the entire survey period, which made it difficult, and in some cases impossible, to record their activities and incomes for significant periods.

The group categories affect the differences strongly. In particular, the group with irrigation from Saturia ADC (group 2.1) consisted entirely of nuclear families (one adult male and female only, or in one case a single adult male); while both those with two extra adult males occurred in group 2.3 (the group not in an irrigated area).

Because the original plan had been to record employment and income by household, this situation, which is usual, compares household totals that are strongly affected by demographic composition and hence quite misleading. For example, household totals of days worked at certain occupations are strongly affected by the number of potential workers, yet dividing totals by this number can be misleading when one or more of the second males are away for part of the year and their activities are not completely reported. Some of the other males were too young for full-time work and hence worked intermittently, for lower wages than the fully adult males. In order to bypass these difficulties, results are on the whole reported only for the respondent.

Land Cultivation

Although the groups supported by Proshika are termed landless, some of their members own, rent, or both, small amounts of land. While some do not even own their house plots, others own these and small areas under homestead cultivation, while yet others own some cultivated land. For reasons explained elsewhere, a self-defined target group approach is used, based on a class analysis of the agrarian structure in Bangladesh, which is broader than those termed landless or even assetless, to include those in imminent risk of becoming so (Wood 1985:459).

Table 8.9 shows the distribution of land. Information on land control is difficult to obtain, and there are many complexities involved. A number of inconsistencies in the data emerged. In some cases, the amount owned was not equal to the sum of that owned and cultivated, plus that sharecropped or mortgaged out. Both the groups in nonirrigated areas had more land on average than the other groups, and very little land was cultivated by members of the group with irrigation assets in Saturia, but this may be due to sample bias. In all the other groups, the respondents included some with agricultural and others with nonagricultural employment income sources. Unfortunately, the survey does not provide information on the cropping patterns on the land cultivated by the groups. The income derived from cultivation depends on whether the land was owned or sharecropped, whether it was irrigated and whether there was access to other necessary inputs such as animal tillage and household labor.

In general, net incomes to the cultivator from sharecropped land are presumed to be less than for owned land. This will depend to some extent on the potential of the land and whether it is irrigated. Tenure by access to irrigation was not reported and the use of the land cannot be accurately inferred from the timing of the labor spent on it (unless the operations done are known).[3] A further problem is that land was sometimes cultivated for only part of the year (for one season only) and in other cases land was cultivated that had not been recorded earlier. Therefore no attempt to impute income from cultivation has been made.[4]

It is often asserted that the introduction of irrigation has led to concentration of land ownership and its loss by weaker sections of the population. There may be good evidence for this hypothesis—and there is, at first glance, some apparent support for it—but it does not, on closer examination, tally with our findings. Most respondents reported fathers having significantly more land than could be inferred from the amounts the respondents reported themselves as owning. The land remaining with the respondents usually bore little relation to their imputed share of their father's land (assuming each brother inherited the same quantity), less the net amount they reported as lost.[5] This suggests either misreporting at some point and/or considerable mobility of land-owning status within generations, as some lose land while others gain it.

Even with such a small sample, on average, about 50 percent of the land cultivated by group members was reported as owned by them in both ADCs. Between households, however, the proportion of cultivated land owned varied from 0 to 100 percent. Most of the land that was not owned was sharecropped, although it is likely that mortgaged land was underreported or reported as owned. The quantity of land cultivated, the proportions owned or sharecropped and the proportions irrigated varied within groups. Five out of the fourteen who sharecropped land did not own any; obviously it was not necessary to own land in order to obtain it as a sharecropper. Without information on previous landholding (or that of close relatives, such as fathers) and livestock ownership, however, it is not possible to say whether those with the least assets can obtain access to land. Furthermore, there was considerable variation over time in the amount of land cultivated by respondents. This was revealed by the visit in 1987, when it was reported that a number of respondents who had been cultivating had given up, or were cultivating less, while others had taken up cultivation, were cultivating more and had even managed to buy some land.[6]

Occupational Patterns

The group with irrigation assets in Saturia differed strongly from the others in consisting almost exclusively of petty entrepreneurs, who owned and cultivated very little land and consequently did not engage in agricultural or nonagricultural laboring. (The petty entrepreneurial activities of these people involve considerable physical exertion.) Most other respondents reported either agricultural or nonagricultural employment, although a number reported both, and in a number of households where one member was reported as pursuing agricultural labor, others were reported as engaged in nonagricultural work. Most of those who cultivated land on their own account also engaged in agricultural labor for others.

Control of land strongly affects the allocation of labor by the respondent (table 8.10, and figure 8.1). Those with land spent more time working on their land than in the various forms of wage or entrepreneurial employment. Hence, as shown in table 8.11, average total recorded non-own-farm incomes declined in proportion to land cultivated. There is a statistically significant negative relation between area cultivated per household and income from employment.

Activities are divided into agricultural and nonagricultural; eighteen respondents reported agricultural labor and own cultivation as their main activities; twenty-six reported nonagricultural labor or entrepreneurial activities; and five reported both agricultural and nonagricultural employment. Some did both agricultural and nonagricultural activities in the same week; others did agricultural labor at one time of year and nonagricultural occupations at another—perhaps migrating for nonagricultural labor, or doing local hand-loom weaving, laboring or petty trading. For the reasons given above it is not wise to attribute differences between the groups to access to irrigation because of the different occupational patterns of each group based on their different access to land and entrepreneurial occupations. Most of those with entrepreneurial occupations do not cultivate land or engage in agricultural laboring, this is, in this sample, due to the influence of the one group in Saturia made up almost entirely of landless petty entrepreneurs. In the other groups, a number of those with land did nonagricultural work, although most did agricultural labor.

Nonagricultural Employment

A breakdown of the daily rates of pay by nonagricultural employment activity shows quite large and significant differences between them (see table 8.12[7]); individuals who did tailoring, van-pulling, milk-selling, masonry and fishing had above-average remuneration rates, while the waiter, driver and hawker had particularly low rates. Attributing these differences to the occupations concerned rather than to the individuals can be misleading, however, because there are not enough representatives of each activity type to provide such a test.[8]

There is no obvious seasonal pattern to nonagricultural employment and wage rates, although the composition of employment varies. In the months of traditionally low agricultural employment in this area—July, August and September—the limited evidence suggests that respondents are more likely to take up seasonal nonagricultural activities such as trading and fishing rather than nonagricultural laboring (such as on roads, brick making, construction and so on). This was the period when laboring opportunities, both agricultural and nonagricultural, were minimal and respondents were most likely to have migrated for work. Rates of remuneration (income per day worked) seem to have been highest at this time, but income per day of the month[9] was lower because fewer days were worked (tables 8.12 and 8.13). The greater frequency of higher-paying activities is misleading because these activities entailed greater expenses —for example, living away from home. Income per day worked from nonagricultural activities was highest from March to June, in part no doubt because this is the peak period for agricultural employment (see below).

Agricultural Employment

Agricultural labor did not on average provide even half the respondents' income and number of working days. Only in one group was income greater from agricultural than from nonagricultural employment; however, for a number of individuals (nineteen), it was the main source of employment and income. Nearly one-third of agricultural employment was on irrigated crops.

An apparent income-per-day differential exists between agricultural and nonagricultural employments. The difference is most striking for Saturia (table 8.14) but can be explained largely by the fact that agricultural wages include meals for the day while nonagricultural employments do not. Thus, for the few occasions in Saturia when payment was by the day, agricultural wages averaged the same as nonagricultural income per day (see table 8.15). The same pattern of difference between agricultural and nonagricultural rates of pay occurs in Ghior but it is not so clear that it can be attributed to the missing meals component in nonagricultural income. A further possibility is that much more agricultural labor is done on a permanent rather than on a daily basis in Ghior, for which payment is more difficult to record.[10] The difference between cash and cash-plus-meal payments is greater for permanently employed agricultural laborers (Tk25 as opposed to Tk20 per day in Ghior) than it is for daily paid labor (both average Tk22 per day).

Types of Labor Contracts

Most labor was employed on a daily basis, although in Ghior, and especially in Ragunathpur, there was a considerable amount of permanent labor (table 8.16). The question arises whether this permanent labor is bonded, with the implication that it is more exploited than daily paid workers. Two hypotheses about the relationship between daily and permanent wage are as follows:

- in semi-feudal conditions, permanent labor may receive less because it is a bonded condition (and may receive some in-kind payments), and
- in more competitive labor market conditions, permanent labor may be offered more employment (although sometimes at lower implicit daily wages) to provide greater incentives to effort and skill, and greater flexibility and lower supervision costs for employers.

The full returns to permanent labor may have been underestimated because they include some in-kind and/or infrequent payments (clothing, money to meet exceptional and emergency needs and so on), or interest and debt repayments (debt to employers was infrequently reported). On the other hand, these returns may have been overestimated because the agreed sums may not have been paid in full, and, especially if the contract is of the more traditional, bonded type, the hours of work may have been considerably longer and more demanding than for daily paid labor, with the laborer very much at the beck and call of the employer. The increase in peak labor demands may also in some circumstances be leading to labor tying, which may appear to have the same form as the traditional bonded labor, but in fact has a more capitalist content, as employers seek to gain preferential access to labor power during such peaks by offering employment above the spot wage rate in off-peak periods. These issues are difficult to investigate, and circumstances may be changing. Confounding factors also exist, such as the age and ability of the laborer, debt or other connections with employers or the coexistence of both types of relationship in the same area.

The apparent absence of a significant difference in the average agricultural wage rate between permanent and daily paid labor in Ghior (table 8.16) is somewhat surprising (there is a difference in Saturia, but the small number of days actually worked and, in one case, the exceptionally high wage reported, suggests that the coding was erroneous). The difference in wage rates is confounded by two factors: differences in the form of payment (cash only or cash plus meals) and the timing of the work under different contractual forms. Some of both daily and permanent labor were paid cash only and others cash and kind (that is, including at least meals). The average daily payment for permanent labor was at the same rate as daily paid labor, but those permanent laborers paid only in cash received slightly more than their daily paid equivalents.[11] In two cases in Ghior, the permanent laborer earned slightly more than the average daily rate but others, who frequently also did daily work as well as permanent, received no more for daily than for permanent labor. Although relatively little contract work was done, the return per day was somewhat higher for this type of work than for daily paid labor, with averages of Tk25 and Tk26 per day in the Saturia and Ghior groups respectively; however, this type of work occurred at times when cash wages for daily paid work were as high[12].

Seasonal factors also affected the difference between the average wages of the two contractual forms.

Seasonal Pattern of Employment and Wages

The availability of agricultural employment is strongly seasonal (table 8.17), reflecting the seasonal pattern of agricultural activities and the impact of irrigation in boosting employment in the winter rice season. Agricultural employment peaked in April, May and June, and was lowest in September, December and August (annual variations, which may be changing from year to year, in the timing of agricultural seasons means that the timing of agricultural labor demand will change from year to year).

Permanent labor occurred most frequently in January, April, May and June. Wages for permanent labor in these months were slightly lower than for the daily rate, although they included meals (table 8.18), and the agricultural wages were lowest at this time. The permanent labor paid cash received the same wages as daily paid labor from December 1985 to March 1986, but the permanent labor paid in cash and meals received less. The low wages in April–July 1985 compared with January–March 1986 may have been due not so much to seasonal factors as to the low price of rice faced by cultivators as a result of the excessive imports following the floods of 1984, which caused less damage than had been estimated.

Thus, the most reasonable interpretation of the slightly lower permanent, compared with daily, labor wages is that while most permanent labor was done in the months of peak labor demand, these months occurred earlier in the survey, when wages were lower.[13] Otherwise, with the exception of payment by cash plus meals, permanent labor did not receive less; in this latter case the difference is probably less than the value of the meals provided. Thus the apparently lower daily wage rate of permanent labor is a statistical artifact and does not lend support to either the labor-tying or semi-feudal hypotheses directly, although it does suggest that wages fluctuate under both payment systems in response to similar factors, which in turn suggests somewhat competitive conditions in the labor market. The coincidence of permanent labor with labor peaks supports the labor-tying hypothesis.

Agricultural Labor and Income

The respondents with the lowest incomes were those dependent on agricultural labor. They also had the most severe seasonal problems with employment and income falling to very low levels, especially in September. In tables 8.18 and 8.19, the sample has been divided into categories according to the proportion of agricultural wage laboring in total employment. Table 8.19 shows the location of these households in the sample groups. The respondents who spent more than 50 percent of their working days in agricultural labor had many days not working (and more days in their own home) between June and October, and lower incomes than other respondents. The increase in categories of work, implying low productivity or income per day, was related to the decline in days of agricultural labor in these months. Respondents who were not so dependent on agricultural laboring maintained higher incomes throughout the year and suffered little, if any, fall in income during these traditionally difficult months.

Employment in Irrigated Agriculture

For some members of three of the groups, there was considerable employment in irrigated agricultural work from December to July (see table 8.17, and figures 8.2 and 8.3). Some work on irrigated crops was reported in the nominally unirrigated area in Saturia, which was the result of short distance migration for such work; there was virtually no work on irrigated crops by the group with irrigation assets in Saturia because, with one exception, they did not do agricultural labor. Higher wages were obtained in irrigated agriculture, at least in Ghior (table 8.14). This suggests increased competition for labor in the irrigation season, but when agricultural wages are broken down by month, this difference occurred only in some months and was due to the coincidence of work on irrigated crops with months of high wages. The difference in average wages in any month of work between irrigated and unirrigated crops was not significant. Thus the apparent difference in the annual average was not an effect of irrigation *per se*, because the work associated with higher wages on irrigated crops occurred later when rice prices were higher, as noted above. Non-agricultural incomes per day do not appear to have been rising toward the end of the survey, although here too one has to look at the type of work being done. Agricultural wages were at their lowest in August and September, when there was least employment (with the exception in these data of December), and incomes per day (that is, income per month divided by number of days in the month) were also lowest at this time.

Conclusions

Care must be taken in collecting and analyzing employment information. Payment terms, contractual forms and seasonal and annual trends have to be taken into account, and the variation in the prevalence of different forms of labor contract by season (and over time?) may well significantly influence their average level. From the evidence presented here, no good explanation for the relative levels of one labor contract compared with another can be inferred, which provides strong evidence against the drawing of simplistic conclusions. Of course we are dealing with small numbers under each payment form and contract type, in a restricted area.

One implication of the seasonal pattern of employment and income is that people who are predominantly dependent on agricultural laboring are short of cash between June and October—precisely the time when members of landless irrigation groups would normally be expected to repay seasonal and capital loans for irrigation equipment. These people will find this cash shortage difficult. Their normal recourse will be to repay loans by selling off their payments-in-kind. In most years, however, there is a significant rise in the paddy price between June and October. Having to repay their loans and therefore sell their kind-payments in June, at the end of the season when prices are low, will be even more difficult. Thus individuals mainly dependent on agricultural labor for their livelihood will find participation in the irrigation program more difficult than will those with other sources of income. Allowing groups to defer payments of season production credit and installments of capital repayments until later in the year in the expectation that paddy prices will rise entails, of course, hazards of nonpayment, (implicit) interest costs and other postharvest losses. A solution might be for Proshika to accept payments-in-kind, sell them when prices are high and debit the irrigation loans before making returns to the groups or individuals. This assumes that the administrative, transport, storage, wastage, selling and other costs would not outweigh the average price rise and that there would be no inefficiency on the part of Proshika staff. Other repayment schedules could be explored.

In conclusion, the survey results suggest that irrigation leads to the following:

- extra employment particularly in the winter rice season, and
- possible higher wages.

Groups in nonirrigated areas had more days of not working and of work in their own homes.[14] The full effects of irrigated agriculture are likely to be much more extensive, because our data do not include migrant labor coming into the irrigated areas (but we record some work on irrigated crops by group members from the area without irrigation). We also do not capture the effects of expenditure of surplus generated by irrigated agriculture but invested elsewhere, except insofar as the degree of integration in the labor market leads to rural wages rising in response to increased employment. This issue is discussed in chapter 10.

Notes

1. In fact, very few STWs and LLPs distributed through KSS are collectively owned.

2. There is a significant difference between the numbers of STWs reported by the MPO and MoA for these *Upazilas*, implying a considerable decline (or problems with the data, this decline is also manifest in other *Upazilas* in Manikganj):

	Saturia	*Ghior*	*Singair*	*Harirampur*
MPO 1983–84	506	343	499	260
MPO 3FYP	684	522	778	220
AST 1985–86	375	238	445	162
AST 1986–87	402	209	444	139

3. The status of land is rapidly changing as the total area irrigated seems to have been rising, and screening of plots in terms of their profitability under different cropping patterns has resulted in some previously irrigated plots ceasing to be irrigated.

4. Further difficulties in imputing income from cultivation in these circumstances arise because not only can we expect input levels and yields to vary, but the terms of sharecropping and interlinked contracts for production consumption and/or credit will mean that different cultivators are left with a different final proportion of the output.

5. No provision was made for recording whether land had been purchased by group members in recent years. The short interviews conducted in 1987 suggest that some members had been able to purchase land.

6. Quantitative information on this is not given because for at least one group (2.3) it was not possible to identify and interview some group members satisfactorily; indeed the group appeared to have become inactive, disbanded, by 1987.

7. Unfortunately, for many cases, the nature of the nonagricultural work was not reported, thus it is not possible to divide households by those engaged primarily in labor and those with substantial entrepreneurial activities (nonagricultural work included both laboring and entrepreneurial activities).

8. The activities of most of the weeks are reported for only six of the fifty-one respondents (all of them in the group of petty entrepreneurs in Saturia 2.1). There were perhaps two factors behind the nonrecording of activities; first, some of the field staff just did not record them, so there are no valid occupation codes for groups 2.3 or 5.1; this may have been because they did not understand that it was wanted (there was no place on the form specifically for this), or because they were disinclined to do so. In either event, lack of supervision by the responsible Proshika staff would have been the cause. Second, when respondents were away for long periods, or engaged in multiple activities in a day, there may have been confusion as to what to enter. Here again, weak design and supervision were ultimately responsible for these missing data.

9. Income per month divided by number of days in the month (rather than days of work in the month). Highest incomes per day worked coincided with lowest incomes per day of the month.

10. The niceties of social relations with profound economic implications may well not be caught in surveys of this type; in this case many permanent laborers are paid in advance (although this did was not reported as indebtedness to employers), and/or in-kind (and/or cheated) so actual income from work may well be underreported.

11. The wage rates in Ghior by type and payment system are as follows: Daily wage is 23 cash, 22 cash and kind; permanent wage is 25 cash, 20 cash and kind.

12. Tables of wage rates by month and form of payment may be obtained from the authors.

13. A further factor was the collapse in the rice price in April 1985, which was noted in chapter 7. This was due to the high stocks held in Government go-downs at the time of the winter rice harvest due then. Stocks were high due to panic imports following the fear of famine induced by the floods of May 1984. Wages are thought to respond closely to rice prices.

14. It is likely that work in own home is in fact productive—house repair, crop processing, craft work and so on. Because of possible confusion between "not working" and "in own home," and because there was no normalization by enumerator (that is,. the same enumerator worked throughout with each group and with no other group), what would have been recorded by one enumerator as "not working" in one ADC may have been recorded by another as work "in own home" in another. If own cultivation had given rise to crop processing in own home, one would have expected group 3 in Saturia to have had a greater total of days worked in own home, as in group 3 in Ghior.

Table 8.1   Number of Sample Farmers and Plots
in Each of the Selected Schemes

Scheme	No. of sample farmers	No. of sample plots
Saturia		
Landless (STW)	19	21
Private (STW)	17	17
Ghior		
Landless (STW)	31	32
Private (STW)	31	32
Kalkini		
Landless (LLP)	26	30
Private (LLP)	25	27

Table 8.2   Average Labor Days Used per Acre of
Winter Rice by Crop Operations in the Selected
Irrigation Schemes

	Saturia		Ghior		Kalkini	
Crop operation	Land-less	Pri-vate	Land-less	Pri-vate	Land-less	Pri-vate
Land improvement and constructing/repairing irrig. channels	5.0	8.4	6.1	5.7	18.6	11.1
Plowing, puddling and seedbed preparation	28.3	30.2	37.8	36.3	21.6	21.6
Transplanting	27.7	29.8	35.3	32.9	53.1	48.7
Weeding	42.4	35.6	44.8	32.7	70.8	51.8
Fertilizer/insecticide application	1.1	0.8	0.2	0.5	1.5	2.4
Preharvest total	104.5	104.8	124.2	108.1	165.6	135.4
Harvesting and threshing	28.7	20.4	20.9	33.1	27.0	30.1
Postharvest operations	5.7	4.4	5.0	8.0	8.7	9.4
Total	138.9	129.6	150.1	149.2	201.3	174.9

Table 8.3 Average Labor Days Used per Acre of
Winter Rice, Paddy and Sex Distribution of Labor

Schemes	Average Preharvest Man-days	Difference Over Private Scheme(%)	% of Labor	
			Male	Female
Saturia				
Landless (STW)	104.5	-0.3	95.6	4.4
Private (STW)	104.8	(0.02)	94.0	6.0
Ghior				
Landless (STW)	124.2	+14.9	96.2	3.8
Private (STW)	108.1	(1.64)	93.7	6.3
Kalkini				
Landless (LLP)	165.6	+22.3	96.2	3.8
Private (LLP)	135.4	(2.44)[1]	93.4	6.6

1 Significant at 1 percent level.
Figures in parentheses indicate estimated t-value.

Table 8.4 Average Family and Hired Labor Days Used per Acre
of Winter Rice Paddy in the Selected Irrigation Schemes

Scheme	Landless			Private		
	Family	Hired	Total	Family	Hired	Total
Saturia						
Man-days	43.1	61.4	104.5	49.7	55.1	104.8
%	41.0	59.0	100.0	47.0	53.0	100.0
Ghior						
Man-days	73.7	50.5	124.2	67.1	41.0	108.1
%	59.0	41.0	100.0	62.0	38.0	100.0
Kalkini						
Man-days	40.7	124.9	165.6	43.3	92.1	135.4
%	25.0	75.0	100.0	32.0	68.0	100.0

Table 8.5 Average Daily Wage Rates by Crop
Operations in Winter Rice Paddy Production in the
Selected Irrigation Schemes

Crop Operation	Saturia		Ghior		Kalkini	
	Landless	Private	Landless	Private	Landless	Private
Land improvement	22.6	20.4	22.0	22.6	20.2	20.0
Plowing	23.1	22.8	24.4	24.4	20.7	20.2
Puddling	25.7	25.7	25.5	25.6	21.5	21.0
Transplanting	25.5	25.5	25.4	25.4	21.4	21.0
Weeding	23.6	22.4	23.6	24.3	20.7	20.3
Harvesting	29.3	32.4	36.5	38.8	1/9[1]	1/10[1]

1   Cropshare.

Table 8.6 Average Preharvest Labor Days Used per
Acre of Winter Rice Paddy by Farmsize Groups in the
Selected Irrigation Schemes

Scheme	Small[1]			Medium[2]			Large[3]		
	Family	Hired	Total	Family	Hired	Total	Family	Hired	Total
Saturia									
Landless	43.6	64.1	107.7	44.0	75.6	119.6	42.1	50.9	93.0
Private	53.8	46.0	99.8	52.6	61.9	114.5	32.2	76.4	108.6
Ghior									
Landless	74.6	43.2	117.8	77.2	56.1	133.3	64.5	54.0	118.5
Private	80.2	33.1	113.3	56.1	45.5	101.6	53.1	50.3	103.4
Kalkini									
Landless	63.8	103.4	167.2	23.3	148.3	171.6	7.7	150.3	158.0
Private	48.5	84.5	133.0	30.6	90.6	121.2	36.2	111.0	147.2

1   Small = up to 2.50 acres of owned land in Saturia and Ghior and up to 2.0 acres in Kalkini.
2   Medium = 2.51–5.00 acres of owned land in Saturia and Ghior and 2.01–4.00 acres in Kalkini.
3   Large = above 5.00 acres of owned land in Saturia and Ghior and above 4.00 acres in Kalkini.
For all the studied schemes, Student-Newman-Keuls (SNK) range tests suggest that no two farmsize groups are significantly different at the 5 percent level with respect to preharvest labor use.

Table 8.7 Average Preharvest Labor Days Used per
Acre of Winter Rice Paddy on Owned
and Sharecropped Land in the Selected Schemes

Scheme	Owned Land			Sharecropped Land		
	Family	*Hired*	*Total*	*Family*	*Hired*	*Total*
Saturia						
Landless	42.4	63.1	105.5	44.9	56.9	101.8
Private	57.3	60.0	117.3	31.5	43.2	74.7
Ghior						
Landless	73.4	51.2	124.6	76.0	45.3	121.3
Private	68.3	42.1	110.4	59.1	32.5	91.6
Kalkini						
Landless	47.2	121.9	169.1	29.6	130.0	159.6
Private	43.8	94.2	138.0	40.0	75.0	115.0

In none of the schemes was the total preharvest labor on owned and sharecropped land significantly different, except in Saturia private scheme, where the difference was significant at the 5 percent level.

Table 8.8 Number of Households per Group

	ADC					
	Saturia			Ghior		
Access to Irrigation	Code	Inter-viewed	in Group	Code	Inter-viewed	in Group
Own STW	2.1	10	20	5.1	12	32
Area of Private						
Irrigation	2.2	9	nk	5.2	6	18
No Irrigation	2.3	8	nk	5.3	6	nk

nk = not known.

Table 8.9 Average Land (acres) Controlled by ADC and Group Category

ADC/ Group Category	Number of Respondents[2]	Cultivated	Owned	Mean of All Households in Group[1]								Father's Land	No Brothers
				Irrigated	Not Irrigated	Share-cropped	Fixed Rent	Mortgaged	Rented Out	Share-cropped	Land Lost		
Saturia													
Own irrigation	3	0.11	0.11	0.04	0.07	—	—	—	—	—	—	0.63	3
Irrigated area	5	0.26	0.09	0.12	0.12	0.15	—	0.03	0.03	0.07	—	0.90	3
Unirrigated area	6	0.77	0.36	0.19	0.46	0.43	0.08	0.04	0.08	0.09	0.02	1.49	3
Total		14	0.36	0.18	0.11	0.21	18.02	0.02	0.03	0.05	0.01	0.98	3
Ghior													
Own irrigation	5	0.36	0.02	0.08	0.25	0.31	—	0.03	0	—	0.08	0.88	3
Irrigated area	3	0.34	0.31	0.28	0.07	0.03	—	—	0	0.19	0.05	0.82	2
Unirrigated area	4	1.10	0.74	—	1.10	0.36	—	—	0	0.24	0.10	2.05	4
Total		12	0.54	0.28	0.11	0.42	0.25	0.02	0	0.11	0.08	1.16	3

1 Not mean per household cultivating.
2 Number of respondents cultivating land.

Table 8.10 Days Worked by the Respondent, by ADC and Group Category

ADC/ Group Category	*Average Number of Days per Respondent*[1]				
	Own Cultivation	*Agricultural Labor*	*Nonagric. Work*	*Other Work*	*Not Working*
Saturia					
Own irrigation	19	2	288	6	4
Irrigated area	13	84	134	12	52
Unirrigated area	26	110	43	10	85
Ghior					
Own irrigation	10	96	138	1	55
Irrigated area	14	54	154	2	70
Unirrigated area	94	44	121	0	25

1 The remainder of days were reported as spent in the respondent's own home.

Table 8.11 Average Land Controlled and Income of Respondent from Different Sources by ADC and Group Category

ADC/ Group Category	*Land Cultivated (ac.)*	*Agric. Labor Income (Tk)*	*Nonagric. Work (Tk)*	*Other Labor Income (Tk)*	*Total Income (Tk)*
Saturia					
Own irrigation	0.11	41	8,017	8,058	—
Irrigated area	0.26	2,302	4,887	503	7,692
Unirrigated area	0.77	4,130	2,106	264	6,500
Total/Average	0.36	2,006	5,222	246	7,474
Ghior					
Own irrigation	0.36	2,561	4,035	23	6,619
Irrigated area	0.34	1,184	5,196	99	6,479
Unirrigated area	1.10	1,024	4,349	—	5,373
Total/Average	0.54	1,833	4,404	36	6,273

Table 8.12 Number of Days and Income from Non-Agricultural Work by Work Type

	Own Irrig. Scheme			Irrigated Area			Unirrig. Area			Total		
	Days Sum	Income Sum	Wage Mean	Days Sum	Income Sum	Wage Mean	Days Sum	Income Sum	Wage Mean	Days Sum	Income Sum	Wage Mean
Saturia												
laborer	71	2,220	31	223	6,599	30	—	—	—	294	8,819	31
fisher	—	—	—	100	3,155	34	—	—	—	100	3,155	34
trader	—	—	—	149	4,262	29	—	—	—	149	4,262	29
mason	556	19,062	34	—	—	—	2	111	56	558	19,173	35
tailor	301	10,850	36	99	3,229	32	—	—	—	400	14,079	35
waiter	273	4,900	18	—	—	—	—	—	—	273	4,900	18
driver	107	2,240	21	—	—	—	—	—	—	107	2,240	21
tea seller	273	7,390	27	—	—	—	—	—	—	273	7,390	27
grocer	297	7,960	27	—	—	—	—	—	—	297	7,960	27
hawker	26	490	19	—	—	—	—	—	—	26	490	19
van puller	—	—	—	147	5,895	40	—	—	—	147	5,895	40
milk seller	84	4,200	50	15	375	25	—	—	—	99	4,575	44
not known	890	20,860	23	473	17,031	36	343	11,894	35	706	49,785	30
Total	2,878	80,172	28	1,206	40,546	34	345	12,005	35	4,429	132,723	31
Ghior												
laborer	—	—	—	312	10,778	34	440	13,386	28	752	24,164	31
weaver	—	—	—	18	680	37	—	—	—	18	680	37
not known	1,657	47,217	29	595	16,878	27	287	8,187	26	2,539	72,282	28
Total	1,657	47,217	29	925	28,336	29	727	21,573	27	3,309	97,126	28

Table 8.13 Non-agricultural Wages of Respondent by ADC, Month, Group and Irrigation (Tk per day)

Month	All Groups			Mean Wages per Day						
	Number of days	Total Income	Income per day	Saturia			Ghior			Total
				Own Irrig. Scheme	Irrigated Area	Unirrigated Area	Own Irrig. Scheme	Irrigated Area	Unirrigated Area	
Apr	1,555	28,400	18	27	34	38	29	33	29	30
May	1,652	30,099	18	27	33	40	27	31	26	29
Jun	1,453	23,685	16	28	31	44	28	29	22	28
Jul	1,548	27,198	18	33	34	31	32	35	30	33
Aug	1,634	25,544	16	32	36	32	30	27	33	31
Sep	1,500	22,644	15	29	34	43	30	30	30	31
Oct	1,602	26,063	16	26	34	44	30	29	32	29
Nov	1,524	25,246	17	27	39	40	27	25	26	29
Dec	1,481	22,302	15	26	36	41	28	31	24	30
Jan	1,659	27,195	16	25	37	31	29	29	24	29
Feb	1,408	24,028	17	26	32	27	27	27	24	28
Mar	1,411	26,799	19	24	30	33	29	28	27	28
Total			17	28	34	35	29	29	27	30

Table 8.14 Wages by ADC, Month, Group and Irrigation (Tk per day)

| | Saturia Crops | | | | | | Ghior Crops | | | | | |
| | Own | | Irrigated Area | | Unirrigated Area | | Own | | Irrigated Area | | Unirrigated Area | |
Wages	Irrig.	Not Irrig.	Irrig.	Not Irrig.	Irrig.	Not Irrig.	Irrig.	Not Irrig.	Irrig.	Not Irrig.	Not Irrig.	Total Mean
Agricultural	(28)¹	12	22	21	22	21	24	21	23	21	20	21
Non-agricultural	28	—	34	—	35	—	29	—	29	—	27	30

¹ Very few cases for this group.

Table 8.15 Agricultural Wages by Labor Contract Type and Payment Form

| | Wages (Tk/day) | | | Number of Days | | |
	Daily	Permanent	Contract	Daily	Permanent	Contract
Saturia						
Cash	28	70¹	—	54	3	9
Cash + kind	—	21	25	152¹	14	0
Kind	—	25	20	0	6	54
Ghior						
Cash	22	25	26	220	250	22
Cash + kind	22	20	—	519	729	0
Kind	—	—	—	0	0	0

¹ This figure probably reflects advances out of wages made to the respondent.

Table 8.16   Agricultural Employment by Labor Contract Type and Month

ADC/Month	Days of Agricultural Labor				Income from Agricultural Labor				Agricultural Wage			
	Daily	Permanent	Contract	Total	Daily	Permanent	Contract	Total	Daily	Permanent	Contract	Mean
Saturia												
Apr	260	3	—	263	5,088	210	—	5,298	20	70	—	21
May	149	6	—	155	3,690	25	—	3,815	25	21	22	24
June	121	10	54	185	2,335	240	1,210	3,785	19	24	—	20
July	131	3	—	134	2,590	60	—	2,650	20	20	—	20
Aug	120	—	—	120	2,264	—	—	2,264	19	—	—	19
Sep	88	1	—	89	1,497	18	—	1,515	18	18	—	18
Oct	168	—	—	168	3,695	—	—	3,695	21	—	—	21
Nov	202	—	3	205	4,500	—	75	4,575	22	—	25	22
Dec	69	—	—	69	1,493	—	—	1,493	22	—	—	22
Jan	137	—	—	137	3,099	—	—	3,099	22	—	—	22
Feb	68	—	—	68	1,461	—	—	1,461	22	—	—	22
Mar	59	—	65	1,345	1,345	—	146	1,491	23	—	24	23
Total	1,575	23	63	1,661	33,122	653	1,431	35,206	21	29	23	21
Ghior												
Apr	86	q	112	—	198	1,606	2,160	3,766	18	19	—	19
May	72	140	—	212	1,474	2,724	—	4,198	20	19	—	20
June	74	105	—	179	1,573	2,095	—	3,668	21	20	—	21
July	59	74	—	133	1,255	1,450	—	2,705	22	20	—	21
Aug	48	63	—	111	860	1,245	—	2,105	18	20	—	19
Sep	42	14	—	56	880	364	—	1,244	21	26	—	21
Oct	76	49	—	125	1,828	1,148	—	2,976	24	23	—	24
Nov	39	58	—	97	839	1,338	—	2,177	22	23	—	22
Dec	35	80	11	126	870	1,905	275	3,050	25	24	25	24
Jan	81	121	—	202	2,022	2,910	—	4,932	25	24	—	25
Feb	78	80	—	158	1,950	1,924	—	3,874	25	24	—	25
Mar	49	83	11	143	1,210	1,987	300	3,497	24	24	27	24
Total	739	979	22	1,740	16,367	21,250	575	38,192	22	22	26	22

Table 8.17 Agricultural Employment by Month and Whether Crops Irrigated

Month	Days of Agricultural Labor			Income from Agricultural Labor (Tk)		
	Work on Crops Irrigated	Not Irrigated	Total	Work on Crops Irrigated	Not Irrigated	Total
Apr	129	332	461	2,636	6,428	9,064
May	115	252	367	2,316	5,696	8,013
June	159	205	364	3,465	3,988	7,453
July	36	231	267	775	4,581	5,355
Aug	2	229	231	40	4,329	4,369
Sep	1	144	145	18	2,741	2,759
Oct	0	293	293	0	6,671	6,671
Nov	4	298	302	92	6,660	6,752
Dec	112	83	195	2,728	1,815	4,543
Jan	229	110	339	5,610	2,421	8,031
Feb	135	91	226	3,313	2,022	5,335
Mar	110	98	208	2,727	2,261	4,988
Total	1,032	2,369	3,401	23,721	49,677	73,398

Table 8.18 Agricultural Labor Income by Labor Categories and Month

Income as % of Agric. Labor	Apr	May	Jun	Jul	Aug	Sep	Oct	Nov	Dec	Jan	Feb	Mar	Average
< 5%	778	692	547	721	687	608	608	609	535	617	570	566	626
5 – 25	383	634	502	615	538	550	502	516	432	469	390	573	509
25 – 50	351	358	388	485	492	502	564	295	412	535	390	381	429
50 – 75	391	577	350	229	228	164	355	391	299	435	396	549	364
> 75	422	447	397	346	280	186	389	436	350	461	404	446	380
Total	556	590	464	533	500	444	511	495	437	533	471	525	504

Table 8.19 Distribution of Respondents by Proportion of Agricultural Labor

% Days Work Spent in Agric. Labor	Own Irrigation		Irrigated Area		Non-irrigated Area		Total
	Saturia	Ghior	Saturia	Ghior	Saturia	Ghior	
<5	9	4	3	3	1	2	22
5 – 25	1	2	1	1	0	1	6
5 – 50	0	2	0	1	5	3	6
0 – 75	0	1	4	0	5	0	10
> 75	0	3	1	1	2	0	7
Total	10	12	9	5	2	6	51

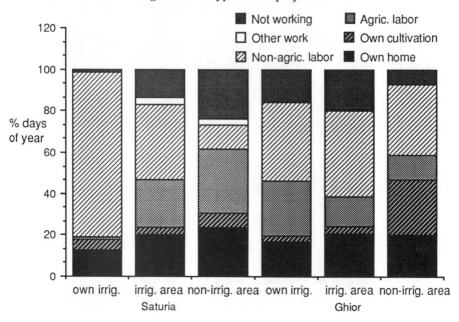

Figure 8.1 Types of Employment

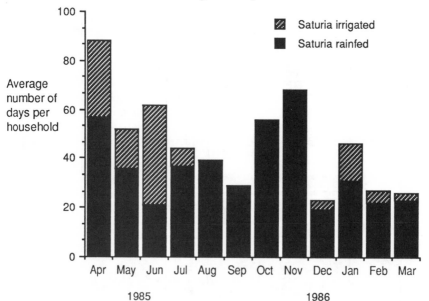

Figure 8.2 Agricultural Labor on Irrigated
and Unirrigated Crops in Saturia

Figure 8.3   Agricultural Labor on Irrigated
and Unirrigated Crops in Ghior

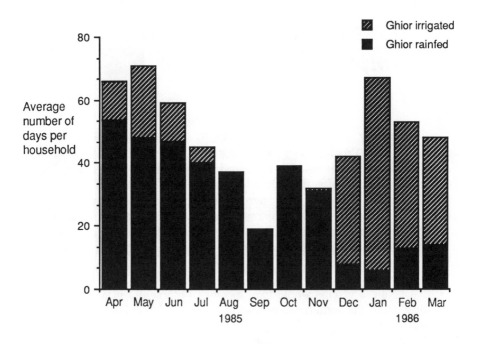

CHAPTER NINE

Lessons and Policy Implications

BEFORE IDENTIFYING THE themes to be discussed in this chapter, we should restate Proshika's irrigation strategy. Under the fragmented but skewed landholding conditions of Bangladesh, with a high proportion of the rural population effectively landless, and in the context of a major national program of expanding the acreage under minor irrigation, Proshika has sought to assist the direct entry of landless groups into agricultural production via the provision of irrigation services to farmers whose plots are scattered around the village and among different command areas. The following was expected:

- that landless groups would gain incomes (and rents) in addition to those from the sometimes precarious and invariably dependent sale of labor,
- that groups would gain greater access to employment opportunities through the leverage and efficiency of their own water selling practices,
- that small farmers would gain improved access to water,
- that the groups' interest in water selling would result in optimal command area sizes and equipment use,
- that groups would benefit from further effects in processing and agricultural service activity (both directly as collective or individual entrepreneurs, or indirectly through enhanced employment prospects),
- that groups would manage direct access relationships with the banking system initially around this activity but extended later to others, and
- that groups would enjoy greater respect and political influence in the local community.

In the attempt to study whether these expectations have been met and simultaneously seek to use the information gained (including information from questions we did not originally ask) to improve the ongoing performance of the groups, many issues have arisen—some with more frequen-

182

cy and significance than others—that have been both technical and organizational, affecting immediate performance as well as having implications for policy within the minor irrigation sector and for broader equity with growth objectives in Bangladesh.

Some of these issues are discussed in this chapter, under the following headings:

- group management and internal group dynamics,
- banking, credit and access,
- technical fixes, organizational forms and economic parameters,
- economic performance,
- hidden subsidies,
- labor markets and employment,
- competition, water markets and state regulation, and
- water rights.

Group Management and Internal Dynamics

The irrigation program as a strategy for income and asset distribution both relied on extant solidarity among the group members as a means to gain entry into the water market and was expected to contribute to the further reinforcement of this solidarity as a basis. The underlying premise of the strategy has been that landless and near-landless villagers are not in a position as individuals to act in an entrepreneurial way and enter these markets. This is partly due to their lack of capital, which can be built up only through collective savings or obtained through loan support that is not dependent upon asset-based collateral (from organizations such as Proshika or Grameen Bank). It is also partly due to members' political weakness and status inferiority, which prevents them from competing with richer farmers and contractors and constrains them in negotiating with other classes over the scale and price of services supplied. The formation of groups has been based upon these principles of action, rather than as a convenient unit of delivery or extension.

From the outset of the program, there was a strong insistence that groups were not to be hastily formed for this purpose and that they would need to display evidence of having worked together and/or having shown collective resilience in local political conflicts with landlords, employers and so on. In this way, the groups would be in a better position to face the severer test of running an irrigation service that involved complex technical and financial management and negotiation with farmers.

Despite the inclusion of extant group solidarity in Proshika's selection criteria, however, that solidarity has clearly remained a variable affecting not only overall performance of a scheme but also questions of equity, participation and accountability among group members. This variable is affected by the composition of the group membership. There are difficulties with simple definitions of target groups, and "landless" is an artificial, observer's term that does not capture the complexity of rural social dynamics and potential allegiances. Proshika staff understand this, and their mobilization of the poor into groups involves those trapped in the same dynamic of poverty, rather than grouping them on the basis of a snapshot of wealth criteria. There is also an element of self-selection through kin and neighborhood networks. This means that group membership may not be simply landless, but may include the near landless, marginal and small peasants *(prantik)*, petty peripatetic traders, migrant workers (either in local or distant agriculture, rural works schemes or temporary urban employment) and poor artisans. If we add to this diversity the possibility of different members being locked in to various kin and/or patronage networks, the threats to group solidarity can be high. Much depends on the objective conditions faced by these group members, and the quality of mobilization achieved by the Proshika field staff. In some cases within the irrigation program, the limitations of group solidarity have been exposed. This situation has several implications, for the management of a scheme, for the way in which income is used and for the long-term viability of the group as a unit of collective activity.

The management issue concerns the extent to which group members really participate in the day-to-day running of the irrigation service. The meaning of a term such as "participate" is ambiguous, and a further question exists about whether participation of group members actually matters. We have encountered situations in which the level of involvement of group members has been nominal outside a committee or clique of group chairman, secretary, driver and lineman and other similar combinations. Ordinary members in these situations have had little idea of the scheme, and there has been little accountability of the committee to them. This bland description, however, may have different meanings.

1. The committee may in effect consist of all the group members left behind in the village during the season, perhaps because they have scraps of land to cultivate or because they have assured employment or artisan/small trading opportunities. We must remember that the irrigation scheme is not in many cases the only economic activity in which the group members are engaged collectively or individually. The committee could therefore be seen as acting on behalf of the group interests, rewarded for the work it contributes with the profit available to the group for a collective decision over its use.

2. Ordinary members may be in the locality during the irrigation season, but may be heavily involved in agricultural work and unable to spare the time to join the committee (that is, participate in day-to-day management), although they contribute voluntary labor for drain construction at the beginning of the season and attend regular group meetings at which the committee presents a report.

3. Paperwork and accounting is involved, so illiterate members of the group are at a disadvantage whether they participate or not. Form should not be mistaken for reality. In these examples, the element of trust is central, together with the difficulty of knowing whether that trust has been misplaced.

4. The limits of accountability may be revealed not by purposive dishonesty but by the incompetence of committees who are themselves illiterate or unfamiliar with bookkeeping.

Even with these explanations of the limits of participation in the context of work habits and literacy, the following two sets of conditions have undermined the solidarity of some irrigating groups.

- The variable of internal social differentiation has sometimes been exacerbated by the availability of income and profit from irrigation.
- The loan source constituted an important external variable, because there is some evidence that internal accountability between the committee and ordinary members was much weaker during the Bangladesh Krishi Bank (BKB) period of the program, and that this accountability improved when the loan arrangements had to be switched to Proshika's Revolving Loan Fund (RLF).

The first situation should not be overstated, despite the case examples that have appeared during the research and ongoing monitoring of the program and that understandably attract considerable discussion. Of the twenty-four groups examined specifically for the ways in which income has been deployed, nineteen stated their clear intention of using any profits gained from the provision of irrigation services in further collective activity (transportation, pisciculture and others). In terms of current behavior, the collective picture is less certain where there has been little net income to distribute. Thirteen of the groups have not really had the choice to distribute net income to individuals after meeting costs and loan repayments and reserving income for next year's operating costs. In six cases, there has been individual distribution of paddy together with the stated intention to pursue further collective activity. Thus five cases out of twenty-four (21 percent) reveal strong individualistic tendencies but, in two of these cases, income was being held by committee members for personal use, until this misuse of group funds was discovered and remedied. When the internal social composition of the group is differentiated by employment and education, the incentive to deploy income for individual use is higher. Small-scale peripatetic traders, for example, will have a strong interest in using income from this source to release them from debt-dependent trading, even though this interest may effectively foreclose the options of other members of the group to engage in group projects.

The second situation of weak financial discipline during the arrangement with BKB has been significant. The unclear division of responsibility between the BKB and Proshika for monitoring and supervising both loan repayment and the maintenance within the groups of accounting records in effect created space for mismanagement, incompetence and even deliberate misuse of loans and gross income (from water users' fees). The Proshika field staffs at the Area Development Center (ADC) level were more concerned about assisting the groups in the resolution of technical problems, supply of fuel, spare parts, mechanical services and ensuring that farmers were paying the groups as agreed. The BKB branch managers had neither the resources, the inclination nor the clear instruction from headquarters to monitor groups closely, partly because they represented a small proportion of the total loan portfolio for their branch and partly because Proshika was acting as a guarantor against default anyway. Under these conditions, the issues of financial accountability within the groups were not initially revealed, and bad practice could develop unchecked. Only when loan support was transferred from BKB to the Proshika RLF were the extent of financial indiscipline and overdue payments revealed. Proshika field staff were now in the position of direct responsibility to ensure that the same problems did not persist under RLF conditions and that past problems were remedied. Thus the whole question of financial accountability between group members came under much closer scrutiny and is now supported by a regular monitoring system that quickly identifies where problems may exist. This development of the RLF program, not only for irrigation but also for many other sectors of group activity, inevitably has an effect on the style of relationship between the field staff and the groups. One could argue, of course, that this new financial realism has had a positive effect on internal group dynamics, in which group members have to make committee members more accountable to the group in the management of the irrigation activity.

Banking, Credit and Access

A major objective in the original program concept was to place landless groups in direct relations with local branches of the BKB, with a longer-term presumption that such relations could be reproduced between other groups engaged in other projects (whether initiated in association with Proshika or not) and local branches of other banks where the BKB was not present. Thus part of the program was a test of the access relations between landless people and the national commercial banks. In this sense, the banks were on trial within a nationally evolving policy framework of credit support for rural business activity among the landless and near-landless. This, of course, represented a departure from their normal practice of loaning to farmers with collateral for cultivation purposes, including the purchase of shallow tubewells (STWs). This policy framework was (and is) evolving under pressure from non-governmental organizations (NGOs) in

Bangladesh, and especially from the experience of the Grameen Bank Project (GBP), which was originally an NGO but is now constituted as a specialist bank with normal deposit and drawing rights with the Bangladesh Bank. More recently, this strategy has also been advocated by bilateral donors (for example, Canadian and Scandinavian) and the World Bank. For Proshika, the significance of this strategy was to preserve Proshika's mobilization and facilitating role in relation to the groups and to avoid extensive financial dependency that might change or undermine that role. There was the further logistical and infrastructural issue that the expansion of business activity among the groups would be restricted by Proshika's own organizational and financial resources, whereas bank branches existed in every *Upazila* and in many unions. Furthermore, because the independence and autonomy of the groups is a long-term objective, it seemed appropriate that they should be encouraged to enter commercial relationships with banks in the same way that they would make contracts with farmers in their command areas. Of course, as explained in the introduction, the BKB was encouraged to participate in such lending (where no collateral would be forthcoming from the groups beyond the amortized value of the purchased irrigation equipment) by guarantee deposits provided out of grants from the Ford Foundation. The long-term intention was to demonstrate to the BKB that the real level of risk would be covered by amortized equipment and interest charges, without the continued support of guarantee funds.

That this part of the experiment has clearly failed. As described earlier, from 1985 the funding of the groups was transferred to Proshika's expanded RLF. The financial analysis, which covers both the BKB and RLF periods, has been presented in chapter 6. The source of funding had to be switched after a frustrating five-year mediation period by Proshika field staff and senior coordinators between the groups and the local BKB branches, together with BKB headquarters. While the BKB staff in Dhaka were enthusiastic about supporting such a program (after all, there was little financial risk and Proshika field staff were providing the extension input), they were unable to supervise and discipline recalcitrant local branch managers. These managers had some genuine problems: lack of proper training and familiarization with the program, lack of briefing on transfer and inadequate information and guidelines from BKB headquarters. As a result, many were reluctant to engage in risky lending without unequivocal authorization from above. In many cases, the senior coordinators in Proshika were explaining the BKB headquarters guidelines to local staff and acting as a line of communication between local managers and their superiors in Dhaka. But alongside this understandable caution, there were many cases of deliberate hindrance by local managers treating with contempt the landless group members who came with correct paperwork to obtain a loan to which they were entitled from earmarked funds. The group members were kept waiting, often for more than a day, in favor of others behind them in line. They were sent away and requested to come on another day many times. They were abused as beggars. Bribes were frequently demanded. This became the reality of access, even with the known support of national-level agreements and Proshika as an organization with an international reputation, which is important in a donor dependent country.

Organizing the landless involvement in minor irrigation had enough technical and social problems without these funding problems. At some point a choice had to be made between securing financing for the groups without unnecessary hassle at the right time to ensure the confidence of the farmers and the viability of the irrigation season, and testing the capacity of local banks and landless groups to enter into autonomous commercial relationships. Also, the Proshika time spent in mediation could be more efficiently spent in administering Proshika's own RLF and providing the necessary extension support for the irrigation activity.

The failure of this dimension of the program and the consequent internalization of this function by Proshika potentially creates a new set of problems, both for Proshika's internal management practices and its relationship to the groups. The danger is that the management of a large RLF, which has been expanded independently of this program to meet demands from the groups for support for other activities, necessarily introduces measures of control between levels of Proshika staff and between ADC field staff and the groups.

Within Proshika, the management of these funds has undoubtedly been assisted by the introduction of microcomputers to RLF accounting and an economic performance monitoring system providing regular, quarterly information on group-level project activity. This enables quick identification of problems and quick remedial action. But there are familiar organizational issues about monopolies of access to information technology —who controls and deploys this information, and is authority in Proshika likely to be shifted centrally as a result? Does the overall organization become more pyramidal in structure? Furthermore, is there a shift in time use of staff from mobilization and extension activity to financial recording and control activity? The answer to all these questions is probably yes. Under such conditions, does an NGO lose its comparative advantage over its bureaucrat cousins among the state apparatuses? In a society where honest people are nervous about the handling of institutional money because the pressures to be corrupt are so strong and the allegations of corruption abound in the normal discourse of institutional politics, procedures become very elaborate with cross-checks and countersignatures defining responsibility, and therefore authority, unambiguously. The place of discretion and personalized knowledge and judgments make way for formal criteria of eligibility that can be inspected by outsiders (such as the roving auditors). The organization can lose its flexibility of response and its comparative advantage of localized, intimate knowledge of potential loanees, or the viability of a project idea in the unique context of local market conditions.

The second issue is the effect of this parallel banking system on the relationships between Proshika's field staff and the groups. The basic problem is the merging of the mobilization, facilitation and extension functions with financial monitoring and management functions. Under such conditions, groups risk becoming clients of a delivery organization. The important difference so far is that groups do not face the same problems of access because the RLF is a dedicated, or targeted, service for them. The access test will occur when the demand among the groups for loans (not necessarily just for irrigation) significantly exceeds the funds available from the RLF. Then waiting will be necessary, along with lines, ranking and prioritization. But at least groups would be restricted to competing with themselves for loans from sympathetic NGO officials, rather than with their employers, landlords and moneylenders, who possess collateral, superior social networks and the ability to bribe. Thus, although we might be able to detect (or at least fear) a shift in the access conditions between groups and the NGO credit service from brokerage to rationed delivery, we should not simply collapse them into a government bureaucracy-client model.

This is not to argue that relationships between Proshika and the groups are not affected after the loan has been granted and received. Here, the merging of extension and financial control functions really occurs. Before, the field staff member could stand alongside the groups and share in their frustrations with the local bank managers, and with other government officials, such as those from the Bangladesh Agricultural Development Corporation (BADC). Now he has to check the account books, insist upon proper repayment of loan installments, check that costs are not being overcharged (to prevent scheme managers from cheating ordinary group members) and check that fees are being received or that yields and cropshares are not underreported as part of a loan repayment avoidance strategy. This is not to imply that groups will perceive Proshika's RLF as an external institution with which they need have no moral relationship, to be outwitted and cheated when possible (a model of government-client relations that applies to official rural credit in Bangladesh). But if the RLF is to be truly revolving, and to enable a wider number of groups to gain access to targeted funds, the maintenance of a credit discipline is essential. Smaller farmers may have a better record of repayments than larger farmers in Bangladesh, but the urgent claims on finance among the poor cannot be ignored, especially if their landlessness actually excludes them from access to local moneylending sources of funds even at high interest rates or with labor bondage. Groups with their own savings to distribute among members for urgent consumption and domestic crises will of course be less tempted to cheat. Responsible and equitable financial management (that is, fairness to repaying groups) requires a set of procedures that can cope with the possibility of cheating. The same procedures will also identify cases of incompetent group financial management (as opposed to deliberate cheating). So standard procedures of accounting and checking cannot responsibly be avoided. The problem is the extent to which the field staff therefore occupy a different role—one of authority and supervision rather than mobilizing and facilitating. A successful experiment with the BKB would have avoided some of these dilemmas of merging the two functions. There are, currently, discussions among several NGOs in Bangladesh to set up an NGO bank (as a distinctive exercise from the Grameen Bank Project, which will only lend to individuals in its own groups, with other members guaranteeing repayments made on fixed schedules irrespective of any project sequence for which the loan was required). These dilemmas should be considered in such plans.

Technical Fixes, Organizational Forms and Economic Parameters

As seen in the preceding chapters, the performance of the program has been dominated by these three dimensions, which have varied in their explanatory significance at different stages in the program's history. We have learned that the program's success cannot be reduced to any one of these dimensions. They are interdependent. Nevertheless, in the formulation period, when the program was being designed before the first season of trial, emphasis was placed on the organizational issues because it was, above all, an institutional innovation involving an experimental relationship between potentially hostile classes. Group solidarity; the history of lack of cooperation among farmers over irrigation; the making of binding agreements with farmers; modes of payment; ensuring adequate access for the groups to loans, supplies and services; reinforcing the groups' own management capacity—all these were prominent areas of concern and therefore debate.

At this early stage the technology itself was considered unproblematic, with well-defined specifications and capacities. Of course, certain potential technical problems were considered at the outset—especially the consequences of machine breakdown and the local shortage of spare parts. This awareness prompted the first specific senior appointment to the program—a roving engineer to monitor the technical performance of the machines, advising on operation and maintenance. This member of the field staff subsequently became a general coordinator for the program. But other technical questions concerning actual water distribution and the physical characteristics of command areas were, at this early stage, secondary. As the program got underway, these technical issues emerged more strongly as problem areas alongside some unforeseen organizational complexities.

The technical issues of water distribution alongside the performance of the machines were also emerging as a whole for the STW part of the minor irrigation sector as the technology entered general use under a variety of organizational conditions. Some of these technical issues concerned the relationship to other irrigation technologies, especially deep tubewells (DTWs), where a faith in the rational allocation capacity of the market was misplaced as the respective technologies were frequently located in areas more appropriate to the other. This problem was partly one of appropriate water tables, with DTWs draining STW aquifers and causing them to dry up before the season was completed. Other soil composition issues emerged, which affected the irrigation capacity of similar installations. This sometimes caused overuse of machines, transferring the problem. But more often the fee structure could not be altered in a locality to reflect the differing economies of scale induced by this variation in soil composition. To a considerable extent, these problems became appreciated for each specific command area only after a season or two of experience (command areas rarely reached full capacity in the first season anyway). Soil surveys were not carried out, partly because the capacity among the groups or the field staff did not exist and partly because many other factors were involved in the determination of a command area, such as farmers' willingness and relationships with the group. As the evidence on machine breakdown, pumping hours, fuel consumption and financial viability began to accumulate, however, more attention clearly had to be given to these technical parameters, such as soil composition and machine efficiency rates (sometimes independent variables—see appendix A). Technical fixes of some kind were therefore necessary to guide a group in the search for extensions to existing command areas, alongside the abandonment where possible, of sandy plots, and in some cases the abandonment, of an entire command area in favor of another location. Under some conditions, this technical advice had to lead to the discontinuation of some group projects. The whole question of feasibility had to be taken more seriously if these problems were to be avoided in the future. By the 1985–86 season, the decision was made to expand this technical capacity among the Proshika field staff to cope with the scale of work involved, and a small cadre of twelve irrigation field staff, with technical qualifications in irrigation engineering and management, was created to service the main Proshika areas of the program. This institutional development within Proshika was made with some reluctance, as specialist field staff are not really within the culture of the organization, but it is a measure of the significance of these technical imperatives for the success of the program that these changes have been forced upon the organization. The development does carry similar implications for the relationships between Proshika field staff and the groups and with the expansion of Proshika's RLF. The significance of professional knowledge has increased within the program, and this carries the dangers of removing decision making (for example, on the location of new schemes) from the groups. Technical criteria, not necessarily appreciated by the groups, will dominate at the feasibility stage; the groups may become dependent upon the specialist field staff for subsequent management advice. There is a difficult trade-off between recognizing the value of technical knowledge and specialist skills to avoid or solve a range of problems that have endangered the program in the past, and some loss of autonomy by the groups in setting up and managing individual schemes. This trade-off, despite mistakes, is an important part of Proshika's broader, long-term, human development objectives. With the appointment of these technical field staff, we can expect fewer discontinuations, improved economic performance and enhanced financial viability of the group schemes. Such improvement is a necessary but not sufficient condition for an agrarian reform strategy of this kind, and Proshika will need to be alert to excessive emphasis on technical fixes within the program.

Reference was made above to "unforeseen organizational complexities." The original organizational concept for the program had been one group (already in existence, with a history of previous collective economic and political activity) running one irrigation scheme. This is still the norm. But some organizational variations emerged in response to different conditions and these should be noted as part of the process of institutional experimentation. First, we have already discussed the internal cohesion of single groups in terms of differentiated social composition, variable work practices and different educational and literacy skills. Thus one potential organizational development, albeit a negative one, is the disintegration of group solidarity. Obviously this is not a process Proshika wishes to encourage, even indirectly, through its support for such programs. There is of course a danger that the stronger working relationships between the irrigation field staff and the group's management committee for the scheme might exacerbate this process. We have also noted that, with the introduction of Proshika RLF support, accountability and therefore participation within the groups will have to improve. Second, and more positively in human development/class solidarity terms, groups have sometimes joined around a scheme. This has often created a problem for our own data recording and accounting requirements; a certain standardized neatness was undermined. Two or even three groups have sometimes established and managed a scheme collectively (though inevitably a managing committee has emerged, with some of the attendant dangers noted above). This has occurred not only for the larger low-lift pump (LLP) command areas but also for some STW schemes. Under LLP conditions, the pressures for groups to join together are stronger: there are more farmers to deal with in a command area; the members of several neighboring groups may have small amounts of land within the single command area and wish therefore to participate directly in the scheme; and the size of the command area (30 to 60 acres) may effectively preclude the possibility of another similar scheme in the locality, so that groups understandably object to the prospect of one group having in effect a monopoly over the opportunity to provide a landless irrigation service in that village. Sometimes a division of labor has occurred, in which one of the participating groups has taken the responsibility to make the loan application and to constitute the legal entity for repayment purposes. Another manages the scheme itself (drain construction, operation of the pumpset and water distribution through the season), and others join in, possibly at the time of drain construction but certainly at harvest time, to secure cropshares or cash fees from the farmers when wider political solidarity is essential. Various permutations have emerged, and of course internal accounting and reward systems for the different functions performed between the groups can be very complicated. Although these organizational variations may have been inconvenient for research, monitoring and accounting, they do reveal a central principle of this strategy for agrarian reform—the development of local institutional practices in response to micro-ecological, political and economic conditions. A further example of this process has been the evolution of arrangements between groups and farmers or water users, especially over payments for water. Modes of payment, especially in LLP areas, have been largely determined by previous practices during the BADC rental period. Mechanized irrigation in STW command areas has been new by definition. The mode of payment in many of these areas was established as a cropshare, which minimized the investment capital required for farmers because water fees were not therefore payable until the end of the season. This did mean, however, that the groups were shouldering all the risk in terms of expenditure not only on capital equipment but also on operating costs. Groups also shared the risk of crop failure. To compensate, the share in many places was set at 33 percent. After a period of learning, some command area farmers considered this share to represent overcompensation when compared either to their own costs of production or to the potential yields obtainable in a good year. Under such conditions, the cropshare has been negotiated downward to 25 percent. This share has become a norm for new schemes too, partly as a result of competing prices offered in the locality by other, private, STWs. There have been other, rarer, conditions, when the cropshare has been increased with the group providing additional services such as fertilizer application. There are many possibilities to extend this principle (through transplanting and weeding services and pesticide spraying), though it would entail more risk for the groups.

There has also been a fine-tuning of cropshare collection practices, with more group members being involved directly in the harvest of plots in the command areas, and therefore being on the spot to supervise the division of the shares between the group and the farmers. This reduces the possibility of cheating and avoids the difficulties of trying to retrieve the share subsequently from the farmer's compound. This process has further advantages, because more group members are actually involved in the physical appropriation of the crop, thus reducing the likelihood of a group's managing committee cheating on its members. But if the crop is taken to individual members' homes for threshing and storage, other problems of managing the common stock arise. The authors, Proshika and the groups have debated endlessly to define a procedure, but local institutional innovation must resolve the issue in a way that reflects location-specific factors such as the availability of threshing floors, storage space, extent of mutual trust among members, loan obligations, proximity to and frequency of local markets and group strategies on the distribution of the product.

Arrangements between groups and farmers have been modified in other ways to adjust the distribution of risk while maintaining incentives for both partners. In many places, pressure has been put on farmers to pay a proportion of the water charge in advance. This has reduced the level of operating costs, which the groups have had to raise before receiving any income. This has been especially important in the early years of a scheme before any capital has been accumulated by the group to be carried over for use in the following irrigation season. Where the mode of payment remains as cropshare, the final share has been reduced. Calculations have to be made, about the value of the cash in hand earlier on in season against the value of the reduced share at harvest time, and these calculations have to include interest rates on outstanding loans and whether groups will need to sell some or all of their share in the immediate, low-priced, post-harvest period. With fixed-cash payment systems, the calculation has been simpler and the arrangement of advanced payments has been more familiar to the farmers. In both situations of advanced payments, attempts by farmers to interfere with equitable water distribution by claiming preferential service have been avoided.

The general conclusion from these examples of organizational modifications is that, even when technical issues of water management appeared to be the dominant problem of performance, institutional practice remained important. The crucial difference is that the process of institutional innovation occurs without specialist troubleshooters but dialectically as a result of groups experiencing problems, analyzing them and solving them. Proshika field staff and the authors were involved in that process, partly to offer groups comparable experience from elsewhere within the landless irrigation program and partly to record the success or failure of different institutional arrangements. This point about the necessity of local problem-solving underlines the importance of groups being mobilized and conscientized across a broad range of issues, so that they are empowered with their own knowledge and assessment of opportunities and constraints. The technical issues of irrigation remain important, but their resolution cannot be a sufficient condition of successful irrigation (whether provided by the landless or not). At the same time, much of the necessary institutional innovation and continual fine-tuning has to be carried out by the actors themselves, often through a process of guided trial and error in which the so-called specialists are onlookers and at best brokers of information, rather than monopolists of it.

The third dimension affecting performance was the economic parameters, which intruded into our explanations in the final research stages of the program. The most difficult period of the program (1984–86) coincided with problems in the agricultural economy as a whole, with an overall decline in the agricultural growth rate. The rate of expansion of irrigated areas rose to 22 percent of cultivated area instead of the intended 32 percent. If we concentrate on the parameters for STWs, their use rose rapidly until 1983–84, when a decline set in for their rate of sale. This decline has been explained in two ways. It may have been due to the removal of subsidies on equipment prices for STWs and related inputs such as fertilizer (urea, which represents 70 percent of high-yield variety (HYV) fertilizer use, rose in price by nearly 150 percent during the Second Five-Year Plan (2FYP) so that input prices outstripped output prices both for jute and rice, which rose by only about 50 percent during the same period. Alternatively, a range of technical and institutional problems (machine breakdowns, lack of cooperation among farmers, inadequate servicing and spare part supplies on aging equipment) may have been responsible for low-capacity utilization and a declining interest in STW irrigation as a direct source of income. However we weigh these explanations (and we can add agronomic problems of declining yield responses to fertilizer and HYVs as a result of increased cropping intensity), they certainly constituted the prevailing conditions within which the landless irrigation service tried to consolidate and expand. Unlike the other two dimensions, these conditions were outside the control of Proshika's field staff or the groups. Together with these parameters affecting the program, we have to recognize that the groups could not benefit in the long term from the hidden subsidies available to other private STW owners through credit indiscipline while the groups were having severe problems of access to credit through the local branches of the BKB.

Economic Performance

Within the program, the financial viability of the groups has been a necessary but not sufficient condition of the value of water selling to the landless. The period 1982–83 to 1984–85 contained many problems of loan management practice as well as economic performance. The economic performance of the schemes was affected both by stochastic external events such as the early floods of 1984, which seriously damaged standing winter rice and prevented many of the groups from receiving water fees, and by structural variables (including external ones such as output prices and input subsidies), which require continual monitoring to place them in locally specific optimal relation to each other. Before these are discussed, the following conditions under which poor temporary economic performance can be tolerated should be noted:

- funding a group's entry into the local water market by adopting a deliberate strategy of the loss leader with a view to raising fees subsequently after proof of efficient performance, and
- environmental fluctuations such as early flooding, which may require spreading risk over several years and accepting losses in the affected year.

Some of these issues are closely connected to internal variables such as the characteristics of command areas. The groups' performance has been affected by size of command area, soil type, quantity and timing of water delivery, farmers' practices with new rice technologies and therefore yields as a dependent variable. Fuel, spares and repairs are the main ingredients in the cost structure, which focuses on improving irrigation management. Achieving optimal command areas, however, depends on successful negotiations with farmers, which are a reflection of competitive markets for water delivery (water fees and reliability, for example) and the groups' bargaining skills. Although command area size is a major variable, the optimum may not be the maximum in terms of yields where water cannot be supplied adequately during the hottest months or late in the season and where machine capacity is overstrained. Such issues stress the need for locally identifying optimal norms through continuous use of monitoring data.

From the inception of the program, the overall performance has fluctuated in response both to these variables and to the degree of learning that has occurred. The first season in 1980–81, located principally in Bhairab, revealed many cost issues, some of which could be instantly recognized and overcome (such as overelaborate housing for the pumpsets, liberal payments to group labor for drain construction, supply of standing water to plots for winter rice cultivation, overgenerous expenses for group members when visiting the bank or taking delivery of equipment and fuel). As a result, the second season, 1981–82, showed a dramatic improvment over the first, although some of the problems with Bhairab persisted and were only later attributed to poor soil types, which reduced productivity and command areas. Elsewhere, the problems had not yet emerged of informally subsidized competitors, decline in fertilizer/yield coefficients, machine breakdowns, availability of spare parts and mechanical services, ambiguity of responsibility between BKB and Proshika for monitoring loan repayments, inappropriate command area sites and early flooding. These problems were identified as potential rather than actual in the 1982 review, and they certainly began to occur during the period from 1982–83 to

1984–85, when many groups discontinued. Our data reveal sharp increases in fuel costs (up by 50 percent) and spare parts alongside a fall in yields (partly due to the flooding in May 1984) and therefore a drop in incomes as rice prices did not rise sufficiently to offset these losses. Since 1984–85, performance has improved steadily, with fewer discontinuations in the first two years of a scheme, partly as a result of more rigorous feasibility assessments by Proshika ADCs. Costs have been further controlled, partly through the use of group voluntary labor in drain construction and partly through improved equipment use as a result of better irrigation management. Yields have increased (as a result of better command area selection and reliable delivery), and paddy prices rose from 1985–86. STW command areas also rose in 1986–87. LLP groups remain a problem in some areas, mainly as a result of increases in fuel costs (diesel and oil), which may be a reflection of inefficient use in the context of difficult water sources and suboptimal command areas. Overall, discontinuations remain a problem although they are not always evidence of failure. We have seen from the analysis in chapter 7 that these discontinuations have not been evenly distributed, by technology or by area, and have been concentrated in two years, 1984–85 and 1987–88. These patterns reveal environmental problems (either chronic or one-off but severe) in some cases; poor monitoring of financial and economic performance by some ADCs; and more recently the efficient use of the newly available central monitoring data to guide ADCs and groups on long-term scheme viability. The current rate of discontinuations (which is no doubt equaled or exceeded in the unresearched private sector) provides supporting evidence (albeit unwelcome) for the continuing volatility of the water market. It raises a wider policy question. Has privatization released ill-informed, anarchic market forces into the expansion of minor irrigation? The cost of many inefficiencies and much expensive learning has been borne by poorer farmers losing crop investments and by credit institutions (national and international) faced with massive defaulting by water speculators and rich, influential farmers. Perhaps the major beneficiaries have been the Japanese multinationals and their commercial and official allies in Bangladesh.

Hidden Subsidies

Hiddens Subsidies to the Private Sector

Action research and this publication have demonstrated that this strategy for agrarian reform, through the provision of irrigation services by the landless, can not only deliver the equity objectives implied by the redistribution of productive assets but can also compete successfully on productivity criteria with the private sector in minor irrigation. We have demonstrated that command areas are larger for the landless programs than for the private sector and that water distribution has been fairer and more reliable. The absence of reliable data sets equivalent to our own for the private sector has made it difficult for us to deploy other indicators such as yields, capital/output ratios, cost structure, employment generation and machine efficiency to demonstrate beyond a doubt the superiority of the landless service. Another dimension to this argument, however, is the conditions under which the different sectors operate.

For the purposes of this discussion, the private sector refers not only to individual contractors (usually themselves farmers) but also to informal and formal groups of farmers. These groups may range from the private cooperatives of water users identified by Glaser (1988) to KSS groups, which may either be fictitious and dominated by one or several leading families or which may reflect a more genuine membership of irrigating farmers. We are therefore including cooperatives as well as individuals in the term "private sector."

The notion of competition between the landless groups and the private sector has the following several dimensions:

- attractiveness of price and service to potential water users, which involves actual competition over control of command areas within a village locality, and
- competition in a national policy sense of maximizing the productivity of the technology consistent with sufficiently attractive rates of return to water sellers.

Groups of irrigating farmers (whether formally registered as cooperatives or not) are obviously both sellers and users, and may compete with the landless service over the control of command areas, especially, where they are subsidized to achieve greater rates of return on their investment. If these subsidies (whether for such groups or single contractors) stimulate underutilization of the equipment and poor service, however, the attractiveness of the subsidized capital costs may be offset for individuals by lower yields on their irrigated plots and for agricultural strategy as a whole (as well as excluded tail-enders) by the smaller command areas served. Both processes represent probable explanations of underachievement in the expansion of irrigated acreage and the slowing of rates of growth in foodgrain production.

In the next chapter, the advantages of the landless service will be contrasted to both single-contractor and group systems of water management. Here we want to point out that the cost structure and the potential rates of return to the private sector appear to be substantially underwritten by national-level credit practices in the agricultural sector. Despite a steady rise in the nominal costs of irrigation equipment during the early 1980s, sales continued to rise until 1982–83. Government policy during this period was to phase out subsidies on STW prices, followed by LLPs, while retaining high levels of subsidy on DTWs. Meanwhile, the BADC retained its rental policy for DTWs and to a lesser extent for LLPs. Formal subsidies were therefore removed totally from STWs and later from purchased LLPs, but this equipment was purchased on formal institutional credit made available for the purpose initially by the International Development Association (IDA). The apparent paradox of a steady rise in the demand for STWs until 1982–83, alongside both the increase in their nominal price and the declining terms of exchange between winter rice output prices and other input prices such as fertilizer, can be explained by the high rates of default on institutional credit in the agricultural sector. We cannot isolate the proportion of this default rate attributable to irrigation equipment and loans for operating costs, but the overall overdues (that is, the proportion of cumulative amounts due but not recovered) were reported as 58.3 percent for FY84, 61.5 percent for FY85 and 73.0 percent for FY86 (World Bank, 1987:78). Thus, assuming that these rates are shared equally by the irrigation subsector, the real costs of equipment purchase and operating costs (mainly diesel fuel) in the private sector have increasingly received a hidden subsidy.

Widespread consensus in Bangladesh is that these rates of default on formal credit are not distributed equally among various classes of farmers. Richer farmers are much higher defaulters than poorer ones, even within credit-allocating institutions such as the Krishi Samabay Samity (KSS). This is often revealed in credit repayment drives, as during 1987, when richer farmers in a KSS put pressure upon their client small farmers-cum-tenants to repay outstanding loans without doing so themselves (according to the World Bank, the recovery rate increased from 27 percent in 1986 to 46 percent in 1987—World Bank, 1987; table 4.3). There is an access corollary too. Small farmer households are made up of nuclear families; richer ones usually consist of extended families. When rates of credit disbursal declined from 1986, as part of the policy on credit tightening, richer households were more likely to maintain access to the shrinking supply of credit with non-defaulting extended family members making fresh loan applications. Recent among the plurality of case-study evidence on these processes are Glaser's findings in Singra, Natore District, where a comparison of local bank records with households in "her" village revealed the pattern for irrigation loans—the wealthier the household, the higher the default. By contrast, the private irrigation cooperatives in the village had a good record of loan repayment (Glaser 1988: chapters 3.4 and 5.2). With the exception of these irrigation cooperatives in Singra, the hidden subsidies to private-sector minor irrigation have not been available to the same extent for landless groups. Also, the financial performance of groups within the Proshika program has been rigorously assessed. This is not to suggest that landless groups have not been defaulters. Our conclusion is that to date, with the most pessimistic assumptions, the default rate for the landless groups within the program does not exceed 30 percent, which compares favorably with the overall default rates for the same time period in the agricultural sector. Of course, these repayment rates have not always been achieved from successful irrigation performance, with sources of repayment sometimes deriving from nonirrigation activities, sales of equipment and rolling over of BKB loans with support from Proshika's RLF. With improved technical inputs into the program, however, these other sources of repayment are seen as temporary devices.

The implications of these variable rates of hidden subsidy to the respective minor irrigation sectors (conceived as private and landless for the purposes of this discussion) *via* defaulting on institutional credit have to be qualified by other dimensions of unaccounted service. On the one hand, the private sector has superior access to local bank branches, BADC and private mechanics and local supplies of diesel and spare parts (including credit facilities). Furthermore, these defaulting practices enable single contractors and formal/informal groups, who are receiving fees or incomes in the form of cropshares, to store and sell paddy at higher prices later in the year rather than at lower harvest prices, because they feel under no immediate obligation to repay due installments. On the other hand, the landless groups within the Proshika program have so far benefited from the services provided by the Proshika field staff at no cost to the groups. These services have included assistance with access to local bank branches and now direct credit support through the RLF at lower interest rates (13 percent); technical assistance (with irrigation management and accounting); and brokerage functions with suppliers (diesel and spare parts) and mechanics. Proshika also represents a more intangible service of general political support in the event of disputes with farmers over payment of fees or the making of agreements. These services are part of Proshika's development role, part of its *raison d'être*, and could not therefore be expected to be a charge on the groups in the early stages of the program. They exist precisely to redress the imbalance in the local political economy between the private sector and the landless groups. With the appointment of the cadre of technical irrigation field staff, these management costs to Proshika have increased, although less general field staff time at the ADC is required as a result. In a sense, hidden subsidies are being replaced by overt ones that can be more directly costed. An estimated charge of 6 percent on loans made for capital and operating costs will be required to cover technical assistance and RLF management costs to sustain the program within Proshika's portfolio. Under these conditions, the groups will no longer be receiving subsidies (even hidden ones), enabling loan capital to be recycled and additional groups to be brought into the program continually.

These variable subsidies between the private sector and the landless groups affect their respective factor endowments to enter the local water markets. Private-sector farmer/contractors are able to contemplate the acquisition of a STW to irrigate what would be suboptimal command areas (in terms of size and soil composition) under full cost conditions. This enables them to irrigate their own land and perhaps that of immediate neighboring plots (possibly of close kin), while excluding, overcharging or offering inferior service to more distant plots. It also enables them to control this subsidized factor of production to gain access or control over other productive land through favorable leasing or mortgaging arrangements (Glaser 1988: chapter 5). Furthermore, it enables them to compete for command area space against landless groups, which are paying nearer to full costs on capital and operation requirements, by undermining the viability of landless command areas in terms of both optimal size and a sustainable price at which the service can be offered to optimize returns to scale. In national policy terms, the two following conclusions for the minor irrigation sector can be drawn from this analysis:

- These hidden subsidies to the private sector are encouraging under-utilization of equipment capacity, which adversely affects the expansion of irrigated area, access of resource-poor farmers to irrigation, potential levels of irrigated output and the efficient use of scarce foreign exchange and external loan sources.
- By comparison, none of these problems occur with the landless service, because groups have a strong incentive to optimize command area size, therefore providing access to resource-poor farmers, and to practice efficient water management, thereby contributing to optimal yields.

A Hidden Subsidy to the Landless Service— Self-Exploitation or Labor Investment?

Hidden subsidy to the landless service concerns the use of unpaid group labor in the schemes, particularly for the construction of the main irrigation channels in a new command area. Further labor is sometimes deployed on the smaller watercourses to farmers' plots and on the annual maintenance of these channels after flood damage. Additional labor is required at harvest and threshing time, or in the collection of cash fees, but its paid/unpaid status is less clear. There are, of course, other labor inputs, such as the pumpset driver and lineman, who are paid formal salaries for the four-month irrigation period. In the first year of the program in Bhairab, these labor services provided by the group members were costed and paid for out of the operating-cost loan. Given the problem of narrow or negative margins experienced in this area, which we subsequently learned were mainly attributable to sandy soils inducing high unit costs, we were concerned with the financial burdens incurred by the groups and sought ways to reduce them.

One of the recommendations made at that time, and subsequently applied across the entire program, was that a group could provide voluntary labor in drain construction. These free labor services were also extended marginally to other activities. This labor contribution by group members may improve the financial figure for net returns to the group from the irrigation service, but are group members foregoing income-earning opportunities elsewhere? A general answer to the question is difficult, because the availability of alternative employment varies along with the work habits of different group members within a locality. But even if the alternative is leisure, is it fair to take advantage and underwrite these costs through the labor of people who are already poor? Is the voluntary labor to be considered as self-exploitation or as an investment? If the scheme is successful, then such voluntary labor is in effect ensuring an entitlement to income (often in the form of paddy) later in the year, while avoiding the costs of potentially expensive capital (that is, interest rates on the incremental operating-cost loan). To be considered as an investment, this voluntary labor should not entail group members entering into personal debt to sustain consumption during the period of foregone income. If the economics of the scheme are precarious, which is more likely in the first year when the command area may not have been optimized but when the main construction labor input is required, then group members are further sharing risk through their voluntary labor contribution, especially if the repayment of due installments has first claim on any gross earnings from the irrigation service. With greater reliance now on Proshika's RLF, there is room to relax these obligations to ensure some return to the labor input and reduce the self-exploitation element. In many of the schemes, this voluntary labor occurs not as a substitute for income-earning activity elsewhere, but as an addition to it in the evenings or early mornings. This represents a heavy burden on manual labor, which is obliged to work long, exhausting hours. In the minds of some of the field staff and group members, this nevertheless functions as a collective commitment to a scheme that is not otherwise conducive to much collective activity until the harvest. In this way, the ordinary members have a stake in the efficient management of the irrigation service and the level of accountability within the group will therefore be improved.

Labor Markets and Employment

Our data on the employment generation of landless irrigation schemes, when compared with the equivalent irrigation technology in the private sector or nonirrigated areas, are statistically inadequate and inconclusive about any possible direct advantages from landless irrigation to employment opportunities for landless labor. The action research operated under various constraints of data collection in terms of resources and the time available for Bangladesh Agricultural University (BAU) staff, and in terms of ADC field staff commitments for the weekly visits to selected group members. Within these limitations of data, we can argue that the main factor in employment generation appears to be irrigated area rather than the intensity of labor use per acre in irrigated areas.

At the outset of the program, we had hypothesized that, with the landless water sellers having a strong incentive (in the absence of subsidies —hidden or otherwise) to maximize production within their command areas, labor intensity per acre would be higher in the landless than in the private-sector schemes. The hypothesis had to be refined for different payment systems. With fixed charges for water (whether cash or kind, though the latter is rare), the farmer benefits directly from additional investment in other inputs and operations (such as labor-intensive weeding). But this incentive to the farmer is neutral with respect to the supplier of water (landless or private) as long as the supply of water is both regular and reliable. Certainly the landless groups provide a more reliable service, but our data do not allow us to conclude yet that such schemes employ more labor per acre than fixed-charge, private-sector schemes. With the cropshare payment system, the landless water sellers have a strong incentive to ensure that farmers maximize the intensity of land use by applying inputs and employing labor. The farmer's propensity to respond will, however, depend on several factors: the cropshare level (33 percent or 25 percent), the farmer's capacity to make the necessary investments and gain access to labor and the importance of winter rice cultivation on the plot to the farm household's overall economic calculations. This will depend on both the existence and characteristics of the farmer's other plots as well as the cropping characteristics (single/double) of the plot in question. To the extent that landless command areas contain a higher proportion of smaller farmers than private-sector schemes, a higher number of farmers might have capital and labor access constraints. This might be counteracted, however, by the increasing significance of winter rice cultivation in a command area to the small farmer's overall production plan. With this complex interaction of variables at work, much larger surveys than ours are necessary to demonstrate any differential patterns of labor use intensity under cropshare payment systems.

With constant labor coefficients per acre between landless and private-sector schemes, the consistently larger command areas in the landless schemes are responsible for generating more employment. At the same time, there is no strong evidence that landless schemes are attracting more labor from the landless group than other private schemes in the locality. Farmers recruit labor in response to wider conditions in the labor market, regardless of the source of water supply. Although the existence of a landless scheme may not lead to improved access for landless group labor within the command area, the corollary is that group members are not denied access to employment on private-sector schemes. It has been the presence of irrigation within a locality, rather than management type, that has therefore been significant in the provision of employment during a hitherto lean season for labor demand. Our data reveal that those group members who used to outmigrate for agricultural work at this time now opt for agricultural employment in the irrigated locality, irrespective of the presence of a landless scheme. But in localities of labor shortage for winter rice, farmers in landless command areas will themselves employ in-migrant laborers, for instance at harvest time. Furthermore, if group members regularly outmigrate for secure, non-equivalent agricultural work (in textile factories, or as part of stable, long-term sharecropping arrangements in traditional winter rice single-cropped areas) these work patterns continue despite the availability of employment in the newly irrigated winter rice lands of the locality. This explains the occasional paradox of outmigration and inmigration in the same locality in the same season. And because inmigrant labor, especially for harvest work, is usually organized in gangs around fixed-price contracts, the price of inmigrant labor is often lower than the local rates for individually recruited casual labor. This acts as a disincentive for local labor to jeopardize secure alternatives that have traditionally existed elsewhere during this season. Of course, such patterns may not persist as local irrigation becomes more stable, and if the circumstances affecting the sources of inmigrant labor change perhaps, too, as a result of irrigation.

Competition, Water Markets and State Regulation

During this program, it has become clear that, even with relatively fixed irrigation installations like STWs, the market for minor irrigation is much more fluid than at first supposed. At the outset of the program, assumptions about water markets were based on comparisons with fixed and immovable capital assets such as DTWs. Once command areas had been established under some form of ownership or organization, it was assumed there would be little competition even under conditions of low-level utilization, as long as the installation remained profitable (directly or indirectly) to the owners.

The LLPs had always been regarded as a more flexible source of irrigation, either where contractors competed annually to rent equipment and supply an established command area or where LLP command areas were impermanent, shifting continually in response to unpredictable sources of supply. Furthermore, under rental agreements for LLPs from the BADC, richer farmers intent on cultivating HYV winter rice would often play a waiting game with the weather, hoping for timely winter rains to avoid or reduce the period of renting a pumpset to irrigate their own land. Farmers with neighboring land who purchased additional capacity from rich farmers' LLPs thus also shared in the seasonal insecurity, adding their land where possible to competing sources of irrigation supply. Although some contractors and richer farmers did effectively acquire monopoly water rights to supply a command area over several irrigation seasons, this could always be challenged through price competition, because long-term agreements were rare. Ecological constraints also intrude, as water sources dry up or change course.

Although their share some of the fixed installation characteristics of the DTW, STWs represented a new form of organizing groundwater irrigation. The earlier DTW programs were formally based on groups of cooperating farmers supplying water to their own plots. STWs, on the other hand, opened up opportunities for individual, private control over groundwater sources with the prospect of monopoly supply to fixed command areas. The problem for us, therefore, at the outset of the program was the extent to which the landless irrigation program was competing for scarce command area territory in a one-off race to capture control over this sector of groundwater irrigation in Bangladesh. We were anxious lest this approach to agrarian reform *via* landless control over irrigation would not have time to be established as a significant program. Our anxieties were further reinforced by the market orientations of the World Bank and its client, the government of Bangladesh. This market orientation was partly prompted by an understandable impatience, both within the Bank and the United States Agency for International Development (USAID), with the state regulation of expanded opportunities in agriculture. Both external agencies could back up their orientation with the provision of liberal credit facilities to individual entrepreneurs, without targeting or even allocating credit quotas to cooperatives, despite the World Bank's virtuous adherence to working with Bangladeshi rural institutions.

Our early fears about these limitations for the landless program were proved wrong. Because the STW water market has remained fluid, the opportunities for expanding the STW landless irrigation service continue to exist. Many variables nevertheless affect the conditions under which this expansion can occur or, to put it another way, they affect the propensity for private owners to sell equipment and abandon command areas:

1. The hidden subsidies to the private sector sustain suboptimal command areas and underutilized equipment in private hands.

2. These subsidies enable private operators to offer lower fees for water, which minimizes users' risk in terms of both water charges and scale of investment to cover other cultivation costs.

3. The cropping characteristics of the command area (elevation, vulnerability to early flooding, soil composition, single/double) affect the intensity with which negotiations over price and delivery are conducted between users and sellers.

4. The motivations of private water sellers vary—for some it is a business that must directly accrue profit and for others it is a bonus above the costs of supplying their own plots, especially when hidden subsidies are available; for yet others, it is a way of achieving economies of scale beyond their own land when subsidies (hidden or otherwise) will not cover costs

(see Glaser, 1988, for a discussion of these motivations).

5. The reliability of the machine affects its running costs and tests the quality of access to spare parts and mechanics.

6. The availability of electricity as a power source reduces the unit costs of water supply and can either reduce the size of viable command areas or reduce the level of water charges and increase the willingness of farmers to buy water.

7. The extent of opportunities for multiple uses of the machine (rice milling, boat or cart transportation, electric generation) will influence the extent of its use for irrigation where use for irrigation alone would not be profitable.

8. Private water sellers are sometimes prepared to provide a non-profitable irrigation service to ensure that their own land in other command areas is irrigated by other water sellers.

9. More viable water sellers may successfully encroach upon the command area, impairing its optimality.

10. Other opportunities for economic diversification may reduce the interest in earning rents and profits from operating a STW.

11. The shifting terms of exchange between input and output prices not only reduces the incentive to invest in irrigation equipment but has also undermined the viability of marginal command areas (marginal in the sense of yield potential as well as size).

These variables have been identified as causes of market fluidity in our research, and are emphasized here as more likely to affect the private sector than they are the landless schemes. This is not to argue, of course, that landless groups have not been selling equipment when their schemes have come under pressure for these or other reasons. Increasingly, however, the landless schemes are avoiding some of these problems through the technical assistance and more rigorous feasibility studies provided by Proshika's technical irrigation field staff. Furthermore, the greater dependence of the groups upon the profitability of their schemes ensures that they are more conscientious about water delivery and optimizing command area, so that they are less likely to be the victims of encroachment or competition through the provision of superior service. At the same time, the threshold of command area viability for the landless schemes (under the conditions of hidden subsidies and some of the other variables noted above) is higher. This partly explains why discontinuations have occurred among landless schemes alongside a large, though unrecorded, number in the private sector. As we have argued throughout, command area size is the most important factor affecting performance, especially for STWs.

All these issues affecting the stability of command areas for LLP and STW minor irrigation represent opportunities as well as problems for the landless irrigation program. Even with relatively location-fixed irrigation technologies, there is no finite and time-bounded race to occupy potential-ly scarce command area territory. It is possible for landless groups to take over DTW command areas, previously in the private sector, which have fallen into partial or complete disuse, and to rehabilitate and extend them where appropriate. This example illustrates a potential danger of landless groups moving without caution into failed private-sector command areas. The reasons for such failure have to be firmly understood and a clear distinction made between problems unique to private-sector management and problems that would undermine the viability of a command area no matter what form of management existed. A significant element in determining such viability is the regulatory practices of the state in the irrigation sector. The open-market orientation of the sponsors of the rapid expansion of minor irrigation, combined with liberal credit supply and lax recovery discipline, has produced a situation of near-anarchy in the location of competing irrigation technologies. There is groundwater competition between DTWs and STWs on both vertical and horizontal dimensions: vertical, with DTWs drawing down STW aquifers and exhausting them before the end of the season; horizontal, with both technologies encroaching on each other's command areas. DTWs have been located in high water-table areas of the northwest, and the Master Plan Organization (MPO) scatter diagrams of STW distribution would seem to indicate that the main determinant of spatial allocation has been proximity to rail heads. STWs have been installed in areas with low water tables and sandy soil.

Furthermore, the zoning restrictions that supposedly set minimum distances between installations and are supposedly administered by the BADC have been an operational farce. The BADC's feasibility certificate should include adherence to the zoning regulations. Normal practice in the private sector, however, is simply to bribe the local BADC official for this piece of documentation. The dilemma here is that, while the opportunities for corruption are obvious (as for any licensing arrangements under such conditions of the Bangladesh political economy), there is a real productive function to be served in ensuring both a rational distribution of different types of irrigation technology and the technically optimal spacing between them to secure viable command areas and adequate aquifers for neighboring schemes. Such a function may run the risk of state guarantees for local water monopolies. Nevertheless, if it had been carried out with any degree of technical competence and responsibility, it would have been possible to avoid the highly expensive learning process of a long market shakedown (made even longer by hidden subsidies) in which many farmers and tubewell operators have in effect gone bankrupt, scarce foreign exchange resources have been wasted, rural institutional credit has been squandered and other linked (and, to the farmer, expensive) agricultural inputs have been unable to realize their full yield potential.

This absence of rational planning in the minor irrigation sector, or deregulation by default, has itself been a source of opportunities for the landless irrigation strategy as well as a source of problems. Some of the group schemes have undoubtedly suffered by not receiving the protection of the zoning regulations to fend off subsidized private-sector competitors, who have encroached on landless scheme command areas and yet still left them underutilized. At the same time, in this context of anarchic competition and keeping in mind the factors noted above, which affect discontinuations, some groups have benefited by extending their command areas into private-sector territory, or by setting up in direct competition with an extant STW irrigation system. The absence of effective zoning has meant that no local water monopoly is safe, and the opportunities for a continuous, steady advance of the landless irrigation strategy therefore remain within the existing areas of minor irrigation in Bangladesh as well as in the new areas of irrigated land as projected in the current Third Five-Year Plan (3FYP). There is no race, just a market—not one of our making but one in which the landless groups can continue to compete.

Water Rights

The issues of markets for irrigation and state regulation are essentially questions of rights to water sources. Such rights are complex in any society, and no less so in Bangladesh where they are more the outcome of practice and power than legislation. Surface and groundwater raise different problems.

With surface water, canals and rivers have to be distinguished from ponds and lakes or *bheels*. Canals and rivers consist of flowing water and therefore have upstream and downstream effects, but otherwise can be regarded as common property. Ponds may be privately owned and access therefore restricted, in contrast to lakes or *bheels*, which can be regarded as common property although government leases sometimes organize access in favor of the local rich. With all surface water sources, however, other variables intrude to determine access and use, such as the proximity of land and capital or the ability to pay labor costs if traditional technologies are used. If capital is required in the form of LLPs, then surface water rights become a function of access to capital or access to rental equipment from the BADC and either the ability to fend off competition through a combination of price and threats or protection from BADC zoning restrictions when leasing out equipment. However, especially in the case of mechanized LLPs with a much larger command area capacity than traditional technologies, such rights are also dependent either on the proximity of a significant amount of the operator's own land to the source of water (which is rare) or on agreements to provide a service with enough farmers to constitute a viable command area.

The advent of mechanized equipment, with perhaps ten times the irrigation capacity of the traditional technologies, does have significant implications for the sharing of surface water rights in a locality. The sources drain more quickly. This may not be a problem (at least for land productivity) as long as more land is irrigated at a reasonable price for the entire season and there is sufficient annual replenishment without long-term silting effects. Monopoly control over fewer access points is likely to develop, however, with farmer/users in a weaker bargaining position. Furthermore, such sources are more likely to dry out before the end of the season, leaving some operators or farmers stranded with no water. With common-property small *bheels,* it has been possible to arrange cooperative use and avoid prisoners' dilemmas. With larger *bheels* and canals and rivers, where the people who can be potentially served by the water sources (either as commercial sellers or farmer/users) are less socially integrated, there is little prospect in obtaining widespread cooperative agreements. With flowing water, intensive irrigation downstream increases the rate of drainage upstream and effectively denies upstream dwellers' water rights. Intensive irrigation upstream reduces the quantity downstream and correspondingly denies those dwellers' rights. Where there is no sense of community to correspond to the common property resource, management is more likely to be the outcome of prisoners' dilemma behavior than of cooperation and sharing. The landless schemes are not isolated from these problems, though clearly any federal relationship between such groups over a wider locality in which landless group schemes significantly dominated could ensure a rationed and collective use of the common-property resource in a way not possible for competing private-sector schemes. The water rights (or in effect rights to an irrigation service) for all farmers in the locality of the common property resource would then in effect be policed by the federation of landless groups operating the service. This form of policing or common property management is even more necessary under certain conditions of land elevation and distance from the water source (such as a large-capacity river), where large-scale lumpy pumping equipment is required alongside a substantial investment in irrigation channels to create a network of smaller water courses for two cubic-foot-per-second (cu.sec) LLP use.

Groundwater presents different issues. The premise for the landless irrigation intervention was that the connection between owning land and having exclusive rights over the aquifers beneath it was an untested and therefore uninstitutionalized legal assumption. The notion of such a connection in Bangladesh was complicated by the extent of fragmentation of holdings, which implies that if farmers were acknowledged to have such exclusive rights over their aquifers, they would have to cooperate to exploit them. In practice, however, such rights were concentrated in the hands of those who had superior access to the capital equipment or to the services derived from it. With the privatization policy for the expansion of STWs, which encouraged the acquisition of such equipment by private operators in order to offer an irrigation service for commercial gain over and above the irrigation requirements of their own land, the state was in effect severing the connection between an owner's land and its corresponding aquifer by endorsing the transfer of rents as well as profits to the STW operator. Through practice, therefore, the principle had been established that rights to groundwater were translated into access to equipment and the finance to pay operating costs, subject to all the variables of competition noted in the previous section. This was the institutional space, the room for maneuver, into which the groups moved.

CHAPTER TEN

Conclusions

DESPITE THE MANY problems encountered in the development of this program, the knowledge that has been acquired and the capacity of Proshika and the groups to respond to that knowledge indicates that the program has a future for the groups associated with Proshika. It is also important, however, to see how far the program could become a wider strategy for Bangladesh both in terms of institutional capacity and the directions of structural change in agriculture and agrarian relations. A glance at contemporary documentation on agricultural policy reveals rhetorical support for landless agricultural laborers, but relies on the non-farm sector (Hossain, 1987) to provide an escape from responsibility (Wood 1986, on sectoralization *inter alia* as an escape from responsibility).

Neither shifts in the sectoral allocation of the labor market nor rates of economic expansion in manufacturing give grounds for optimism. The 1981 Bangladesh Census reported that among active males for Bangladesh as a whole 58 percent were in cultivation, 4 percent in manufacture and 11 percent in business. Contrasting the 1974 census with the 1983–84 Labor Force Survey shows a 30 percent increase in the employed male population, and it is true that none of this increase went into agriculture (suggesting the limits to labor absorption capacity directly in agriculture). Actually, shops absorbed about 40 percent of the increase, and manufacturing, transportation and services took about 15 percent each of the increase. Since independence, agriculture has fallen only from 55 percent to 47 percent (at constant prices) as a proportion of the gross domestic product (GDP). There has not been an equivalent rise in manufacturing, which has expanded its share by only 0.4 percent. During the 1970s, there was an annual 6 percent rate of growth in GDP (starting from a devastated low base). During the 1980s, this has slowed to 3 percent. The rate of growth in manufacturing might have been expected to be faster but in fact has only been at 4 percent, with services not much higher, although there is likely to be a significant unrecorded element in transportation (a rapid expansion of rickshaws, buses and trucks—the last due in part to the expansion of agricultural activity). The international terms of trade have worked against Bangladesh to the extent that from 1973 to 1983, the movement in import and export prices has virtually halved export buying power. At independence, raw jute and jute products accounted for about 90 percent of export earnings. This has now declined to 70 percent at constant prices but to 50 percent at current prices. Leather exports initially rose quickly but have now tapered off. Tea exports have grown steadily but international prices are unstable. The expansion of garments and frozen seafood as an export component has been dramatic: from 7 percent to 31 percent in the ten-year period, but from a low base. The export of garments could probably have been much higher had it not been for import restrictions in the United States and Western Europe.

The World Bank projects the growth of the labor force at 3.2 percent per year for 1985–90, rising marginally thereafter to 3.5 percent by the end of the century, which would add about one million to the labor force each year. But if we look at the constraints to the expansion of the non-farm sectors, we can see that solutions to this projected growth in the labor force have to be found directly or indirectly within food-related agriculture. Because the need to grow food constrains the expansion of non-food agricultural products such as jute and tobacco—0.85 million acres have been diverted from jute to rain-fed cereals during the Second Five-Year Plan (2FYP) period—limits are therefore set to the utilization of such raw materials in manufacturing. And although there has been an exportable surplus of agricultural goods such as jute, tea and leather, it seems clear from the terms of trade discussion above that the only room for maneuver in generating non-farm employment has been restricted to garments, services and construction. The problem of course is to enter sectors where output can be traded at internationally competitive prices and/or supply an expanding domestic market. But here the constraints are severe, with an average of 70 percent of rural household income spent on food.

No linkage is recognized between a strategy for growth in agriculture and an opportunity for fair rent-seeking by the landless in that process. But, as argued before, under the conditions of rural landlessness in Bangladesh and the consequent high proportion of the rural (therefore total) population dependent on purchasing food, unless that purchasing power exists in the form of rents and incomes, an incentive price for agricultural output would be difficult to sustain. The existence of food for work and the vulnerable group-feeding programs (with all the attendant labeling problems—see Wood 1985) may provide distribution and crucial periods of employment, for some, but they are also reliant on distributors of food aid, which undermines the objective of incentive prices for farmers. In the context of a reduced level of manifest, as opposed to latent, subsidies on agricultural inputs, the maintenance of output prices on farm products is essential, but this can be achieved only if the level of effective demand in the domestic food markets is sufficiently buoyant. Reliance on the food-aided non-farm sector undermines the level of effective demand for domestic food production rather than contributing to it.

At the same time, the trickle-down or "Cadillac" approach to agricultural growth is limited by declining rates of labor absorption, notwithstanding the short-term rise in real wages in 1985–86, which the World Bank (1988:7) and Hossain (1987:4,195) saw as heralding the success of the green revolution strategy. In short, we cannot rely on the non-farm sector or rises in agricultural employment alone to sustain levels of effective demand in the domestic food market to maintain incentive prices to farmers to invest in nonsubsidized inputs. Under such conditions, the landless actual and potential purchasers of food must have access to rents and profits from expanded agricultural production—not just access, for some, to higher incomes from the acknowledged but inadequate increase in agricultural laboring opportunities. This argument is the economic basis for the landless irrigation strategy as an example of the necessary link between growth and distribution/equity. We are not just arguing that equity (in the sense of fair rent-seeking by the landless from expanded agricultural production) can be consistent with growth. We argue that equity strategies are necessary for growth through the medium of effective demand and incentive prices.

From 1980, the irrigation strategy with Proshika was developed on the basis of these principles and to demonstrate that they could be translated into practice. Irrigation could be regarded as an experimental example for these purposes, showing the way for the landless involvement in other sets of opportunities offered by the expanded investment in agriculture (food processing, tillage, supply of inputs, transportation, marketing, repair and maintenance). Even as a demonstration, however, the program is more significant because minor irrigation has been the leading subsector in agriculture since 1980 (and will continue to be so if the arguments contained in the Ministry of Agriculture's "Floods 1987: Medium Term Recovery Program" hold water). An irrigation-led solution to the expansion of agricultural production and the target of food self-sufficiency remains the centerpiece of agricultural policy, and further investment will be applied to this sector. Water development—drainage or flood control plus minor irrigation and surface water schemes—has attracted an investment of US$1.2 billion since 1977, representing about 55 percent of development expenditure directly in agriculture. Further irrigation-related expenditure occurs through the support of irrigated crops.

A survey of performance over the 2FYP period shows that agriculture production as a whole grew at about 3 percent per year, with foodgrain output slightly higher at 3.2 percent (but in contrast to the 6.5 percent planned). But performance has declined since 1985 to nearer 2.5 percent. The more input-dependent crops, such as wheat and high-yield variety (HYV) winter rice, which have been responsible for the expansion since 1980, have shown signs of losing momentum (due to irrigation failures, farmers' preferences for rotations, decline in fertilizer/yield coefficients, early flooding of late harvested winter rice/*braus* crops and a dip in output prices. The growth rate might therefore decline further to around 2 percent, contrasted to the Third Five-Year Plan (3FYP) target of 4 percent. A major explanation in the slow rate of growth in foodgrain production is the below-targeted rate of expansion of irrigated area, which has risen to 22 percent of cultivated area (from 11 percent) instead of reaching 32 percent. The opportunities for including the landless irrigation strategy in this scenario continue, therefore, and are further reinforced by our awareness of the fluidity of water markets and competition for water provision and use. Such markets create both problems and opportunities for landless water sellers, not only undermining any security in water rights independent of performance/efficiency criteria but also preventing the establishment of permanent water monopolies and the long-term denial of access to command areas.

While recognizing the problems of efficient water use and irrigation management, we advocate the direct involvement of the landless in expanded agricultural production through the provision of irrigation services, encouraged by our awareness that these problems are not disproportionately distributed to the landless water sellers and that opportunities for the landless entry into water markets will persist. But the problem remains whether non-governmental organizations (NGOs) enjoy special advantages over government in assisting the rural poor in this way and whether, therefore, government should endorse the further expansion of NGO activity in irrigation as part of its own policy stance rather than attempt to replicate the strategy through its own institutions.

In this chapter, we will consider the following issues:

- the comparative advantages of landless irrigation services—reconciling growth and equity objectives,
- action research—location-specific problem solving and monitoring for management,
- effects of employment and income-generating (EIG) activities on group solidarity and local politics, and
- implications for agrarian reforms strategies—NGOs and government.

The Comparative Advantages of Landless Services

The landless irrigation initiative seized the opportunity offered by the *de facto* separation between land ownership and rights to water under the conditions of highly fragmented farm holdings in Bangladesh. Fragmentation occurs mainly as an outcome of multiple inheritance practices under conditions of restricted income-earning opportunities outside cultivation, so that agricultural land remains a precious asset. Although women have formal rights to inherited land, these rights are normally waived in favor of movable dowry goods, so that fragmentation is mainly explained in terms of division between sons. (This is not to suggest that women are exercising independent choice or that they gain independent access to the dowry attached to them—see White 1988.) Furthermore, the attributes of land are soil composition and elevation as well as surface area, so that multiple inheritance involves not just the equal allocation of plots but the division of each scattered plot. Under the conditions of labor- and bullock-intensive traditional agricultural technologies, this intensity of fragmentation has not required the plotholders to cooperate extensivly with neighbors (who may of course be kin). It has certainly entailed management problems for owners. For the richer ones, these problems have been resolved in the past by leasing out some plots to sharecroppers, and this logic still remains for traditional, especially broadcast *aman* cultivation (see Glaser, 1988, for findings from seven villages in Rajshahi District). However, with HYV-irrigated cultivation, neighboring plots have to be brought into some kind of relation to secure the potential levels of productivity from the technology.

One principle for such a relationship is to match plural ownership of plots in a given area with collective rights to the water that serves that area (either surface water sources, or the corresponding groundwater aquifers) to constitute an irrigation cooperative of the member farmers. The difficulty with this principle is that member farmers are not equal, either with reference to the size of their plots in the command area or with reference to their overall landholdings and therefore leverage in the community. This has led to the familiar pattern of domination of command areas, reported extensively in the literature (Boyce 1987, and Glaser 1988). The further complication is that individual farmers, especially large ones, have their land scattered across many command areas, each requiring cooperation. This institutional option of cooperatively managed command areas has remained the prevailing organizational model for deep tubewells (DTWs), but has not overcome problems of underutilization and inefficiency (see Boyce, 1987:228–248). The options for DTW management are limited because DTWs are a lumpy and fixed technology, and with approximately 50-acre command areas, rich farmers cannot realistically consolidate through purchase, mortgaging-in or reverse tenancies to reach optimal private command areas. Similar problems exist for low-lift pumps (LLPs), but investment costs are considerably lower and, because the technology is movable, richer farmers have more scope for underutilization with profit and for private use just by supplying different areas of their overall holding. If concern for principles of equity alongside efficiency exists, either the cooperative strategy must be pursued with DTWs and made to work, or some form of irrigation service must be provided. This can be done either through public-sector management, with all the dangers attendant on it in a society like Bangladesh, or through specialist irrigation companies with a commercial interest in providing a good service in the sense that command area sizes are optimized and equitable delivery thereby ensured. The cooperative option remains the dominant policy, despite the social constraints to efficient and equitable water distribution that are reinforced to the level of contradiction by the strong subsidy element.

The organizational options for shallow tubewell (STW) management differ from DTWs for the following reasons:

- The technology is not immovable once installed, although some loss is incurred for the boring.
- Command areas are smaller, thus reducing the scale of cooperation required between farmers owning constituent plots.
- With no formal subsidy, there is more pressure on operators to utilize equipment efficiently than there is for DTWs, although hidden subsidies can offset this.

With STWs, therefore, individual private operators and some richer farmers have more scope to move pumping equipment between several boring sites to irrigate different parts of the farm holding. The technology is sufficiently flexible to enable operators to engage in substantial bargaining with potential users, because the option of moving the STW to another site is always credible. Under these conditions, however, private operators have fewer incentives to provide a comprehensive and equitable service and to optimize command areas.

These reasons do not constitute a strong set of advantages for farmers who wish to irrigate their land but who are unable to become STW operators themselves. Despite the smaller command areas, however, the cooperative option for such farmers is hardly less complicated than for DTWs, especially because their land is likely to be distributed across more separate command areas in STW than in DTW areas. We must nevertheless accept that the prospects for cooperation among farmer-users in STW command areas are greater than for the larger DTW areas. Because smaller numbers of farmers will be involved, there will be more trust and personal connection between them, and kin may tie a greater proportion of them together. But even though the potential for cooperation may be higher in STW command areas (as compared to DTW command areas), most findings indicate that effective command areas are much smaller than the notional ones, and that dominant families prevail over water distribution so that tail-enders abound. (One exception to this picture has been found by Glaser in Singra, Rajshahi, which is why she called "her" village Samitigram, but even she could not find a similar picture in the neighboring seven villages she examined.)

Thus both of these options for STW irrigation—private operation and cooperatives—have disadvantages for most classes of farmers under the Bangladeshi conditions of intense fragmentation of holdings. But because the nonsubsidized private operator solution could be more readily applied to STW irrigation, and was indeed positively encouraged by the World Bank at the beginning of the 2FYP, there has been less alternative pressure from the Government of Bangladesh (GOB) and foreign donors to persist with the cooperative option for STW command areas. In this context, then, the commercial landless irrigation service offers several comparative advantages.

First, at the public policy level for minor irrigation, the landless irrigation service is superior to private operation or actually existing cooperatives on efficiency and equity criteria. It can operate commercially without subsidy support, optimizing command area size and providing irrigation to all classes of farmers. In this sense, mechanized irrigation can be rendered neutral to scale for water users. One set of conditions exists when it is not in the commercial interest of the landless service to provide water to poorer farmers—namely when the water fee is in the form of cropshare, and ecological and social options exist to optimize the command area toward richer farmer-users who are more able to maximize yields through applying a full package of inputs. Even under these conditions, however, there may be social and political reasons for not discriminating against poorer farmers, especially if they are group members. Furthermore, if the poor farmers' problems are those of access to credit to apply fertilizer and pay for weeding labor, then the landless irrigation service can take on the additional function of supplying credit to its poorer clientele.

Second, the commercial incentives for equitable distribution among farmers, virtually regardless of class, maximize the use of all the scarce foreign exchange commodities involved in capitalized agriculture—not only irrigation equipment, spare parts and fuel but also imported chemical fertilizer and pesticides or, indirectly, the imported capital goods that underpin domestic fertilizer production. At the same time, different classes of farmers are paying equitable shares of these costs in proportion to their size of holdings under mechanized irrigation by virtue of the landless irrigation service rather than the distorted financial burdens that appear under the conditions of hidden subsidies noted in the previous chapter. Some distortion remains, however, through non-repayment of fertilizer credit, but even this could be eliminated if landless groups supplied fertilizer with the cost incorporated into a joint water/fertilizer fee.

Third, by removing the problems of cooperation (in either privately operated or cooperative schemes) between farmers over such issues as fair water distribution, labor inputs on channel construction, payment of operating costs and loan repayments on capital, potential arenas of conflict between farmers are reduced. By externalizing the service, farmers do not need to dispute between themselves as service suppliers, because they have more common interests as customers. Poorer farmers, or those with plots on the edge of command areas, need never become tail-enders or losers in the process of negotiation itself.

Fourth, the landless irrigation service does provide advantages to the landless that they do not receive through schemes organized in other ways, although we have been unable to demonstrate clear advantages for employment generation. The groups are gaining incomes through rents and profits. They are gaining leverage to bargain with farmers (as land-lords, employers and moneylenders) over other issues. They are able to reinvest in other collective income-generating activity (including additional irrigation schemes). Where collective funds have been developed, individual members gain some security against unforeseen disasters. Where dividends have been distributed as paddy for storage to members, this has reduced their dependency on cash purchases of high-priced paddy later in the season. They are gaining direct management experience, which can be transferred to other business activities. They are interacting directly with other actors in the local and regional economic system, and are thus able to develop other networks for potential service delivery in agriculture.

Action Research: Location-specific
Problem Solving and Monitoring for Management

This program has clearly been an exercise in action research. At its inception, the social and organizational innovations, along with the relatively unknown performance characteristics of the mechanized STW technologies under Bangladesh conditions, excluded the possibility of available models for imitation or reference. The program was founded on an understanding of the contradictions of macroeconomic and agricultural policy in Bangladesh, and on some understanding of agrarian social structure in which room for maneuver could be identified for this strategy. But beyond this, there was little choice but to be tentative and experimental and to learn from the experience of trying to introduce the approach. At first, therefore, our learning was unstructured, based on the sharing of experience at the site level in trying to solve problems as they arose. After the first season, the significance of various categories of data could be more readily appreciated and organized in a more standard way with checklists, pro formas and questionnaires. As far as possible, the data headings reflected the way in which group members recorded information as part of their management of the irrigation activity. In this way, it was hoped that group members would not lose touch with their own data and that they would readily understand the comparisons drawn between their own performance and those of other schemes. The methodology for the 1982 report tried to retain the principles of participatory action research, though recognizing that a hierarchy had developed with groups providing information, field staff processing it and central program staff writing it up to present an analysis.

The phrase "participatory action research" could become merely bemusing rhetoric. In fact, it reflects the important principle of avoiding monopolies of knowledge and the directive styles of management that follow. It was attempted to overcome the ignorance of those involved centrally in the program alongside a quickly emerging recognition of the diversity of local conditions in rural Bangladesh (ecology, social structure and water market practices) that crucially affect the optimal strategies groups can adopt.

Despite the existence of an initial master project proposal, few program-wide norms can be established—for example, size of command area, rates of machine use and forms as well as value of payments. At the same time, gaining an understanding of how such variables (along with others) interact in order to maximize the returns to a group in each specific situation was important. The second phase of action research has been designed, in part, to achieve this objective. Of course, it has also been designed to convey the overall financial performance of the program, and to describe, where possible, the comparative advantages of this strategy for minor irrigation over other private-sector formulas. Despite the various weaknesses of method that have emerged in the research, some success can be claimed in producing an overall framework of analysis that has been transferred to Proshika as a regular and continual monitoring instrument for overall management purposes but that allows the space for location-specific problem solving.

In addressing these dual objectives, it is essential to develop and preserve the local capacity for adaptive research among the technical irrigation field staff, the field staff at the Area Development Center (ADC) level and as far as possible among the groups themselves. Such capacity requires the confidence of central coordination staff in the field staff, and styles of monitoring and management based more on principles of reciprocity between central and field staff than on pyramidal structures of hierarchical authority. These sets of principles are difficult for government bureaucracies to follow, especially in seniority-preoccupied societies such as Bangladesh, where standardized instructions flow from the center with only the possibility of feedback from the field (which can always be discounted) to modify them.

This becomes an important, wider issue of project management and development administration connected to familiar distinctions between process and blueprint planning. Rural development in particular is sensitive to the activity of local variables, in which the exercise of central authority, even through apparently decentralized units of administration, is inappropriate because it is locally insensitive to the specific interaction of such variables. This program of irrigation services by the landless depends crucially on the capacity for independent analysis in the location of the schemes.

Such analysis is required to establish the technical, social and financial feasibility of a scheme proposal, involving the joint knowledge of the groups (about possible command areas, social composition of potential farmer-irrigators, existence or likelihood of competing schemes and the group's own solidarity) and the field staff (soil types, availability of supporting services, projected discharge rates, cost structures and necessary payment values). The same expertise is necessary for subsequent problem solving, which may involve renegotiating agreements with farmers, changing the command area layout and so on. The field staff also have a role in establishing local norms (as for command area size, value of payment or diesel consumption) based on an understanding of soil types, local cropping patterns, and competitive pricing. These norms can function more as guide to feasibility and what counts locally as strong or weak performance.

In the development of this capacity for adaptive local research, the relationship between the technical cadre of field staff and the general program field staff in the ADC must also be reciprocal rather than hierarchical. Such a principle is always difficult to preserve when one of the partners has, by definition, more specialist knowledge than the other. But of course, the general field staff member has knowledge that the technical specialist requires. (This issue does not apply only to irrigation, of course.) In such a context, one function of central management is to monitor local experience, rather than seek to standardize it, and to transfer that local experience where appropriate into other locations. The other function of central monitoring is to use key indicators such as loan repayments and net returns to ensure that schemes in particular localities are not getting into difficulty systematically because locally optimal solutions are not being found. Such monitoring is necessary to protect the overall position of the Revolving Loan Fund (RLF), because high defaults would constrain future lending in irrigation and in other sectors. Groups must also be discouraged from entering adventurist projects, from which extrication could be long and painful.

Effects of EIG Activities on Group Solidarity and Local Politics

The purported tension between employment- and income-generating (EIG) activities and the political radicalism of the rural poor in Bangladesh has become a dividing issue between NGOs of different persuasions, as well as between NGOs, intellectual radicals and academic nationalists. The propositions of this debate have become difficult to disentangle from the sets of vested interests at stake behind different positions. The discourse is tinged with hypocrisy, as the codes are elaborated to disguise jealousies, factions, personal animosities and so on. Some of the criticisms should not, however, be dismissed on this account and have therefore prompted extensive discussions within Proshika as well as raising issues of more general significance concerning the place of NGOs in the development of Bangladesh.

The case against the NGOs in general, and EIG activities in particular, is that they are counterrevolutionary and indeed revisionist and neoimperialist, the last a reflection of their reliance on donor funding. Different statements are being made here. The neoimperialist allegation is a favorite both of intellectual radicals and academic nationalists, but the latter point out the artificiality of NGO humanitarianism because it involves salaries and careers rather than personal sacrifice, whereas the former also see deep conspiracy in the availability of donor funds to sap the radical strength of potential cadres of revolutionary activists and divert it into a pseudoprofessionalism of alternative rural development. These are not issues to be discussed here, though to place them in perspective it should be recognized that 80 percent of the government's development budget is funded by foreign aid of one kind or another, but only 1 percent of donor funds are received by NGOs. Academic nationalists in particular have often enjoyed the fruits of donor support through consultancies, sabbatical years abroad and so on.

The issues concerning the counterrevolutionary and revisionist tendencies of EIG activities have to be taken more seriously by NGOs like Proshika, which have a strongly political analysis of poverty in which the power of the organized poor is an essential part of any strategy for the improvement of their material well-being as well as their civil rights. This question of revisionism is also, more surprisingly, raised by some Western development academics who derive significant sources of personal income from training and advisory work on income-generating projects for the poor, while turning their backs on the virtues of entrepreneurialism in the comfort of their university seminars. Proshika's philosophy has always been based on the premise that poor and hungry people cannot be mobilized around campaigns that involve only conflict with exploiting classes and state authority. Given the complex social structure of rural household survival, landless and near-landless households cannot be expected to place all their tenuous links to resources at risk in wage struggles, sharecropper movements and the occupation of *khas* land and *bheels*. These links require some material substitution in the form of EIG activities before they can be challenged, modified or discarded. Poor households organized in groups can create mutual assistance funds out of savings and collectively earned income. They can create sources of employment that may keep them from dependence on extortionate loans during lean periods of agricultural labor demand. They can acquire rents and profits from business activity rather than just incomes from selling their labor.

The issue that arises from this justification of EIG activities is whether the premise involving the substitution of hierarchical survival links between different classes is itself contradictory in that it prompts the development of individual entrepreneurial behavior among the poor, thus reproducing the structures that have historically been responsible for poverty and inequality. If such a contradiction existed, the charge of revisionism would have some foundation. But a distinction should be drawn between entrepreneurial behavior of a productive kind, in which goods and services are exchanged in open markets, and other forms of entrepreneurial behavior that rely on interlocked factor markets to realize and concentrate surplus from production and services. The latter form of entrepreneurialism reflects the familiar structures of exploitation through monopolies over land and employment opportunities and through the operation of merchant capital in the countryside. Proshika is eager to avoid any development of the latter form of entrepreneurialism among the groups that it supports. Such developments would constitute a failure in the process of conscientization in which groups of landless and near-landless should appreciate that their own advancement, and that of their class generally, depends on the disappearance of these exploitative economic relations from the society as a whole. Their own imitation of them for short-term advantage would undermine this process in the long run. Were groups or individuals to try to reproduce such structures (through using incomes for usurious moneylending, for example), they would quickly isolate themselves from the fellowship of the poor in the locality. It is therefore unlikely that they could sustain such behavior for long.

This returns us to the former category of productive entrepreneurialism. The landless irrigation program mainly conforms to this definition, though references have been made to leverage over water to secure employment opportunities or to provide other services such as fertilizer supply or pesticide spraying. The first issue to resolve is whether such entrepreneurialism is emerging in individual or in collective form. The model for Proshika has, in effect, been to advocate forms of collective entrepreneurialism, where the degrees of collectivity vary according to the type of economic activity. Single groups may operate a STW service, but many groups in the program collaborate in LLP and DTW schemes, as well as in the occasional STW scheme. This collaboration may occur at different stages of the activity—in the making of initial agreements, in the construction of field channels, or in the collection of water fees—with income distributed to reflect work contributed. Other levels of collaboration can purchase diesel fuel or retain mechanic services. And of course, because the need for continuing technical support is becoming more apparent, federations of groups at *Upazila* level may undertake the management of rural workshops and extension services.

But even within single groups, individuals cannot easily go it alone. This is not an option within the program itself, unless a group member acting as a manager or driver is actually cheating the group. Again, such cheating would reveal weaknesses for the conscientization side of Proshika's work in overcoming the strong temptations that exist when new resources enter a poor society. Outside the program, can individual group members take their share of collective income and set up in business alone? There are no formal rules to prevent this, and such rules would anyway constitute an infringement of civil rights and imply a direction over group member behavior that is not part of Proshika's philosophy. It is difficult for a single group member to move beyond existing petty trading or artisanal activity and become an individual contractor or dealer, or to acquire land to become a strong farmer. To upgrade one's personal fortunes through individual economic activity requires, in rural Bangladesh, participation in many interlocking networks. Processes of agrarian entrepreneurialism are developing in the country (Wood 1988a) but the actors involved are already well placed in these networks through urban and rural property, and through long-established kin and other relations in commercial, professional and official sectors. We would therefore conclude that the prospects for *individual* entrepreneurialism among the landless and near-landless remain unlikely outside existing low turnover activity. At the same time, part of Proshika's strategy is to understand the processes of agrarian entrepreneurialism occurring in the society and to identify the opportunities for the landless to participate through collective organization to overcome the social limitations of their exclusion as individuals from the social and economic networks.

The second issue to resolve is whether such collective entrepreneurialism turns the groups inward, toward business management preoccupations and profit seeking, and diverts them from wider forms of social action not only on their own behalf but in conjunction with others sharing similar class positions. This issue is perhaps the most central part of the revisionist criticism and is where Proshika's premise concerning the mutual reinforcement between material security (achieved through EIG activities) and political participation is most severely tested. The main evidence that can be offered at this stage is that, in the Proshika areas where group use of RLF credit is highest, the recent history of group involvement in social action has been strongest. This is correlated with the irrigation program where capital requirements are the highest of any EIG activity within Proshika. In such areas, irrigation groups have been extensively engaged in wage struggles and successful attempts to occupy *khas* land and *bheels*. The formation of federations of groups at village, union and *Upazila* level has also made more progress in these areas, enabling Proshika (as a facilitating organization) to start withdrawing some of its staff presence from these areas. The groups, through various committees, are slowly beginning to take over some of the mobilizing and monitoring functions normally undertaken by Proshika field staff. In some of these areas, federations of groups have pooled part of their incomes to set up primary schools, realizing the value of education for their children but also realizing the difficulties of sustaining access to state or private schools. Such evidence corroborates Proshika's philosophical stance on the positive rather than negative association between EIG activities and a sense of consciousness and commitment to collective social action. It connects well with many other theses that argue that immiseration is not a sufficient condition for the development of class awareness, and that poor people engage in progressive (as opposed to fascist) social movements when their own status is rising and producing contradictions in the treatment received from other social groups. But we should not be complacent about this evidence or about the criticisms that prompted the reference to it. Constant vigilance and monitoring of this issue are necessary.

It is difficult to leave this discussion without some countercriticism. The revisionist allegation is favored by the category labeled here as intellectual radicals. These are the writers and theoreticians of the various political parties in Bangladesh who adopt some kind of Marxian analysis of the contradictions in Bangladesh society and derive their political programs accordingly. Most of these writers and party leaders share urban backgrounds with NGO leaders and senior staff. Perhaps this is inevitable in such a society, where educational institutions beyond school age are exclusively urban. The difference, though, between such political parties and NGO leaders is their stance toward the countryside. The radical political parties in Bangladesh are culpable in their neglect of any serious program of consciousness-raising among the rural poor, but expect the poor to make some conceptual leap into Marxian theoretical positions and vote for them. Their past intellectual and cultural arrogance has left them stranded on the political sidelines. Meanwhile, some NGOs have entered the space thus vacated, with programs that offer an immediate prospect of greater material security, at a time of changing structural relations when entitlements to the means of survival are becoming more precarious for many. Even if the charge of revisionism were true, revisionism might be justified. But the onus is on the critics to put their own house in order.

Implications for Agrarian Reform
Strategies—NGOs and Government

A principal purpose in writing this book has been to develop a policy argument about agrarian reform that is appropriate to the special conditions of Bangladesh, characterized by extensive landlessness, vigorous agricultural growth strategies based on the expansion of irrigated area and the inability of other sectors to absorb significant amounts of underemployed surplus labor in the economy. The existence of NGOs like Proshika represents a further set of special development institutions, which have combined the ideas of Paolo Freire with an analysis of the political economy of Bangladesh to create distinctive programs of work with the rural poor. This work has perhaps gained more significance both in scale and technical content in Bangladesh than in other Third World societies through the support of the donor community. The work of NGOs has also gained prominence through comparisons with state-administered programs, which have been beset by the inherited problems from the 1947–71 period, the disruptions of the early 1970s and the problems (such as inefficiency and corruption) that arise from a monopoly position over various sectors of the economy—especially agriculture. The rural development innovations during the 1960s at Comilla created a climate of institutional experimentation that stimulated the rise of NGOs from the mid 1970s in the immediate aftermath of liberation, dislocation and relief programs. Now, some of these NGO strategies (especially in EIG activities and skill training) have been recognized and supported by the major donors (both bilateral and multilateral). Such recognition, along with the criticisms noted in the previous section and the suspicious attitude of government, constitutes the ideological climate within which NGOs like Proshika must operate. There are both dangers and opportunities in this situation.

The first issue is the extent to which a program such as irrigation services by the landless can be regarded as a model to be adopted by government through the Rural Poor Program (RPP) in the Bangladesh Rural Development Board (BRDB). A transfer of the strategy into the RPP has already been attempted, supported by the Ford Foundation. The evaluation of this program by Hakim from the Rural Development Academy at Bogra (Hakim 1986) indicated many weaknesses, some them arising from official management and supervision, but most stemming from the process of group formation within the RPP. Such evidence confirmed other studies (for example, Wood 1984, Wood 1988b) on RPP landless groups, which indicated that they were fictitious or dominated by individuals linked to the dominant families in the village. The RPP is not organized to devote the same attention to the preparation of groups through programs of conscientization. Yet we have claimed in various parts of this text that the solidarity of groups is a necessary condition of the success of an EIG activity that involves continuous interaction with the landowning, employing, moneylending classes. This example shows the limitations of using a program located within one institutional structure as a model for simple transfer to another that is organized on different principles, both in relation to its clients and the degree of participation of its staff. In considering this approach to agrarian reform as a general policy initiative in Bangladesh, the narrow content of a program cannot be detached from the institutional culture through which it is implemented. The broader institutional context has to be regarded as part of the model.

If this is accepted, we should be neither utopian nor optimistic about the extent to which approaches of this kind, which involve the diversion of significant rural means of production toward the landless and near-landless, can be absorbed into mainstream government programs. At the same time, these institutional issues raise questions about the nature of administrative reform appropriate to the development needs of the poor in a society such as Bangladesh, which is also characterized by much ecological and social diversity. In particular, this refers us again to the action research style of programs of this kind, where an investment in local problem-solving capacity is required that, at the same time, curtails the domination of those more senior and central in the official hierarchy to conduct analysis and formulate policy.

In the meantime, until the significance of the management *style* of NGOs like Proshika for government administrative practice is recognized, a second issue remains: how far NGOs themselves can carry the burden of implementing these programs in a *routine* rather than *experimental* way? Are they to be substitutes for government, performing delivery functions in sectors of governmental weakness? These are the dangers referred to above, because it does appear that both bilateral and multilateral donors are increasingly seeing NGOs as delivery arms of the government especially in programs for the poor, where private-sector solutions do not resolve problems of entry and access. The dangers are not just restricted to radical NGOs becoming incorporated into ideological support for a non-benign government. The dangers extend to the administrative capacity of NGOs to sustain large programs and retain their distinctive organizational style. These problems have been discussed in relation to Proshika's management of the RLF and the appointment of technical field staff for a number of EIG sectors within Proshika. If this kind of constraint exists on scale, alongside the difficulties of transferring strategies into incompatible institutional contexts (that is, from Proshika to government), then the replication of the landless irrigation program would appear possible only through other similar organizations. Indeed, the Bangladesh Rural Advancement Committee (BRAC) and the Grameen Bank have been involved in smaller versions of the program since its second year, and both are now strongly committed to the Landless Operated Tubewell Users Service (LOTUS) program in which BRAC, Grameen Bank and Proshika are collaborating with the Committee for American Relief Everywhere (CARE). The involvement of such established organizations, and the *non*-involvement of many other smaller ones, reflects the increasing technical and managerial competence required to support programs of this kind. Both technical competence in determining feasibility and on-site monitoring of agronomic and economic performance, as well as managerial competence in monitoring and supervising credit support are needed. The plethora of smaller NGOs in Bangladesh are not realistically able to replicate programs of this kind.

Do we therefore have a program that, although it addresses the contradictions of agricultural growth strategies in the conditions of Bangladesh, cannot be significantly expanded because of these institutional constraints? There are several responses to this apparent dilemma. First, a return to some fundamental principles of Proshika's philosophy as a *facilitating* organization. If the following were true:

- the objective of collective entrepreneurialism by the landless is to be achieved in the space provided by the privatization initiatives and the problems of farmers managing their own collective good (Mandal has found cases of individuals bidding to operate DTWs owned by the KSS Farmers' Cooperative), and
- the notion of technology is exploded (Lewis 1989) to acknowledge chains of activity reflecting multiple points of entry at different economies of scale for different sizes of corporate entity,

then groups themselves, sometimes operating jointly with others, become responsible for their expansion into these opportunities. They have to be empowered through their capacity to analyze the changing local political economy and assess the opportunities offered by it. They have to be empowered through their acquisition of technical and accounting skills. They have to be empowered through their networking with other groups to exchange goods and services and through their collective strength as consumers to insist on fair prices for inputs, spare parts, equipment and specialist services outside their own abilities. They have to be empowered through their ability to control scarce means of production and to provide high-quality service or goods at competitive rates. This empowerment is a process. Once it was the ability to fatten livestock, now it is the provision of an irrigation service, tomorrow it could be the operation of rural work-shops servicing all the mechanized irrigation, milling, threshing and small-scale transportation equipment in a locality. Once it was two or three households working together, then single groups, then two or three groups. Soon it will be more organized federations of groups operating in different units at different economies of scale. In this process, it is the organization of the groups that expands, not Proshika.

The existence of thousands of such groups (not just supported by Proshika) all over the country has increased the significance of new kinds of organizations with more narrowly conceived technical support functions. There is a strong sense now that their time has come. Groups and federations already mobilized through other organizations now constitute an effective demand for various advisory services and credit support to enter at one point or another these chains of activity—for example, production of spare parts, mechanical services, production of small capital goods equipment such as lathes and looms, processing of food products, textile production and garment making and so on. Some of these organizations, such as Micro-Industries Development Association (MIDAS), are essentially private-sector organizations; others, like the Sericulture Board or Bangladesh Small and Cottage Industries Corporation (BSCIC), are quasi-government agencies; others are government departments, such as the Directorates of Livestock and Fisheries, which assists with vaccines and the allocation of open-water fishing grounds. Thus we can envisage the process moving from one of initiation and mobilization by outsiders toward groups demanding services from a range of external agencies. This process therefore relaxes the institutional constraints noted above.

Finally, the knowledge and expertise gained within Proshika on the development of minor irrigation (and reflected to some extent in this book) becomes itself a resource available to other organizations and groups mobilized by them. The cadre of irrigation field staff, together with the central coordination team, can provide these advisory services on demand. The other NGOs involved in the provision of irrigation services by the landless also have expertise and experience to contribute to this process. This experience should be more centrally included in the future planning of groundwater irrigation strategies in Bangladesh, and the principles that underlie this approach to agrarian reform should be acknowledged as an organizational form for such development.

Technical and Management Aspects of Landless Irrigation Schemes

THE MAIN PURPOSE of this study was to help Proshika to advise the groups on their performance with machine operation and maintenance, channel design and layout. The study focuses on pump operation, the conveyance system and water distribution. The research resources available and the detail required confined the study to three group schemes from Saturia (shallow tubewells (STWs)), Ghior (STWs) and Kalkini (low-lift pumps (LLPs)). These locations were selected partially to cope with the logistical problems faced by fieldworkers from the Bangladesh Agricultural University (BAU) and partially to coincide with schemes that were being selected for the studies conducted by Proshika in order to pool and maximize information on the case studies. In each location, the studies had a common interest in selecting those schemes with command areas nearer to the average command area for the locality in 1984. Each technical study is obviously organized within the context of the general performance-monitoring data in order to offer an account of the technical and management variables in explanations of financial returns, command area size and so on. The study is therefore organized around the following headings: topography, soil properties, installations and engine characteristics, water level and pump characteristics, channels, water loss, use of irrigation units, command area efficiency, irrigation efficiency, management of schemes, water distribution system and irrigation costs and returns.

This study analyzes the technical and management aspects of Proshika landless irrigation schemes on the basis of field surveys conducted on three selected sites. It examines the current practices of pump operation, water distribution and conveyance system, cost of irrigation and water charge collection. Its primary intent is to suggest guidelines on these topics that will be helpful not only to the Proshika project in Bangladesh but to similar projects elsewhere.

Methodology

Data relating to the technical and management aspects were collected through intensive field surveys on the following three schemes:

1. Attigram Gorib Unnayan Samity STW scheme in Saturia;
2. Ragunathpur Bhumihin Samity STW scheme in Ghior; and
3. Char-Daulat Kha/Jagorani Samity LLP scheme in Kalkini.

This investigation was carried out in the first week of April 1985. Additional data were collected from the Proshika field workers at the end of the irrigation season. The investigation covered three interrelated components: the physical characteristics of the command area, the engineering aspects of irrigation units and the water distribution and management of the schemes.

In the absence of complete and time-consuming contour mapping, an overall idea of the topography of the command areas was obtained by combining eye estimation and field measurements. Two soil samples located at two different points at a depth of 0–15 centimeters (cm) were collected from each of the schemes, on the basis of each scheme manager's report regarding the water-retaining capabilities of the soils in the selected spots. The soil samples were collected in polythene bags and taken to the Soil Science Laboratory of BAU, where their textural classifications were tested. Within the context of these classifications, water-holding capacity, infiltration rate, percolation rate, bulk density and porosity were estimated from relevant literature.

On the basis of the collected field-level data, a number of interrelated issues are discussed. These include the operation, maintenance and pumping costs of the units; their pump and engine characteristics; and their installation and reliability. This information was collected from the scheme managers through survey questionnaires. Data on pump and engine characteristics were collected from relevant literature and also from measurement in the field. The pump discharge was measured by using a 15x60 cm cutthroat flume placed as close to the units as possible. In the LLP scheme, a trajectory method was applied to measure the pump discharge because of the existence of a long, wide creek that is used for irrigation as well as for domestic water supplies. An Avometer (Ampare-Volt-Ohm) was used to measure the static water level in the STW schemes, and for the LLP scheme, trigonometrical rule was applied. To determine water losses in the canals, the measurements were taken from only one of the main canals of a scheme because of time constraints. Data on water distribution methods and command areas were collected from scheme managers as well as from the farmers concerned.

Background History of the Schemes

Attigram Gorib Unnayan Sanchoy Samity STW scheme

This scheme has been functioning since 1981–82 under the control and management of the landless group. The group consisted of twenty members, none of whom had any land, owned or sharecropped, in the command area. There were sixteen sharecroppers in the scheme cultivating 33.8 percent of the command area. The usual sharecropping arrangements in this area were payment of the stipulated cropshare, usually one-fourth, as water fees. The tenants paid half of the remaining output to their landowners, who in some cases shared a part of the production costs.

The group collected one-third of the crop as water fees for the first three years, in accordance with the written contract, but then had to reduce water charges to five-sixteenths in 1983–84 and to one-fourth in 1984–85 because of the pressure from the landowning farmers in the command area. The tubewell was located on the land of a non-member who owned 0.71 hectare (ha) in the command area and who was exempted from paying water fees in the first year.

According to the agreement, the group members were responsible for the construction of the main canals on a voluntary basis, but the construction and maintenance of field channels were the responsibility of the water users. In this particular scheme, the manager himself was the driver of the machine and received constant advice from the Committee for American Relief Everywhere (CARE) on pump operation and maintenance. Furthermore, group action was reflected in the management decisions on water distribution and canal maintenance. For example, each member of the landless group had to volunteer two hours of labor per day for ten days for canal maintenance work in the 1984–85 season, and anyone failing to provide labor according to the schedule was charged Tk5 as compensation to the group.

Ragunathpur Bhumihin Samity STW Scheme

The landless group started operating this scheme in the 1984–85 irrigation season. Before Proshika's involvement, this command area was irrigated by two private machines, one operated by Mr. Shaha in the 1981–82 and 1982–83 irrigation seasons and another by Mr. Tainuddin in the 1983–84 season. Mr. Shaha withdrew his machine because of farmers' non-cooperation following the crop failure in some parts of the command area, and he used the same machine to start a rice-husking mill. Mr. Tainuddin wanted to run the scheme for three years, but had to withdraw after only one year following a serious disagreement with one of the landless group members (Mr. Hanif), who was then the cashier of the group. In the 1984–85 season, the scheme was run by a machine that was previously used by the same group on the nearby Sharbovoum STW scheme, currently operated by twin STWs managed and controlled by the group's former driver.

There are thirty-two members in the Ragunathpur landless group. Eight of them cultivated 1.12 ha (23 percent of the command area). The Sheikh lineage in the village dominates management decisions on water distribution and machine operation, because two of their own people are represented in the five-member managing committee, one of them as cashier. Most of the plots in the command area were owned by the kin of group members. For example, the father-in-law and cousins of the landless group cashier owned about one-half of the command area. Indeed, the group could not make any written water contract with the landowning farmers because of the strong kinship relations that prevailed, although Proshika had issued guidelines that such agreements should be completed.

There was neither training nor a designated driver in this scheme in the 1984–85 season, and therefore mishandling of machinery caused frequent breakdowns. In an emergency, the previous driver was consulted, although he also lacked any formal training as a mechanic, but his services were not always available because he was involved with his own machines in Sharbovoum.

Char-Daulat Kha/Jagorani Samity LLP Scheme

This command area was previously irrigated by a loose farmers' group using a LLP rented from the Bangladesh Agricultural Development Committee (BADC). The pump broke down in the 1983–84 season and there were conflicts over water distribution. Against this background, the Jagorani Samity took over the responsibility for irrigating the command area. The samity used a bank loan to purchase a LLP previously operated by another Proshika landless group, Khilgaon Udayan Samity, which had to stop its scheme because the surface water source was inadequate.

There were twelve members in the Jagorani landless group and one of them owned 0.4 ha in the present command area. Two of the group members also sharecropped a little land in this command area. Seven share-croppers in this scheme cultivated 1.2 ha in the command area.

Of thirty-six farmers in the command area, twenty-five contracted to receive water from the group. A few farmers neither negotiated with the group nor paid a fee for water, but claimed water forcibly from the line-man. The water charge in this scheme varied from Tk2,224 to Tk5,187 per ha depending on the type and location of plots.

Physical Characteristics of the Command Areas

Topography and Land Classification

The topography of Attigram STW scheme is relatively flat, having medium lowland (seasonally flooded up to 1.5–2.5 meters), which is gently sloped from the west to the east with an elongation from south to the north, while the flatter land in the eastern portion terminates in a low-lying area. The topography of Ragunathpur STW scheme is uneven, combining medium lowland and upland (relatively elevated land), which has a variation in elevation of 0.5–1.0 meters. The lowland slopes from the north to the south, and the upland slopes from the east to the west. This scheme is elongated in a north-south direction, with about 60 percent of medium lowland in the eastern portion and about 40 percent of medium highland (seasonally flooded up to 0.3–1.0 meters) in the western portion.

The Char-Daulat Kha LLP scheme slopes from the north to the south, and the topography may be classified as flat with medium-lowland. The command area was limited to a relatively low-lying area in the southern portion of the scheme. There are quite a few nonirrigated plots by the side of the main canal, but these could not be brought under the scheme because of the non-cooperation of the owners of these lands. For example, a part of such land was covered by the scheme but the owners' nonpayment of water fees, their attempts to construct an illegal water course and their frequent intimidation of the linemen (including physical assault) created such an uncongenial atmosphere that the scheme authority decided to stop delivering water to these plots.

Soil Properties

Soils in the Char-Daulat Kha LLP scheme were clay loam; the soils in the Attigram STW and Ragunathpur STW schemes varied from clay to clay loam (table A.1). The water-holding capacity of clay and clay loam ranges from 31–39 percent and 20–30 percent respectively, because of the dominance of clay particles. These soils are capable of retaining water to a higher degree, and the infiltration rate (ranging from less than 0.25 cm/hour for clay, and 0.25–0.50 cm/hour for clay loam) indicate that the rates of both entry of water into the soils and movement of water through them range from slow to very slow. This implies that these soils are quite suitable for growing lowland crops such as winter rice. Table A.1 also shows that the porosity of the soil (50–56 percent for clay and 47–51 percent for clay loam) in the schemes is of a higher degree, giving more space to conserve water for the crops. The bulk density (1.20–1.30 grams per cubic centimeter (gm/cc) for clay, and 1.30–1.40 gm/cc for clay loam) of the soils, however, is of relatively high magnitude, due to intensive cultivation practices.

Canal Characteristics

In the Char-Daulat Kha LLP scheme, water was conveyed to the irrigated fields by a small creek 367 meters long, which linked the canal intake and the single irrigation main canal in the field. This creek was also used as a source of water for domestic use. In general, the width of the main canals was larger than required in all the areas. The canals were not designed according to flow, soil and other surrounding conditions but, as expected, the bed slopes of the canals were constructed without following any standard rule. The cross-sectional area of the main canal in the Char-Daulat Kha LLP scheme was unnecessarily large for the designated discharge, but the canals in the Attigram STW scheme maintained a reasonable range of cross-sectional area. All the main canals in Attigram STW scheme were raised high above the paddy level, whereas the only main canal at Char-Daulat Kha was a dug one. Both raised and dug canals existed in the Ragunathpur STW scheme.

Canal density (expressed as the length of canal required to serve one ha) for the main canals was 70.7, 81.9 and 101.4 meters per hectare (m/ha) in Attigram STW, Ragunathpur STW and Char-Daulat Kha LLP schemes, respectively (table A.2). There were four main canals in Attigram, two in Ragunathpur and only one in Char-Daulat Kha. The higher value of canal density in Char-Daulat Kha indicates a higher magnitude of total water loss, and the higher number of main canals in Attigram indicates a high magnitude of total filling loss. Canal layout was more or less well aligned in the Attigram STW scheme. The main canals cover 58 percent, 69 percent and 64 percent of the total length of the canals in Attigram, Ragunathpur and Char-Daulat Kha, respectively. The effect of microtopographical settings of the plots on the canal density could not be evaluated here, as the lack of easy communication and the absence of the necessary material facilities made it impossible to carry out the required contour survey.

Water Loss

The water loss in the main canal conveyance system tabulated in table A.3 shows that the water loss per 100 meters of the main canal was 30.7 percent, 28.7 percent and 12.9 percent in Attigram, Ragunathpur and Char-Daulat Kha, respectively. About 30–50 percent of the water lost in the process of seepage, leakage, breakage and bank overflow could be used by the crop, especially by crops in the lower portion of the scheme. As the length of the single main canal in Char-Daulat Kha was 780 meters, the total water loss was extremely high. On the other hand, the lengths of the main canal varied from only 50–173 meters in the Attigram STW scheme and from 140–258 meters in the Ragunathpur LLP scheme, so that the total water loss in these two schemes was relatively low. In all the studied areas the reported depth of the given irrigation water was less and the irrigation interval was higher for the low-lying plots, as there was an inflow of water from higher land. The relatively high land required frequent irrigation, resulting in a high amount of irrigation supply at higher cost. A flat rate of water charge was collected in the schemes irrespective of the type and location of land, except in the Char-Daulat Kha LLP scheme.

Water Distribution

In the Attigram STW scheme, a rotational block irrigation system was followed. Four different irrigation blocks received irrigation at four- or five-day intervals, with an average depth of irrigation supply of four to five cm. In this area, the canal layout improved water distribution. Moreover, the soil's high water-holding capacity helped the irrigation schedule function smoothly. When this survey was conducted, the plots had standing water to the desirable level.

In the Ragunathpur STW scheme, rotational water distribution was followed in four different blocks with a rotation period of two to three days. The depth of irrigation was supposed to be maintained in the field from 5–7.5 cm but, because of the frequent breakdown of the engine, two blocks in the higher land faced serious stress from lack of adequate water supply.

In the Char-Daulat Kha LLP scheme, there was no definite block system for distributing water to the fields; plots were irrigated sequentially from the end of a canal to the head end. The main canal had to take a long course because the water source was so far from the fragmented, scattered plots. The lack of cooperation on the part of a few influential farmers also created practical problems, making it impossible to construct straight, shorter canals. Water in the unusually long canal took longer to reach the tail-end plots (about two hours to travel only 780 meters) and this, in turn, gave rise to conflicts over water distribution. Furthermore, a southern part of the landless group command area was encroached by the flow from an adjacent LLP, which aggravated the problem of canal construction and water distribution to the plots left out in this portion. In spite of this problem of longer canal length, irrigation water was delivered to the plots at a depth of 5–10 cm with a rotation period of five to seven days, which represents a high interval of irrigation per unit of land.

Technical Characteristics of the Installations

Installation and Engine Characteristics

Table A.4 presents evidence on installation and engine characteristics; table A.5 shows that the static water levels in the Attigram STW and Ragunathpur STW schemes were 3.35 and 4.09 meters, respectively. These provided good indications regarding the suitability of irrigation by STW. The lowest value of pump discharge, in the case of the Ragunathpur STW unit, was due to its low discharge capacity, which caused serious water stress to the crops; consequently, the average yield was as low as 2,150 kilograms per hectare (kg/ha). The lower value in the Char-Daulat Kha LLP scheme was due to both low command area and low pump discharge. In all the areas, pump discharges were well below the desired levels (the ideal level is at least 80 percent) and in particular the value obtained for the STW scheme at Ragunathpur was alarmingly low (46.7 percent).

Utilization of Irrigation Units

Table A.6 shows that the STW at Attigram was operated for 105 days with 20 days of breakdown, making an irrigation period of 125 days (December

26, 1984 to April 30, 1985), while the STW at Ragunathpur was operated for 102 days plus 42 days of breakdown, making an irrigation period of 144 days (December 18, 1984 to May 10, 1985). The LLP at Char-Daulat Kha was operated for 73 days with 32 days of breakdown, the total irrigation period being 105 days (January 3 to April 17, 1985). The irrigation period was therefore relatively high in the Ragunathpur STW scheme. The reason was that the engine had continual serious breakdowns, especially during the peak period of March–April. As the crop was at the flowering stage at that time, serious water stress caused severe damage. Careless operation and maintenance of the unit at this site further aggravated the problems. The irrigation periods at both Attigram STW scheme and Char-Daulat Kha LLP scheme were reasonable. The highest average operating hour per day was observed in the Attigram STW scheme (13.15 hours), while the lowest value was observed at Char-Daulat Kha LLP scheme (7.72 hours). Total operating hours per ha were 168.6, 229.0 and 71.0 at the Attigram STW scheme, Ragunathpur STW scheme and Char-Daulat Kha LLP scheme, respectively.

The average available operating hours per day is assumed to be eighteen hours for the STWs and twelve hours for the LLP scheme (as the flow of water in this case is controlled by periodical tidal flow in Char-Daulat Kha LLP scheme), so utilization of the units (average operating hours per day divided by the average available operating hours per day) attains a maximum value of 0.66 in the Attigram STW scheme, and a minimum value of 0.55 in the Ragunathpur STW scheme. The relatively low value of reliability in the Ragunathpur STW scheme resulted from the breakdowns of the engine, indicating inefficiency and poor organizational standards in the landless group.

Command Area Efficiency

To determine the potential command area, it is necessary to know the existing/rated discharge of the unit, the crop water requirement and the estimated efficiency. Jenkins (1981) reported that the command area may be based on peak monthly crop water requirements, 70 percent irrigation efficiency (actual crop evapotranspiration divided by water delivered by the pump) and twenty hours per day pump operation. In the case of the LLP scheme at Char-Daulat Kha, the operating hours per day were assumed to be twelve. In order to determine the crop water requirement, the highest values of monthly evapotranspiration and dependable rainfall and the highest value of crop coefficient within the base period (time from showing/transplanting to maturity) of the crop are necessary. The irrigation interval (time between two consecutive irrigation applications) in minor irrigation schemes is usually small, so the matter of dependable rainfall is neglected. The crop water requirement was calculated using the reference data from Jenkins on potential evapotranspiration (the amount of water evaporated and transpired by an actively growing, thick cover of grass that is not short of water) and crop coefficient (ratio of evapotranspiration of the specific crop to the potential evapotranspiration).

In this study, the maximum monthly evapotranspiration (in the month of March within the actual base period) was estimated to be 16.8 cm in Char-Daulat Kha and 17.3 cm in Attigram and Ragunathpur. However, the crop coefficient was assumed to be 1.25 (applicable for high-yield variety (HYV) flooded rice). Once these data were integrated, the potential command areas based on actual pump discharge were found to be 10.74, 7.23 and 17.25 ha in Attigram, Ragunathpur and Char-Daulat Kha, respectively; potential command areas based on the rated discharge were found to be 15.48 ha in Attigram and Ragunathpur and 25.16 ha in Char-Daulat Kha. Table A.7 also shows that the command area efficiencies based on both existing and rated pump discharges were found respectively to be 76 percent and 53 percent in Attigram, 67 percent and 31 percent in Ragunathpur and 45 percent and 31 percent in Char-Daulat Kha. These results reveal that the equipment still had immense technical capacities to increase the command area under all the schemes by improving the pump discharges. The social factors such as these encountered in Char-Daulat Kha may not allow further expansion of command areas in spite of the unused technical capabilities of the equipment.

Irrigation Efficiency

Jenkins (1981) reported that irrigation efficiency for the small systems can be defined as the actual crop evapotranspiration divided by the water delivered by the pump. Reference data was used to determine the actual crop water requirement, which was 55.27, 62.57 and 46.36 cm of water (based on the irrigation period in each area) in the Attigram STW, Ragunathpur STW and Char-Daulat Kha LLP schemes, respectively (table A.8). Irrigation efficiency was 62 percent in the Attigram STW scheme, 77 percent in the Ragunathpur STW scheme and 45 percent in the Char-Daulat Kha LLP scheme. In the Ragunathpur STW scheme, although the irrigation efficiency was relatively high, its frequent breakdown, often for long periods, during the irrigation season (144 days) resulted in an irregular and erratic supply of irrigation water to the fields. This interrupted and insufficient application of water created a continual stress on the crop at the critical stage, however, which frustrated both farmers and group members. Rainfall at the later part of the flowering stage provided a rainfed contribution to the crop. Due to comparatively higher actual water requirement and low water delivery, the irrigation efficiency was higher. On the other hand, water delivered by the LLP at Char-Daulat Kha was relatively high to fulfill the crop water requirement. The table also shows that the crop water use efficiency (crop yield per ha for one cm of consumptive use of water, which may be taken as equal to crop water requirement) was 46.5, 26.4 and 65.1 kilograms per hectare per centimeter of irrigation water applied (kg/ha/cm) in the Attigram STW, Ragunathpur STW and Char-Daulat Kha LLP schemes, respectively. The lower value at Ragunathpur resulted from serious stress on the crop due to the inadequate and irregular supply of water by the pump.

Irrigation Costs and Returns

The operation and maintenance cost of the irrigation units was Tk2,351 per ha in the Attigram STW scheme, Tk3724 per ha in the Ragunathpur STW scheme and Tk2,907 per ha in the Char-Daulat Kha LLP scheme (table A.9). The unusually high cost in the Ragunathpur STW scheme was due to the low pump discharge, which resulted in a low command area. In the Attigram STW scheme, the technical intervention and advice provided by CARE for the water distribution system helped in reducing the operation and maintenance costs of the scheme.

The irrigation cost per ha was estimated to be Tk2,920, Tk4,972 and Tk3,643 in the Attigram STW, Ragunathpur STW and Char-Daulat Kha LLP schemes, respectively (see table A.10). In calculating irrigation costs, the irrigation units were assumed to have ten years of serviceable life with 20 percent of the purchase price as the scrap value. The irrigation cost per ha was highest in the Ragunathpur STW scheme because of the high operation and maintenance costs per ha (see table A.9).

Although total irrigation cost in Ragunathpur was relatively low, the cost per ha was the highest due to the low coverage of the irrigation unit resulting from low pump discharge and poor management of the scheme, while the total cost incurred in the Attigram STW scheme was quite reasonable and the increased command area reduced the irrigation cost per ha.

Table A.11 shows that the cost of irrigation water per cubic meters (m^3) was Tk0.33, Tk0.61 and Tk0.36 in the Attigram STW, Ragunathpur STW and Char-Daulat Kha LLP schemes, respectively. By withdrawing only 52.9 m^3 of water per hour, the STW scheme at Attigram covered an area larger than that under the Char-Daulat Kha LLP scheme, where the amount of pumped water was estimated to be 140 m^3 per hour. The higher value of irrigation water in the Ragunathpur STW scheme resulted from higher operation and maintenance costs per ha, combined with the low irrigation coverage. The reduced cost of water per hour of pumping in the Attigram scheme again demonstrates that the maintenance of the equipment and management of the scheme were improved because of the involvement of CARE in 1984–85.

In both the Attigram STW and Ragunathpur STW schemes, the water charge was collected in terms of a one-fourth cropshare. The paddy obtained from the cropshare was 866 kg/ha in the Attigram STW scheme (a total collection of 7,091 kg of paddy out of 8.19 ha), and 538 kg/ha in the Ragunathpur STW scheme (a total collection of 2,612 kg of paddy out of 4.86 ha). In the Char-Daulat Kha LLP scheme, the water fee was Tk2,965 per ha (table A.12). The return over operation and maintenance costs per ha was Tk1,476, -Tk1,348 and Tk59 in the Attigram STW, Ragunathpur STW and Char-Daulat Kha LLP schemes, respectively. As the return was calculated over total irrigation costs, both Ragunathpur STW and Char-Daulat Kha LLP schemes had a negative return, whereas the return was positive in the Attigram STW scheme. The negative return in the Ragunathpur scheme was caused by higher pumping costs resulting from low discharge and longer hours of pumping per unit of land. In the Char-Daulat Kha LLP scheme, it was due to the underutilization of pumped water (table A.12).

Summary of Findings

1. The pump discharges were, in general, well below the rated one, seriously so in the case of the Ragunathpur STW scheme, resulting in extremely low irrigation coverage. To increase the efficiencies of the irrigation units, it is necessary to check the matching of the pump to the engine, rated revolutions per minute (rpm) of the pump and engine and alignment of the pump with the engine. The matching of the strainer with the aquifer characteristics (in the cases of STWs) also has to be checked.

2. The command area under the Attigram STW scheme was optimum, whereas the command area in both the Ragunathpur STW scheme and the Char-Daulat Kha LLP scheme was well below the potential command area. This situation could be improved through better management of the schemes.

3. Command area efficiency and water use efficiency are unsatisfactory in both the Char-Daulat Kha LLP scheme and the Ragunathpur STW scheme. A better understanding between the farmers and the group is necessary to expand irrigation facilities bring more area under command.

4. The canal layouts in the Ragunathpur STW and Char-Daulat Kha LLP schemes were not well aligned. Furthermore, the cross sections of the canals were unusually large. Though CARE intervened in the water distribution system in the Attigram STW scheme, the canals were not of the required cross section and were not properly sloped. Hence, engineering surveys are necessary to design well-distributed canal networks in all the schemes.

5. Water distribution through rotation by block was well practiced in the Attigram STW scheme, but in the Ragunathpur STW scheme the water distribution through the rotational block system was not properly maintained. In the Char-Daulat Kha LLP scheme, sequential water distribution (from tail end to head end of a canal) method was followed, together with the method of irrigation on demand. To improve the water distribution system in all the areas, an irrigation schedule based on crops, soil, climate and the pump discharge must be developed.

6. Water losses were high in both the STW schemes because of uncompacted raised canals, whereas the loss was low in the Char-Daulat Kha LLP

scheme because of the dug canal. To reduce water loss in the conveyance system and to improve water distribution, it is necessary to align the canals properly, based on an engineering survey. The canals must be constructed so that the level of flowing water in the canals remains above the paddy level; in order to reduce water loss, the canals should be well compacted.

7. When an engine is out of order for a long time, especially during land preparation and/or in the flowering stage of the crops, the schemes as a whole suffer through low yield per unit of land. Because the farmers depended on the mechanic to get the engine repaired, they faced many difficulties when he failed to repair it immediately. It was therefore necessary to train the driver to do repairs so that engines could be repaired as soon as possible to avoid disturbing the irrigation schedule and causing damage to crops.

8. Operation and maintenance costs and also the total cost of irrigation water per ha were lowest for the Attigram STW scheme and highest for the Ragunathpur STW scheme. The reduction of costs in the Attigram scheme is mainly attributed to the technical intervention and advice provided by CARE.

9. Returns over operation and maintenance cost were negative for the Ragunathpur STW scheme but highly positive for Attigram. The low return in Char-Daulat Kha indicates serious underutilization of pumped water due to its low command area; in the Ragunathpur scheme, negative returns were caused by the higher pumping costs arising from low discharge.

Table A.1 Some Physical Properties of Soil

Item with Unit	Attigram STW Scheme		Ragunathpur STW		Chara-Dulat Kha LLP	
	Spot-1	Spot-2	Spot-1	Spot-2	Spot-1	Spot-2
Soil Texture (sand:silt:clay)	Clay (41:17:42)	Clay Loam (41:21:38)	Clay (41:19:40)	Clay Loam (41:22:37)	Clay Loam (41:29:30)	Clay Loam (40:29:31)
Water holding capacity (%)	31–39	20–30	31–39	20–30	20–30	20–30
Infiltration rate cm/hr.	<0.25	0.25–0.50	<0.25	0.25–0.50	0.25–0.50	0.25–0.50
Percolation rate cm/hr.	<0.25	1.00	<0.25	1.00	1.00	1.00
Porosity (%)	50–56	47–51	50–56	47–51	47–51	47–51
Bulk density gm/cc	1.20–1.30	1.30–1.40	1.20–1.30	1.30–1.40	1.30–1.40	1.30–1.40

Spot-1: Soil retaining water for a longer duration.
Spot-2: Soil retaining water for a relatively short duration.

Table A.2 Canal Density

ADC	Command No. of Area	Total Length of Main Canals (ha)	(m)	Total Length of All Canals (m)	Density of Main Canal (m/ha)	Density of All Canals (m/ha)	Percent Covered by Main Canal (%)	Percent Covered by All Canals (%)
Attigram STW scheme	8.19	4	579	1,002	70.7	122	58	42
Ragunathpur STW scheme	4.86	2	398	575	81.9	118	69	31
Char-Daulat Kha LLP scheme	7.69	1	780	1,215	101.4	158	64	36

m = meters, ha = hectare.

Table A.3 Conveyance Loss in the Main Canals

ADC	Actual Pump Discharge (l/s)	Distance of Discharge Measuring Point from Pump (m)	Discharge at Measuring Point (l/s)	Water Loss in the Main Canal (l/s)	Water Loss per 100 Meters of the Main Canal (%)
Attigram STW scheme	14.7	49	12.49	2.21	30.7
Ragunathpur STW scheme	9.9	43	8.68	1.22	28.7
Char-Daulat Kha LLP scheme	38.8	314	23.04	15.76	12.9

l/s = liters/second, m = meters

Table A.4 Installation and Engine Characteristics

ADC	Installation (m) Blind Pipe	Filter	Model	Fuel Consumption (l/hr.)	Mobil Consumption (l/hr.)	Engine bhp	Rated rpm
Attigram STW scheme	18.30	9.15	Yanmar TS70C	0.71	0.045	6	2,200
Ragunathpur STW scheme	18.30	12.20	Yanmar S70C	0.76	0.045	6	2,200
Char-Daulat Kha LLP scheme	6.10	—	Yanmar TS220CP	1.17	0.085	18	2,200

Table A.5 Water Level and Pump Characteristics

ADC	Command Area (ha)	Pump Characteristics				Water Level (m)	Actual Pumping (l/s)	Area Covered (ha/1/s)	Percent of the Rated Discharge %
		Type	Rated Discharge (l/s)	Lift (m)	Rate (rpm)				
Attigram STW scheme	8.19	KSB ETA 80-20	21.2	7.3	2,200	3.35	14.7	0.56	69.3
Ragunathpur STW scheme	4.86	KSB ETA 80-30	21.2	6.8	2,200	4.09	9.9	0.49	46.7
Char-Daulat Kha LLP scheme	7.69	KSB EAA 125-20	56.6	6.1	2,200	1.00	38.8	0.20	68.6

Table A.6 Utilization of the Irrigation Units for 1985 Winter Rice Production

ADC	Command Area (ha)	Irrigation Period (days)	Operating Days	Breakdown Days	Total Operation Hours	Avg. Operating Hours per Day	Avg. Operating Hours per ha	Use of Unit (ratio)
Attigram STW scheme	8.19	125	105	20	1,380.5	13.15	168.6	0.66
Ragunathpur STW scheme	4.86	144	102	42	1,112.0	10.90	229.0	0.55
Char-Daulat Kha LLP scheme	7.69	105	73	32	564.0	7.72	71.0	0.64

Table A.7 Command Area Efficiency

ADC	Actual Command Area (ha)	Actual Pump Discharge (l/s)	Rated Pump Discharge (l/s)	Crop Water Requirement[2] (cm/day)	Potential Based on Actual Pump Discharge[3]	Command Area (ha)		Efficiency (%)[1]
						Rated Discharge[3]	Actual Discharge	Based on Rated Pump Discharge
Attigram STW scheme	8.19	14.7	21.2	0.69	10.74	15.48	76	53
Ragunathpur STW Scheme	4.86	9.9	21.2	0.69	7.23	15.48	67	31
Char Daulat Kha LLP scheme	7.69	38.8	56.6	0.68	17.25	25.16	45	31

1 Irrigation efficiency (70%)/crop water requirement.
2 Crop water requirement (cm/day) = Maximum monthly ETP(cm) x 1.25 / No. of days in a month.
3 Potential command area (ha) = Pump discharge x average daily operating hour.

Table A.8 Irrigation efficiency and crop water use efficiency

ADC	Actual Command Area (ha)	Water Crop Water Requirement (cm)	Delivered by Pump (cm)	Average Irrigation Efficiency (%)	Crop Yield of Crop (kg/ha)	Water Use Efficiency (%)
Attigram STW scheme	8.19	55.27	89.2	62	4150	46.5
Ragunathpur STW scheme	4.86	62.57	81.5	77	2150	26.4
Char Daulat Kha LLP scheme	7.69	46.36	102.0	45	6640	65.1

Table A.9 Operation and Maintenance Cost (Tk)

ADC	Diesel		Mobil		Spare Parts	Mechanic	Canal Construction	Salary		Incidentals	Total	Total/ha
	Liters	Amount	Liters	Amount				Manager	Driver			
Attigram STW scheme	1,090	8,468	50	1,635	3,257	400	—	—	3,000	2,500	19,260	2,351
Ragunathpur STW scheme	1,199	9,350	36	1,100	2,900	400	—	—	2,800	550	18,100	3,724
Char-Daulat Kha LLP scheme	1,280	10,096	86	2,302	3,220	725	1,323	1,200	2,000	1,485	22,351	2,907

Table A.10 Irrigation Cost per Annum (Tk)

ADC	Purchase price of equipment	Install- ation cost	Total Capital Invest- ment	Interest on Capital Invest- ment@15%	Deprecia- tion[1]	O and M	Total Irriga- tion	Irrigation/ha
Attigram STW scheme	2,000	360	20,360	3,054	1,600	19,260	23,914	2,920
Ragunathpur STW scheme	26,113	400	26,513	3,977	2,089	18,100	24,166	4,972
Char-Daulat Kha LLP scheme	25,000	—	25,000	3,750	2,000	22,351	28,018	3,643

1 Depreciation = Purchase price x 0.80 / (Serviceable life of the unit)

Table A.11 Estimated Cost per Unit of Water

ADC	Command Area (ha)	Actual Discharge Capacity (1/s)	Total Oper-ation (hours)	Total Vol. of Water (m³)	Volume of Water Lift (m³/hr)	Volume of Water Supplied (m³/hr)	Depth of Irrigation (cm/ha)	Total Cost (Tk)	Irrigation Price per Hour (Tk/hr)	Water Price (Tk/m³)
Attigram STW scheme	8.19	14.7	1,380	73,056	52.9	8,920	89.2	23,914	17.32	0.33
Ragunathpur STW scheme	4.86	9.9	1,120	39,632	35.6	8,155	81.5	24,166	21.58	0.61
Char-Daulat Kha LLP scheme	7.69	38.8	564	78,780	140.0	10,244	102.0	28,018	49.68	0.36

m³ = cubic meters.

Table A.12   Irrigation Costs and Returns

ADC	Command Area (ha)	Paddy Charge[1] (kg/ha)	Water Charge Cash (Tk/ha)	Total Collection of Water Charge (Tk)	O and M Cost (Tk)	Total Irrigation Cost (Tk)	Return over Irrigation Cost (Tk)	Return over Total O and M Cost (Tk)
Attigram STW scheme	8.19	866	3,828	31,350	19,260	23,914 (1,476)	12,090 (908)	7,436
Ragunathpur STW scheme	4.86	538	2,376	11,550	18,100	24,166 (-1,348)	-6,550 (-2,596)	-12,616
Char-Daulat Kha LLP scheme	7.69	—	2,965	22,802	22,351	28,018 (59)	451 (-678)	-5,216

1   Goverment paddy procurement price of Tk4.42/kg was used for this calculation.
Figures in parentheses refer to return per ha of land

Use of Income by Groups

THE ISSUE OF how the groups deploy their income from selling water is crucial to the long-term goals of altering the structure of dependency between the group members and other dominant classes in the locality. This aspect of the research is a specific component of the broader concern with the relations with other classes. It is important to distinguish between two main categories in the use of income—where the structures of dependency are not challenged by its use, and where there are implications for structural change. It is very easy to understand the pressures from poor group members for an immediate share of the joint income for urgent household consumption needs. No-one outside those groups is in a position to judge those needs harshly. Certain kinds of immediate consumption may also have implications for structural dependency. If, by consuming profits in the form of household rice consumption, the group member releases himself and his family from an annual reliance upon an advance of paddy or rice from an employer (which is usually paid off in the peak season for labor, thus undermining the landless worker's capacity to bargain over wages), then clearly part of the relations of structural dependency have been altered. This use of income would be a minor individual challenge to the structure but will not have direct implications for redistributing control over productive assets in the local society. If, on the other hand, income was used by households to enter other forms of hitherto foreclosed expenditure such as daughters' dowries, ceremonial expenses, house improvements or additional clothing, then such expenditure would be structurally less significant even though we could not judge it to be illegitimate by the norms of society or human entitlement. Proshika is not engaged in a value judgment about the use of income but with an analysis of its structural significance. It is difficult to ask the *poor* to defer gratification for the sake of a longer-term, distant improvement in their structural position. But there can be little doubt that the two forms of income use should be contrasted.

Structurally significant income use refers more to group decisions about collective expenditure that could be crucial to the fortunes of individual members and their families. We have to ask therefore whether it is possible for groups to deploy their incomes from selling water in such a way as to release their members from specific dependency relations such as indebtedness, mortgaged land, bonded labor service, insecure tenancy arrangements, inflated rent or share obligations and low wages (for example, through a strike fund or through individual advances administered by the group)? Are incomes being deployed to create alternative patterns of ownership or control over land through the setting up of informal land mortgage banks, sharecropping cooperatives, joint land purchasing and the capture of other services and technological levels in the agricultural system?

Because we could not guarantee in advance that the groups from which our individual respondents were drawn would be the receivers of significant income, we finally collected information on twenty-four groups in Ghior (5), Saturia (7), Madaripur (3), Mirzapur (3), Gabtoli (3) and Shibganj (3). These groups were selected to coincide with the group respondents for the study on relations with other classes.

Dakkhin Aynapur Palli Unnayan Samity, Saturia

Start Year 1981–82   *12 Group Members*

Year	1981–82	1982–83	1983–84	1984–85	1985–86	Mean
Net Margin	4,399	-1,291	-6,274	-5,542	-5,814	-2,904
Net Income	491	-8,176	-916	1,133	1,426	-1,208

In the first two years, the operating-cost loan and capital installment were paid back, but there was no deposit to the group fund. But in 1983–84 and 1984–85, due to crop damage by flood, the group could not pay back its due capital installment and operating loan in full to BKB and Proshika RLF. So the group became a defaulter and made no deposit to the group fund. Only during 1983–84, thirty-six mounds of paddy were distributed to group members (three mounds each). The group plans to use future income to lease in land and cultivate jointly.

Attigram Gorib Unnayan Samity, Saturia

Start Year 1981–82   *20 Group Members*

Year	1981–82	1982–83	1983–84	1984–85	1985–86	Mean
Net Margin	22,628	12,678	25,343	4,102	3,648	13,680
Net Income	19,024	9,135	18,146	10,181	22,082	15,714

In the first season, the group paid back its entire capital loan and due operating cost plus interest to BKB. Tk2,000 was distributed to group members (Tk100 each). In 1982–83, 1983–84 and 1984–85, the group took and operating loan from BKB and at the end of each season paid back loan and interest to BKB. In 1982–83, 180 mounds of paddy were distributed among group members (9 mounds each), and in 1983–84, 170 mounds were distributed (7 per head). No money from the income was kept in the group fund. In 1984–85, after repaying its operating-cost loan, Tk8,500 was deposited in the group's bank account, which was used as part of group's operating expenses in the following season. Nothing was distributed among group members in 1985. The group plans to invest in a mini-truck and scooter with future earnings.

Danga-Shimulia Samanaya Samity, Saturia

Start year 1982–83   *20 Group Members*

Year	1982–83	1983–84	1984–85	1985–86	Mean
Net Margin	6,150	-3,822	-9,927	—	-2,533
Net Income	3,430	-4,300	-885	—	-585

In 1982–83, the group had net savings of Tk4,000, after repaying its capital installment and operating-cost loans. This money was used as part of operating expenses in 1983–84. But in following years, due to crop failure, the group defaulted to BKB, and was unable to repay further capital installments. The group would like to use any future income in a joint venture.

Char Moheshpur Biplab Samity, Saturia

Start Year 1983–84   *26 Group Members*

Year	1983–84	1984–85	1985–86	Mean
Net Margin	-8,755	-9,340	3,914	-4,727
Net Income	-10,597	1,930	11,801	1,045

In 1983–84, severe flood damage meant the group could not repay its due capital installment and operating loan to BKB. Although fifty-one maunds of paddy were distributed to group members with idea that individual members would pay for it later at Tk140 per maund, this was never paid back. In 1984–85, out of total receipts, operating loans were paid back to Proshika RLF and the previous year's overdue capital installment to BKB was paid. The current year's due capital installment to BKB could not be paid, and the group therefore became a defaulter to BKB. No paddy or money was distributed to group members this year, and nothing was deposited in the group fund. If possible, the group will invest in profit-making activity, but it also wishes to create a welfare fund to assist members in distress.

Sarkarpara Bhumihin Krishak Samity, Saturia

Start Year	1983–84	20 Group Members		
Year	1983–84	1984–85	1985–86	Mean
Net Margin	-15,363	-4,628	8,775	-9,589
Net Income	-10,597	1,930	11,801	1,045

In 1983–84, the severe flood damage prevented repayment of the entire capital installment and 50 percent of the operating loan. No paddy or cash was distributed to group members. In 1984–85, Tk17,200 was obtained and kept in a bank account. This will be paid back to BKB as the previous year's due and the present year's capital installment. The group remains in default to Proshika for not repaying 1984–85's operating loan of Tk10,000.

If income is available from the scheme in the future, the group wishes to invest in a new irrigation scheme and lease in land for collective farming.

Mirzanagar Jubo Unnayan Samity, Saturia

Start Year 1983–84   *20 Group Members*

Year	1983–84	1984–85	1985–86	Mean
Net Margin	-5,647	-3,674	-2,500	-3,940
Net Income	-6,755	7,500	12,602	4,449

In 1983–84, the crop was damaged by flood, so only the operating-cost loan was repaid to BKB. But twenty mounds paddy were distributed to group members. In 1984–85, from total paddy proceeds of Tk12,600, Tk8,500 was repaid to the BKB as the previous year's overdue capital installment and a part of the current year's due capital installment. Thus, BKB was not fully repaid. In 1984–85, the group took an operating-cost loan from Proshika RLF of Tk10,000. The Proshika RLF loan was not repaid, while the group kept Tk4,100 in its fund. And the group distributed fifteen mounds paddy to individual members this year. It intends to invest in joint business and collective farming.

Rajnagar Gorib Unnayan Samity, Saturia

Start Year 1983–88   *16 Group Members*

Year	1983–84	1984–85	1985–86	Mean
Net Margin	-25,283	7,169	-5,990	-8,035
Net Income	-24,620	18,589	8,270	746

In 1983–84, the crop was damaged before harvest, and a small amount of bad quality paddy was obtained. Fifty mounds of paddy were distributed to group members. The due capital installment and operating loan to BKB and Proshika RLF (BKB Tk10,000 and Proshika RLF Tk2,000) could not be paid, and only Tk2,000 was repaid to BKB. In 1984–85, out of total receipt of 266 mounds of paddy, 48 mounds were distributed to individual group members. The remaining paddy was sold for Tk31,000. From this, Tk20,000 was repaid to BKB for the previous year's operating loan and the current year's due operating loan (the current year's operating loan to BKB was Tk9,000) and to Proshika RLF Tk5,000 for the current year's operating costs. The remaining TK6,000 was kept in the group's fund. Capital installments were not repaid. The group intends to go into joint business and collective farming.

Ganasingjuri Samaj Kallayan Samity, Ghior

Start Year 1981–82   *32 Group Members*

Year	1981–82	1982–83	1983–84	1984—85	1985–86	Mean
Net Margin	12,566	8,379	8,352	-3,395	3,463	5,873
Net Income	11,541	8,891	12,020	-1,5295	12,750	5,981

In 1981–82, the capital installment and operating loan due to BKB was repaid. Twenty-two maunds of paddy were distributed to group members and Tk6,000 was deposited in group funds. In 1982–83, twenty-seven maunds of paddy were distributed to group members. Operating costs were based mainly on the group fund(previous year's deposit plus other group savings), and Tk2,000 was from Proshika RLF. Out of total sales proceeds, the entire capital loan to BKB was repaid, plus a Tk2,000 operating loan to Proshika RLF. In 1983–84, the entire operating loan of Tk11,000 was obtained from private sources. Out of the total paddy received, 105 maunds were distributed to individual group members, the remaining paddy was sold and the operating loan plus interest was repaid. No cash was kept in the group fund. The group could have had substantial savings in 1983–84, but instead distributed the paddy among themselves. In 1984–85, the operating loan was Tk13,000, of which Tk11,000 was from private sources and Tk2,000 was from Proshika. Out of sale proceeds of Tk15,500, the operating loan was repaid, and Tk1,300 was kept in a group fund to be used as individual loans to group members. No paddy or cash was distributed among the group members. With future income, the group intends to start a joint pisciculture venture.

Ragunathpur Bhumihin Samity, Ghior

Start year 1982–83   *28 Group Members*

Year	1982-83	1983-84	1984-85	1985-86	Mean
Net Margin	3,565	-37	-3,875	-3,439	-947
Net Income	1,103	-2,080	13,200	-5,071	1,788

In 1982–83, the operating cost was Tk12,500 (BKB Tk8,000 plus group fund Tk3,500 plus private source Tk1,000). The group had total sales proceeds of Tk19,700. After paying Tk1,000 to a private lender, the group paid the remaining Tk18,700 to BKB as due capital installment and operating loan repayment plus interest, and some capital installment paid in advance. In 1983–84, financial mismanagement took place. From the total sales proceeds, Tk1,000 was misappropriated by the paddy dealer, BKB was paid only Tk1,800 against the due operating loan and Tk2,000 was paid back to a private lender. Instead of paying back the due capital installment and full operating loan to BKB, the cashier kept Tk11,200 and used it for private purposes; this money was used for operating expenses in 1984–85. In 1984–85, operating costs were too high (Tk16,000) due to mismanagement and repeated mechanical problems, which caused crop damage. Only sixty maunds of paddy were received, so that total sales proceeds were only Tk9,000, which did not even cover the operating-cost loan. The group became a defaulter to BKB for the previous due, the current year's due and its capital installment.

Parmastul Bhumihin and Prantik Chashi Samity, Ghior

Start Year 83–84		*22 Group Members*			
Year	*1982–83*	*1983–84*	*1984—85*	*1985–86*	*Mean*
Net Margin	-972	3,658	-5,408		-907
Net Income	-730	2,745	-3,700		-562

In 1983–84, the group had a gross return of Tk16,300, from which the BKB was paid Tk13,250 against the due capital installment and operating loan of Tk8,000. The remaining Tk3,050 was kept in the group fund. The group contributed Tk4,300 to the operating cost of 1983–84 from its own savings. So should this deposit of Tk3,050 be considered as net income? In 1984–85, the total sales proceeds, the due capital installment and the operating loan was paid back to BKB and Tk6,600 was distributed among the group members at Tk300 each. No cash was deposited in the group fund. The group made a contribution of Tk5,100 to operating costs from its own group savings, which was not refunded to the group fund. The group is interested in collective farming.

Poyla Prantik Chashi Samity, Ghior

Start Year 1983–84		*19 Group Members*		
Year	*1983–84*	*1984–85*	*1985–86*	*Mean*
Net Margin	-2,803	-5,840	-7,364	-5,336
Net Income	-5,371	2,567	2,581	-74

In 1983–84, from sale proceeds, the group paid to BKB a due capital installment and a operating loan repayment to BKB and to a private lender. No paddy was distributed to group members, and no money was kept in the group fund. In 1984–85, from sale proceeds the group could repay only operating loans to BKB and Proshika RLF. The due capital installment to BKB was not repaid. No paddy or cash was distributed to group members. The group has Tk600 that will be used for loan repayment. The group would like to buy a passenger-carrying engine boat for use during monsoon season.

Bangala Bhumihin and Prantik Samity, Ghior

Start Year 1983–84		*18 Group Members*		
Year	*1983–84*	*1984–85*	*1985–86*	*Mean*
Net Margin	-1,945	1,601	-2,801	-1,048
Net Income	-3,365	660	3,115	137

In 1983–84, the crop was damaged by flood. Due capital installment and operating cost of Tk8,000 plus interest was repaid to BKB, and the group's own contribution of Tk3,500 was partly repaid to the group fund (Tk2,000). Therefore, there was no net deposit made to the group fund. In 1984–85, the group paid due capital installment and operating-cost loans of Tk8,000 to BKB and Tk3,000 to Proshika RLF (for operating cost). The group contributed Tk5,330 from its own savings and this could not be repaid into the savings fund. A deposit of Tk3,000 was made to this fund, but can this be called net income? The group would like to use funds for beef fattening and collective farming.

Unnamed Group, Ghior (to protect anonymity)

Start Year 1982–83   *16 Group Members*

Year	*1982–83*	*1983–84*	*1984–85*	*1985–86*	*Mean*
Net Margin	874	6,517	1,310	-5,380	830
Net Income	-3,904	499	40,136	9,080	11,453

In 1982–83, total sales proceeds were Tk15,000 and the entire amount was paid to BKB against the due capital installment and operating loan. In 1983–84, total sales proceeds were Tk33,000. The group could have had substantial savings this time, but instead the group paid the full amount to BKB against due capital installment, operating costs and interest and an advance payment against the capital loan. The group therefore did not deposit cash to the group fund, nor was there a distribution of paddy among the group members. In 1984–85, the group obtained another machine that had been transferred from another group at cost of Tk15,000 from Proshika RLF. It operated both of the machines by expanding the existing command area. The group had an operating loan of Tk30,000 (BKB Tk25,000, Proshika RLF Tk5,000). This year total sales proceeds were Tk37,000. Proshika was paid back Tk5,000, but only Tk16,400 out of Tk25,000 was repaid to BKB. The remaining operating-cost loan of Tk8,600 plus interest was not paid back to BKB. Even Proshika's due capital installment for the second machine was not paid. The remaining Tk16,100 of sales proceeds was kept in the hands of five group members (chairman, secretary, cashier and two others), who used the money for personal purposes. This created confusion and conflict within the group. They have now a commitment to refund the money before the beginning of the next irrigation season so that it can be used for operating costs. The group wishes to invest in another machine and a stock business.

Bharuapara Jubo Kallayan Samity, Madaripur

Start Year 1983–84   *10 Group Members*

Year	*1983–84*	*1984–85*	*1985–86*	*Mean*
Net Margin	na	5,566	-7,176	-805
Net Income		na	10,020	10,020

na = not available

In 1983–84, the group got the machine transferred from another group under the Proshika RLF of Tk25,000. The group took an operating loan of Tk15,000 from BKB. Out of total sales proceeds of Tk29,000, Tk22,900 was paid back to BKB and Proshika RLF against the operating-cost loan and the due capital installment, respectively. Tk7,000 was deposited in the group fund. Also, eighteen maunds of paddy were distributed to group members. In 1984–85, twenty-eight maunds of paddy were distributed to group members and the rest was sold for Tk21,680, of which Tk9,000 was paid back to BKB against the operating-cost loan and interest, and Tk11,000 was paid back to Proshika RLF against the due capital installment and an advance payment of the capital loan. The remaining Tk1,680 was deposited in the group fund. In future, part of the income will be distributed to group members, and the rest will be deposited in the group fund to be used for a collective seasonal stock business, such as molasses.

Mahmudshi Khudra Chashi Samity, Madaripur

Start Year 1983–84   *10 Group Members*

Year	1983–84	1984–85	1985–86	Mean
Net Margin	na	-3,252	-13,789	-8,521
Net Income	na	472	2,307	1,390

In 1983–84, the crop was partly damaged by flood, but the group received 150 maunds of paddy. Total sales proceeds were Tk23,282. The group had an operating loan of Tk14,750 from BKB. Tk16,282 was paid back to BKB against operating loan and interest. Instead of paying back the due capital installment to BKB, the remaining Tk7,000 was kept in the hands of a few group members and used for personal purposes. At the end of the year, the money was refunded to the group and was used as part of the operating cost for 1984–85. But the group remained a defaulter to the BKB during the 1983–84 season for not paying back the due capital installment. So should this deposit of Tk7,000 be considered as group income? In 1984–85, the group had an operating loan of Tk9,000 from the BKB and the 1983–84 proceeds of Tk7,000 were also used for operating costs. Due to crop damage, the group received Tk15,000 from sales, which was paid back to BKB against an operating loan of 1984–85 plus interest and overdue capital installment of the previous year. The group is still a defaulter to the BKB for not being able to pay back the due capital installment of 1984–85. With future income, the group wants to do collective farming.

Purba Pouli Tati Samity, Mirzapur

Start Year 1981–82   *16 Group Members*

Year	1981–82	1982–83	1983–84	1984–85	1985–86	Mean
Net Margin	2,916	-1,525	-4,287	-3,701	6,859	52
Net Income	5,042	4,429	2,983	-8,407	12,212	3,252

In 1981–82, fourteen maunds of paddy were distributed to group members. From sales receipts, the due capital installment and operating loan were paid back to BKB and Tk600 was deposited to the group fund. In 1982–83, from sales receipts, the due capital installment and operating-cost loan were paid back to BKB plus interest, and Tk3,131 was deposited in the group fund. Nothing was distributed among group members. In

1983–84, there was severe flood damage to the crop and the BKB due capital installment and operating-cost loan could not be paid fully—only Tk6,000. The group was therefore a defaulter, with no money deposited in the group fund. In 1984–85, a hailstorm severely damaged the crop, and sales receipts were insufficient to cover the previous year's overdue loan to BKB and the 1984–85 capital installment and operating-cost loan. Nothing went to the group fund. The group would like to do collective fish farming and lease in land for collective cultivation.

Singairdak Dak Khanapara Chashi Samity, Mirzapur

Start Year 1981–82			21 Group Members			
Year	1981–82	1982–83	1983–84	1984–85	1985–86	Mean
Net Margin	-16,247	-2,801	3,539	1,605	11,582	-464
Net Income	-16,498	3,532	8,275	1,583	10,869	1,552

The water fee is paid in cash. Each year, from the farmers' payment after meeting operating expenses and paying back the due capital installment and interest to BKB, there had been a small savings deposit to the group fund. During 1983–84, Tk300 was distributed to each of the group members. The group wishes to set up another irrigation scheme.

Purba Pouli Bhumihin Samity, Mirzapur

Start Year 1983–84		23 Group Members	
Year	1983–84	1984–85	1985–86	Mean
Net Margin	-7,218	-3,529	5,790	-1,652
Net Income	2,723	6,520	-21,220	-3,992

Due to severe crop damage and hailstorms for two consecutive years, the group could not pay back its outstanding capital installment, operating loan and interest for two years and therefore has defaulted. The group would like to invest in collective fish farming and agriculture.

Dehrapara Bhumihin Samity, Shibganj

Start Year 1981–82			9 Group Members			
Year	1981–82	1982–83	1983–84	1984–85	1985–86	Mean
Net Margin	2,520	1,252	-354	458	6,073	1,990
Net Income	4,540	6,404	5,798	4,052	8,153	5,789

In 1981–82 the fee was in cash. Operating costs were met out of farmers' fees the BKB was paid its due capital installment and each group member received Tk100. No money was deposited in the group fund. In 1982–83, it was the same story but, in addition, Tk900 was paid into the group fund. In 1983–84, it was the same story but Tk1,500 was paid into the group fund. In 1984–85, after repayments, there was nothing to distribute or pay into the group fund. The group wishes to invest in leasing a *khas* pond for fishing and also in collective cattle rearing.

Atahar Bhumihin Samity, Shibganj

Start Year 1981-82   17 Group Members

Year	1981–82	1982–83	1983–84	1984—85	1985–86	Mean
Net Margin	1,623	-579	-1,668	-929	2,998	289
Net Income	3,277	4,724	4,998	2,364	5,431	4,159

The water fee was paid in cash by farmers in three to four installments. During the first three years, after meeting operating costs through farmers' advances and paying due capital installments to BKB, group members received Tk150–200 each. No money was kept in the group's fund during these years. This picture persisted in 1984–85, except that some farmers were late in paying so repayment to BKB was delayed and no money was distributed or placed in the group fund. The group would like to use funds to expand into another irrigation scheme.

Bihar Chunatapara Bhumihin Samity, Shibganj

Start Year 1982–83   37 Group Members

Year	1982–83	1983–84	1984—85	1985–86	Mean
Net Margin	-4,038	-7,651	-4,612	na	-5,434
Net Income	2,803	751	-1,201	na	784

After meeting operating costs and due capital installments to BKB, over the three years no money could be deposited in the group fund. The group wishes to invest in a joint seasonal stock business such as potatoes in cold storage.

Nepaltali Mollahpara Bhumihin Samity, Gabtoli

Start Year 1982–83   12 Group Members

Year	1982–83	1983–84	1984—85	1985–86	Mean
Net Margin	na	na	7,901	12,730	10,316
Net Income	6,575	3,669	149	14,959	6,338

In 1982–83, the group had receipts of Tk25,000 from sale of paddy, and in 1983–84 receipts were Tk27,000, but in both years, instead of distributing to individuals or depositing in the group fund, surplus balances were also paid to BKB as advance against the capital loan. In 1984–85, the group had 145 maunds of paddy in its store, and receipts were Tk18,850. The due payment to BKB for operating and remaining capital is Tk16,000. A surplus of Tk2,850 was deposited in the group fund. The group wishes to lease or mortgage in land in the command area, and some members want to buy a minibus.

Nepaltali Khetmajur Samity, Gabtoli

Start Year 1983–84   20 Group Members

Year	1983–84	1984—85	1985–86	Mean
Net Margin	na	5,892	8,981	7,437
Net Income	2,398	523	-2,771	50

In 1983–84, total sales receipts were Tk23,190. The group had an operating loan from BKB of Tk9,000. The due capital installment, operating loan and interest was paid back to BKB. The group chose to pay its remaining money to BKB as an advance on its capital loan, instead of saving. Only Tk150 was deposited in the group fund. No paddy or cash was distributed to group members. In 1984–85, 142 maunds of paddy were brought into the group's store. Receipts became Tk18,460 at Tk130 per maund. The group will pay off its annual operating and capital loan obligations and pay the rest as an advance on the capital loan. Operating costs remained at Tk9,000. The group would like to lease in land from the command area for collective cultivation.

Chakmallah Prantik Chashi Samity, Gabtoli

Start Year 1983–84   *13 Group Members*

Year	1983–84	1984–85	1985–86	Mean
Net Margin	5,543	7,403	13,927	8,958
Net Income	5,697	-3,548	13,271	5,140

In 1983–84, the group had an operating loan of Tk9,000. From receipts, the due capital installment, operating-cost loan and advance on the capital loan were paid and Tk7,748 was deposited in the group fund. No paddy or cash was distributed to group members. In 1984–85, the water fee arrangement was partly in cash and partly in kind. Farmers from forty-five *bighas* paid in cash, and farmers from seven *bighas* paid in kind. There was a small operating loan of Tk4,000 from BKB, with Tk6,500 received as farmers' advance and Tk2,148 contributed from the group's previous fund to make up operating costs. Forty maunds in the group's store are worth Tk5,200. From this, Tk4,000 will be repaid to BKB and Tk1,200 will be paid to group's fund. There is a further Tk10,000 unpaid by member cultivators who did not pay anything in advance. This will be deposited in the group fund. The group wishes to invest in a power tiller and in seasonal business.

APPENDIX C

Some Notes on
Data and Methodology

AT MANY POINTS in this work we have mentioned difficulties
with knowing and understanding what happened to the landless irrigation
program because of the data or resources available. The issue of action
research is dealt with elsewhere; here we are concerned mainly with the
quantitative dimensions of the data we have tried to produce and use.
Nevertheless, the difficulties of combining action with research were a
large part of the deficiences touched on here. What follows is not a comprehensive analysis of the data quality; this has been presented elsewhere
(Palmer-Jones, 1986), and would be out of place here.

Landless Irrigation Monitoring Data

An extended discussion of the quality of the data, as far as it can be determined from internal consistency checks, has been provided in a separate
report (Palmer-Jones 1985) as well as earlier in this publication. What we
intend to report here is the potential number of cases and the pattern of
missing data. This will also allow simplification of the tables given later.

Table C.1 shows the number of groups that were irrigating with equipment and/or operating costs funded with loans in the program, and the
incidence of missing information for a number of key variables. Table C.2
shows that a higher proportion of information is missing for the last year
of operation of the group. Each group should have a set of data for each
year in which it operated; this group year is the basic unit of evaluation of
performance, and the total number of these cases is 31 for deep tubewells
(DTWs), 556 for shallow tubewells (STWs) and 163 for low-lift pumps
(LLPs). For STWs, the command area is known (with quite a high proba-
bility of accuracy[1]) for 83 percent of cases; the number of pumping hours
are known only for 73 percent of STW cases. The net margin for STW is
known in 84 percent of cases that were not the final year it is known for
only 67 percent of final STW years. Table C.3 shows the number of operating groups by ADC and year, which can be compared with the number of
valid cases reported for individual statistics in later tables. This shows a
considerable variation in the proportion of information available; for ex-

ample, we know operating costs in only 37 percent of potential STW cases in Bhairab; for Saturia the proportion is 92 percent.

Drawing up the master list of operating groups took a surprising amount of time, and at the time of writing there are a number of cases where it is not clear whether a group should have been recorded as working in a year or not. This is partly because a group may not discontinue until after a considerable amount of preparation for the forthcoming irrigation season has been made and pro formas have been completed, in part or in full. With the passage of time, it has not been possible to check data for the early years and to determine whether the group really operated in that year when data from later in the season is missing, or whether the group discontinued irrigation. Both groups and Proshika were reluctant to cease irrigation, and a considerable time often elapsed before the affairs of some groups were wound up. As a result, the missing data are more frequent in the final year of operation; this is likely to bias some statistics.

Employment Data

The One-off Survey

The original design consisted of a one-off questionnaire, conducted in September 1984, on household characteristics—demographic composition, employment patterns and landholding status before and after the introduction of irrigation and perceived impact of irrigation. This was followed by weekly interviews starting in April 1985 and continuing for a year.

The one-off survey provided useful information on the landholding status of the respondents (or their fathers in the two cases where the group members were not household heads). On the matter of changes in employment patterns, however, the responses were much less satisfactory. This was partly because of the design of the questionnaire and partly because of the way it was completed. The questions about employment before and after irrigation provided more possible categories of employment for after than before (that is, respondents were asked about agricultural labor before the advent of irrigation, and about agricultural labor in irrigated crops in their own and private schemes and in unirrigated areas; this meant that because they were asked only whether they did this type of work rather than how frequently—which would not have been a sensible question—there were more responses about labor after irrigation than before). Because the time when irrigation was introduced was not specified, and because irrigation grew rapidly in the years immediately preceding the survey, there was probably some ambiguity in all areas about when irrigation started; but this ambiguity was most evident in the groups in unirrigated areas where there was no response to the question "did you do agricultural work before the introduction of irrigation?" or to the question "do you work in irrigated areas?" Yet, as we will see, a number of respondents did in fact do so. Because there was no baseline for the incidence of work before irrigation for these groups, the before/after comparison could not be made.[2] Other questions, particularly those about the impact of irrigation on employment and on land, probably required more detailed and careful study, because the answers were frequently incomplete and often revealed inconsistencies. Such research is unfortunately intensive in its skill requirements and is not easy to implement with the staff and resources available. It remains to be seen what type of data production and research facility will satisfactorily support this type of program, or whether such a facility is strictly necessary for an organization like Proshika; this is an issue to which we return.

In the year-long survey, the Proshika field staff questioned the senior male of the household of the chosen group member about his activities (all were male), the activities of other adult members of the household over the previous week and the incomes they received from wage work. Income from own cultivation was excluded, which, as will be apparent, means that income levels cannot be compared. The structured survey forms divided activities into five categories: own cultivation (OWNCULT), days worked on others' farms (DOTF), days worked in own home (OWN-HOME), days not working (NOTWORK), days of nonagricultural work (DNAGWK) and days work in others' home (DWOTH). Responses were recorded in terms of whole days worked since the last interview, roughly one week previously. Apart from the obviously unsatisfactory nature of asking one person about the activities of others, and of using recall over a week or more, for non-registered activities the whole-day categorization is likely to have picked up only the main activity of the day, possibly missing the parts of days worked at other occupations, and income derived from these parts is likely to have been underreported. Furthermore, the importance of part-day working may not be independent of the land access and occupational patterns of the respondent; these differ systematically between the groups, is this is likely to be a further source of bias.[3] Also, we have no clear picture of how the occupational pattern affects the distribution of time and income from those activities that are fitted around the major activities of a day, so it is not really possible to substitute for the missing values; this may be particularly important for income derived from own cultivation and part-time craft, trading, and so on. It is not even known whether these are generally likely to contribute relatively little compared to the main sources of income.

Another problem concerns the validity of reports of income from entrepreneurial activities when it is not clear whether net or gross returns are being reported; here reporting of net incomes was intended, and it is not clear how accurately expenses were deducted. Also in cases of migration for work, the absence of information on search, travel, and accommodation costs means that wage rates and incomes from this type of work are not strictly comparable. When someone is away for a considerable period, there must be some doubts stemming from recall problems about the accuracy of reports of days worked and income received over that period. In some cases, employed members of the household ceased to be recorded if they were absent for long periods, but in others their information was completed at some time.

A number of other methodological problems occurred, which necessitates caution in the use and interpretation of the results and makes some of the data unusable. Some of these problems have been discussed before (Palmer-Jones 1985); here, to avoid repetition, we emphasize that the sampling of only six groups from three categories means there are only two members of each category; thus it is extremely unlikely that differences in employment and income characteristics between groups can be attributed to the categories (access to irrigation) rather than to the characteristics of the group, which are to some extent independent of their access to irrigation.[4]

Given the aim of assessing the impact of irrigation and the ownership of irrigation assets on the employment of the group members, it was unfortunate that the sample groups chosen were quite different from each other in terms of both landholding and occupation, both of which had important effects on employment patterns. Most significant were, first, the predominance of self-employed petty traders in the 2.1 group, who gained most of their income from these sources and engaged only to a negligible extent in wage labor and cultivation on their own account; second, several members of both groups in the nonirrigated areas owned and cultivated significant amounts of land, with consequent effects on their labor allocation and incomes. This was doubly unfortunate in that income from own cultivation was not recorded, for reasons of practicality; this means that for those group members concentrated in the groups in unirrigated areas, welfare cannot be compared with those whose welfare depends predominantly on selling their labor or on petty entrepreneurship (see Table 5.2 for land cultivation and access).

A further complication lies in the particular choice of group members from each group, because it is not known how representative of the group they are. In a number of groups, the members do not have the same activity patterns and, unless they are representative of the group, the averages of, say, days' employment in particular activities from the sample cannot be considered representative of the group or category of group as a whole. Thus the simple averages conceal the fact that in all groups there were some respondents with no land and some that cultivated no land, while some did own and or cultivate land. It also disguises the fact that cultivation of land changed over time as respondents changed their access to land (it would have been better to have questioned about land cultivated in specific seasons of the previous agricultural year, and to have updated the amounts cultivated as the seasons passed). For example, there is no simple relation between days spent on own cultivation and the amount of land reported in the one-off survey as cultivated. This is not surprising, in that labor inputs will vary between plots, and the use of others' labor is quite common even among the very poor; but, if the amount of land recorded as cultivated is wrong, further complications arise.

Some Problems of the Financial Data

Financial viability for groups cannot, unfortunately, be determined at the group level because sufficient data on loan repayment has not been available, for reasons that are discussed elsewhere. The financial repayments reported for groups are inconsistent with the aggregate loan repayment reported by the Bangladesh Krishi Bank (BKB) in the earlier years of the project and up to the present. For reasons pointed out above, this lack of an up-to-date picture of the financial position of irrigation groups could lead to economic problems. The written records of financial payments kept by Proshika sometimes reported actual financial payments to BKB and sometimes, apparently where these financial records were not available on time, reported estimated payments based on depreciation and nominal operating loan financial charges. The exception to this is the forty-two BKB loans currently outstanding. The availability of information on the RLF loans is better but, because of the failure to monitor the performance of loans by group until very recently, it has only just become possible to link each RLF irrigation loan to a specific group. Also, only an up-to-date statement of the RLF account is available, rather than the timing of disbursements and repayments, which would give a better picture of group finances.

General Questions

The first year of the project was almost exclusively taken up with initiating the action, in an atmosphere of considerable pressure. As noted previously, it was believed that the mass installation of STWs and, to a lesser extent, LLPs, presented a once-and-for-all opportunity to establish water rights. In the next year, an ambitious monitoring program was undertaken and the results analyzed in some detail. The data consisted of two pro formas that were to be completed by the responsible field staff. After this, the data continued to be produced but no use was made of the formal data, as it was felt that some years should pass before another thorough analysis was warranted. But no definite practice of collecting the pro formas was instituted. When it was time to analyze the pro formas they were not all available, and many of those that were eventually located had missing or erroneous data on them. This was not initially obvious, in part because assurances were given that the pro formas would be found, and in part because most of them were in Bangla and therefore unreadable by the main analyst. This led to further problems as, under the impression that the data would turn out to be of good quality and relatively complete, an ambitious computerized data-processing approach was used. This was despite a trial run or pilot test of the data-processing approach with the available data; but because the pro formas that were produced for the trial run were in English and of good quality, the result was quite misleading.

In a way this aspect of the project represented classic pilot project symptoms, initially highly successful data production and analysis under intense supervision, with ample high class inputs that deteriorated rapidly when left to the normal course of events. Without doubt there was a lot to be learned about the establishment and operation of such a monitoring system. There were a number of underlying problems. First, and most importantly, no master list of irrigation projects and their status was kept, so reports of the numbers of projects started, working and discontinued could never be definitive, and no register of pro formas required and completed could be kept. Even in 1987, one could visit ADCs that had had irrigation programs for many years and there would be no count or list of the active numbers; workers would have to name them from memory, counting on the joints of their fingers, not even attempting to write them down. Only very recently have files been kept. This deficiency is not confined to irrigation. Most of the other RLF activities do not have lists of groups involved in activities.

A related problem has been the lack of maps. When visits to schemes became necessary, there were no maps showing where they were. Maps are the beginning of organized data collection for geographically dispersed activities. They provide an essential framework and structure for collating information, especially where the quality of environmental resources, and of local and economic variables, is geographically contingent. As we have noted, the soil and water qualities are probably crucial to the success of irrigation even in apparently superficially similar environments, and these can best be gathered on maps. There should be maps at each ADC showing the location of projects and giving some description of the soil and water characteristics.

This problem of lists partly reflected the second problem, namely that of categories. It was not known for some projects whether they discontinued in a year because success was uncertain. In a project of this type, the commitment to it leads to the hope that it will succeed, and so when groups got into difficulties, solutions were sought that meant either restarting in another site or transferring the equipment to another group (it was suggested that the only discontinuations were where machines, rather than groups, had ceased operation).

The difficulties caused by categories extend to many dimensions; did groups/schemes continue or not? Many occurences did not readily fit the categories of the original pro formas; what was happening was new, and it could hardly be expected that the pro formas would remain appropriate over many years in such dynamically changing circumstances as the water market in Bangladesh in the 1980s. There are numerous cases of category confusion. What is the command area? the area in the original contract? the area that is prepared for irrigation? or that receives any irrigation? or the area harvested? or the area for which the group receives payment? What is the group's income? the amount it should have received (and may yet if pressure can be kept up on cultivators to pay what they owe)? or what is actually received? by what date? What is the water contract—that specified in the agreement with the cultivators, which often turned out to be a fiction, or the way in which most of the cultivators paid for water (because in many cases some paid by cash and others by a share)? For the data set to be of use later these issues would have had to have been identified, their importance for subsequent analysis realized and appropriate action taken to ensure a reasonably complete and consistent data set.

It is not clear what, if anything, should have been done about these deficiencies. After all, the project has passed the survivor test. But given a commitment to monitoring, what would need to be done to enhance the perfomance of this aspect? First, more resources would have to be allocated to it, and there is a question of whether specialized staff with different qualifications from those currently available should be employed. Then there is the question of the perception of the importance of these data and a structure to generate and make use of them. There is no doubt that bad news—discontinuations and financial arrears—have been pushed into the background. But this is not all. There is a conflict between flexible management and seemingly inflexible hard data. At one point it was suggested that monitoring would be done better if its usefulness was demonstrated. There are two aspects to this perception. Either the usefulness was not demonstrated, or it was not perceived. If it was not perceived, it was not useful, or perhaps it was not in the interests of individual members of the staff to perceive it as such. There is a chicken-and-egg problem here. If the perception of benefits is not there by those who produce and would use the data, then they will be inadequate, and if the data are inadequate then their usefulness will be hard to demonstrate.

But this is not all there is to it; a problem that has not been generally acknowledged within Proshika is the possibility that staff and workers have their own interests, which may, at times, conflict with the ostensible aims and interests of the organization. This incentive problem is particularly hard to acknowledge because of the ethos of Proshika as a facilitator for the poor. Unlike firms whose aim is to make money, where there is no disjunction between the pursuit of private gain by individuals within the firm and the aims of the firm, this is not the case for an organization like Proshika whose aim is to serve other, deprived, people or collective interests. But, while more committed and less self-serving patterns of motivation and behavior may have characterized staff and groups, in the earlier days following the trauma and crisis of independence, it seems more reasonable to suppose that self-interest of a fairly material type is now more general, not only within Proshika and the groups but also between groups and Proshika. Under these circumstances, monitoring of performance by staff and groups of some sort will be essential, and this will require resources rather than relying entirely on commitment.

Proshika has adapted to circumstances to some extent by establishing a position for monitoring of the RLF and also by appointing irrigation extension workers whose task definitely includes the quantitative monitoring of the program. The technical educational qualifications and general literacy in English is a help, but there are still problems in ensuring the understanding of the pro formas and their relation to the particular circumstances of different ADCs and groups. Also, no manager of the irrigation program can be held responsible either for its performance or for the monitoring. Many people are involved who bear some collective responsibility; apart from the headquarters worker and the irrigation extension workers at some ADCs, the ADC and regional coordinators seem to have some responsibility. This diffusion of accountability among people and the lack of clear criteria for judging performance provide ample opportunities for confusion about reporting and responsibility. Their responsibility for monitoring also puts those responsible for the action in control of information about it. Our suggestion, as far as monitoring is concerned, is that a headquarters officer is required to organize, operate and maintain the system. But this runs counter to the practice and ethos of avoiding monopolization by collective responsibility and nonspecialization of roles. This is a common conflict to which there is no simple solution. But recognition of the difficulties that lack of specialized skills and straightforward accountability has or would have created, if applied to monitoring the performance of RLF projects as opposed to their financial aspects, is a step in the right direction.

Notes

1. For a number of variables that were estimated in different ways, such as the command area, there was often considerable divergence; in these cases, the most reliable figure has been used, although in some cases no such figure could be identified and the variable set was missing.

2. The possible responses were as follows:

	before	after
With irrigation assets	Y	Y
In irrigated area	Y	Y
In unirrigated area	N	Y

Thus, it is not possible to say whether the changes between before and after that are common to the groups in irrigated areas are due to irrigation or to time, because there is no comparison with the group in a nonirrigated area. Of course the pattern of changes over time could have been different between the areas anyway, partially independent of irrigation, due say to differential growth of population, changes in cropping patterns and so on, hence even the complete with/without before/after combination could not unambiguously answer the question of what changes were due to irrigation.

3. Systematic differences in the occupational pattern of group members between groups is likely, given the self-selection of group members; it is frequently reflected in the name chosen for the group (*Prantik Chashi* = "poor and marginal farmers" as opposed to *Bhumihin* = "landless" or "assetless").

4. But not perhaps entirely independent, because some characteristics of the group may determine their access to irrigation; for example, those who have obtained irrigation assets may be more entrepreneurial or better off in some way. Or circumstances in nonirrigated areas may be somewhat different, for example, population density or landlessness may be less, with consequent implications for employment and wages.

Table C.1 Potential and Actual Valid Data by Year

		Valid Numbers							
Technology/ Year	Total Cases	Command Area	Gross Income	Oper. Costs	Gross Margin	Net Margin	Diesel Used	Pump Hours	Water Contract
DTW									
1985–86	11	9	9	9	9	9	9	7	11
1986–87	20	20	20	20	20	20	20	18	20
Total	31	29	29	29	29	29	29	25	31
STW									
1980–81	16								16
1981–82	52	50	49	46	46	46	48	48	52
1982–83	71	54	63	54	54	54	51	52	71
1983–84	98	81	80	72	72	72	68	68	98
1984–85	96	89	88	90	89	89	84	79	96
1985–86	115	96	97	96	96	96	94	70	115
1986–87	108	94	96	95	95	95	93	86	108
Total	556	464	473	453	452	452	438	403	556
LLP									
1980–81	10								10
1981–82	31	31	30	30	30	30	30	30	31
1982–83	26	18	22	20	20	20	3	3	26
1983–84	24	16	18	17	17	17	17	8	24
1984–85	15	11	12	12	12	12	10	8	15
1985–86	22	16	16	16	16	16	15	13	22
1986–87	35	31	31	31	31	31	29	28	35
Total	163	123	129	126	126	126	104	90	163

Table C.2 Number of Cases and Missing Data by Whether Last Year

		Valid Numbers							
Technology/ Year	Total Cases	Gross Income	Oper. Costs	Gross Margin	Net Margin	Command Area	Water Contract	Diesel Used	Pump Hours
DTW									
Not last year	28	27	27	27	27	27	28	27	23
Last year	3	2	2	2	2	2	2	2	2
Total	31	29	29	29	29	29	31	29	25
STW									
Not last year	478	415	401	400	400	413	478	391	361
Last year	78	58	52	52	52	51	78	47	42
Total	556	473	453	452	452	464	556	438	403
LLP									
Not last year	103	83	83	83	83	84	103	75	67
Last year	60	46	43	43	43	39	60	29	23
Total	163	129	126	126	126	123	163	104	90

Table C.3   Number of Cases and Missing Data for Key Variables by ADC

Technology/ Year	Total Cases	Valid Numbers							
		Gross Income	Oper. Costs	Gross Margin	Net Margin	Command Area	Water Contract	Diesel Used	Pump Hours
DTW									
Mirzapu	9	9	9		9	9	9	9	8
Sreepur	18	16	16	16	16	16	18	16	16
Serajgonj	1	1	1	1	1	1	1	1	1
Dhamrai	3	3	3	3	3	3	3	3	
Total	31	29	29	29	29	29	31	29	25
STW									
Bhairab	67	45	25	25	25	31	67	28	27
Saturia	92	84	85	85	85	83	92	83	67
Singair	30	29	29	29	29	29	30	29	26
Harirampur	25	24	24	24	24	23	25	23	22
Ghior	51	47	48	47	47	48	51	48	44
Nagarpur	28	22	22	22	22	20	28	16	16
Madaripur	43	32	31	31	31	34	43	30	28
Mirzapur	52	45	45	45	45	47	52	39	36
Shibgonj	69	61	61	61	61	65	69	65	64
Gabtoli	50	49	49	49	49	49	50	48	49
Kaliakoir	4	3	3	3	3	2	4		3
Atpara	5	3	3	3	3	3	5	3	3
Sreepur	3	3	3	3	3	3	3	3	3
Chatalpar							1		
Domar	4	2	2	2	2	2	4	2	
Kuliarchar	5	1	1	1	1	2	5	1	1
Serajgonj	10	10	10	10	10	10	10	10	9
Muksudpur	3	3	3	3	3	3	3	3	1
Debigonj	2	1	1	1	1	1	2	1	1
Bhanga	6	6	6	6	6	6	6	6	3
Brahmanbaria	2	2				2	2		
Narail	2	1	2	2	2	1	2		
Total	556	473	453	452	452	464	556	438	403
LLP									
Bhairab	4	3	3	3	3	3	3	4	
Ulania	27	15	13	13	13	13	27	9	8
Khaliajuri	36	20	19	19	19	25	36	12	12
Kalkini	19	18	18	18	18	17	19	17	8
Madaripur	15	15	15	15	15	15	15	15	14
Mirzapur	6	6	6	6	6	6	6	6	6
Atpara	4	2	2	2	2	2	4	2	2
Sreepur	4	3	3	3	3	3	4	3	3
Chatalpar	27	27	27	27	27	19	27	20	20
Gournadi	7	7	7	7	7	7	7	7	5
Serajgonj	1	1	1	1	1	1	1	1	1
Muksudpur	2	2	2	2	2	2	2	2	1
Brahmanbaria	2	2	2	2	2	2	2	2	2
Bhola	8	7	7	7	7	7	8	7	7
Ulipur	1	1	1	1	1	1	1	1	
Total	163	129	126	126	126	123	163	104	90

References

Ali, S.A. 1986. *A Comparative Economic Study of Irrigation under Private and Land-less Group-owned Shallow Tubewell Schemes in a Selected Area of Manikganj District.* Msc Paper, Department of Agricultural Economics. Mymensingh: Bangladesh Agricultural University.

Arthur, W. and G. McNicholl. 1978. "An Analytical Survey of Population and Development in Bangladesh." *Population and Development Review* 4: 1 23–80.

ASR. 1989. *Bangladesh Agricultural Sector Review Main Report.* Dhaka: UNDP.

AST *Minor Irrigation Review.* 1987. Agricultural Sector Team, Canadian International Development Agency and Ministry of Agriculture. Dhaka: Government of Bangladesh.

Bailey, F. G. 1963. "Closed Social Stratification in India." *Archives of European Sociology* 4: 107–124.

Bailey, F. G. 1968. *Stratagems and Spoils.* Oxford: Blackwell.

BAU. 1985. *Evaluating the Role of Institution in Irrigation: Some Preliminary Findings.* IWM-11, Department of Irrigation and Water Management. Mymensingh: Bangladesh Agricultural University.

BAU. 1986. *Water Market in Bangladesh: Inefficient and Inequitable?* IWN-12, Department of Irrigation and Water Management. Mymensingh: Bangladesh Agricultural University.

Bertocci, P. 1972. "Community Structure and Social Rank in Two Villages in Bangladesh." *Contributions to Indian Sociology,* New Series VI (Dec.), 28–52.

Bertocci, P. 1977. "Structural Fragmentation and Peasant Classes in Bangladesh." *Journal of Social Studies* 5: 43–60.

Biggs, S. D., and J. Griffith. 1987. "Irrigation in Bangladesh." In F. Stewart (ed.), *Macro-Policies for Appropriate Technology in Developing Countries.* Boulder, CO: Westview Press.

Bottrall, A. F. 1983. *Review of Minor Irrigation Management Practices in Bangladesh.* Mimeo report. Dhaka: Center for Development Studies.

Boyce, J. K. 1987. *Agrarian Impasse in Bengal: Institutional Constraints to Technological Change.* Oxford: Oxford University Press.

Clay, E. J. 1978. *Employment Effects of the HYV Strategy in Bangladesh: A Rejoinder.* Mimeo report. Dhaka: Centre for Development Studies.

Gill, G. J. 1983. "The Demand for Tubewell Equipment in Relation to Groundwater Availability in Bangladesh." *Agricultural Economics and Rural Social Science Papers* No. 13. Dhaka: Bangladesh Agricultural Research Council.

Glaser, M. 1988. *Water to the Swamp: Patterns of Accumulation from Irrigation in Rajshahi Villages.* Unpublished doctoral dissertation, Bath University.

Hakim, M. A. 1986. "Irrigation Assets for Landless Groups: An Evaluation of the Ford Foundation-assisted BRDB Programme for the Rural Poor." Mimeo report, Dhaka.

Hamid, M. A. 1982. *Shallow Tubewells under IDA Credit in North West Bangladesh.* Department of Economics, Rajshahil University.

Hirschman, A. 1970. *Exit, Voice and Loyalty*. Cambridge, MA: Harvard University Press.

Hossain, M. 1984. "Credit for the Rural Poor: The Grameen Bank in Bangladesh." *Research Monograph* No. 4. Dhaka: Bangladesh Institute of Development Studies.

Hossain, M. 1987. *Green Revolution in Bangladesh: Its Nature and Impact on Income Distribution*. BIDS Working Paper No. 4. October.

Hossain, M., and S. Jones. 1983. "Production, Poverty, and the Cooperative Ideal: Contradictions in Bangladesh Rural Development" in D. A. M. Lea and D. P. Chaudhuri (eds.), *Rural Development and the State*. London: Metheun.

Howes, M. 1985. *Whose Water?* Dhaka: Bangladesh Institute of Development Studies.

IRBD. 1979. *Bangladesh: Food Policy Issues*. Report No. 2761–BD. Washington, DC: International Bank for Reconstruction and Development (World Bank).

ILO. 1977. *Poverty and Landlessness in Rural Asia*. Geneva: International Labor Organization.

Jenkins, D. 1981. *Irrigation Water Distribution Systems for Tubewells and Low-Lift Pumps in Bangladesh*. Mimeo report. Dhaka: USAID.

Lewis, D. 1981. *Technologies and Transactions: A Study of the Interaction between New Technology and Agrarian Structure in Bangladesh*. Unpublished doctoral dissertation, Bath University.

Lipton, M. 1987. "Limits of Price Policy in Africa: Which Way for the World Bank?" *Development Policy Review*, 5.

Lukes, S. 1974. *Power: A Radical View*. New York: Macmillan.

Mandal, M. A. S., 1986. *Changes in Irrigation Schemes: Findings from a Follow-up Survey in Ghatail-Kalihati Areas of Tangail District*. Mymensingh: Bangladesh Agricultural University.

Mandal, M. A. S., and R. W. Palmer-Jones. 1987. *Access of the Poor to Groundwater Irrigation in Bangladesh*. Paper presented at Workshop on Common Property Resources with special reference to access of the poor, Roorkee University, February.

Mendoza, S. T. 1989. *An Analysis of Yield Estimates and Benefits to Participants in the LOTUS Project, 1987/8*. Dhaka: CARE-Bangladesh.

McGregor, J. A., and B. Wilkinson. 1986. *Production and Employment Programme: Establishment of a Banking Plan*. Dhaka: Swedish International Development Authority.

MoA. 1987. *Floods 1987: Medium Term Recovery Programme*. Draft report, Ministry of Agriculture, Government of Bangladesh, November.

MPO. 1986. *National Water Plan*. Three volumes. Dhaka: Master Plan Organization.

Osmani, S. R., and M. A. Quasem. 1985. *Pricing and Subsidy Policies for Bangladesh Agriculture*. Dhaka: Bangladesh Institute of Development Studies.

Palmer-Jones, R. W. 1985. *Report on the Monitoring of the Landless Irrigation Programme of Proshika*. Mimeo report. Dhaka: Proshika.

Palmer-Jones, R. W., and M. A. S. Mandal. 1987. "Irrigation Groups in Bangladesh." ODI/IIMI *Irrigation Management Network Paper* No. 87/2c.

Palmer-Jones, R. W. 1988. *Multi-User Schemes and the Theory of Clubs*. Draft. Oxford: Queen Elizabeth House.

Palmer-Jones, R. W. 1988. *Optimal Capacity of Multi-User Irrigation Schemes*. Mimeo report. Oxford: Queen Elizabeth House.

Quasem, M. A. 1985. "Impact of the New System of Distribution of Irrigation Machines in Bangladesh." *Bangladesh Development Studies* 13 (3&4):127–140.

Rahman, A., ed. 1985. *Special Issue on Agricultural Inputs in Bangladesh:*

Bangladesh Development Studies 13 (3&4).

Rahman, A. 1986. *Demand and Marketing Aspects of the Grameen Bank.* Dhaka: University Press.

White, S. 1988. *In the Teeth of the Crocodile: Class and Gender in Rural Bangladesh.* Unpublished doctoral dissertation, Bath University.

Wood, G. D. 1974. "A Peasantry and the State." *Development and Change* 5:2:45–75.

Wood, G. D. 1976. "The Political Process in Bangladesh—A Research Note." In A. Huq (ed.) *Exploitation and the Rural Poor,* 16–58.

Wood, G. D. 1980. "The Rural Poor in Bangladesh: A New Framework?" *Journal of Social Studies* (10 October), 22–46.

Wood, G. D. 1981. "Rural Class Formation in Bangladesh 1940–80." *Bulletin of Concerned Asian Scholars* 13:4, December.

Wood, G. D. 1982. *The Socialisation of Minor Irrigation in Bangladesh.* Dhaka: Proshika.

Wood, G. D. 1984. "Provision of Irrigation Services by the Landless." *Agricultural Administration* 17:2:55–80.

Wood, G. D. 1984. *Government Approaches to the Rural Poor in Bangladesh.* Dhaka: Swedish International Development Authority Report.

Wood, G. D. 1985. "Politics of Development Policy Labelling." In G. Wood (ed.), *Labelling in Development Policy.* Newbury Park, CA: Sage.

Wood, G. D. 1985. "Targets Strike Back: Rural Works Claimants in Bangladesh." In G. Wood (ed.), *Labelling in Development Policy.* Newbury Park, CA: Sage.

Wood, G. D. 1986. "Don't Give Them My Telephone Number—Applicants and Clients: Limits to Public Responsibility." *Public Administration and Development* (Oct.-Dec.) 4:6 475–484.

Wood, G. D. 1988a. *Agrarian Entrepreneurialism in Bangladesh.* Keynote address to 22nd Bengal Studies Conference, June. Lewisburg, PA: Bucknell University.

Wood, G. D. 1988b. *Sirs and Sahibs: Group Mobilisation and BRDB/TA Relations.* Dhaka: Swedish International Development Authority, December.

Wood, G. D., and R. W. Palmer-Jones. 1988. *Social Entrepreneurialism in Bangladesh: Water Selling by the Landless.* Dhaka: Proshika.

World Bank. 1982. *World Development Report.* Washington, DC: International Bank for Reconstruction and Development.

World Bank. 1983. *Selected Issues in Rural Employment.* Country Report for Bangladesh. Washington: IBRD.

World Bank. 1986. *Bangladesh: Country Report.* Washington: IBRD.

World Bank. 1987. *Bangladesh: Promoting Higher Growth and Human Development.* Washington: IBRD.

World Bank. 1988. *Bangladesh: Adjustments in the Eighties and Short-Term Prospects.* Country Report 7105–BD. Washington: IBRD.

World Bank. 1989. "Selected Issues in Agricultural Development." Working Papers for the Special Aid Group Meeting on Bangladesh Agriculture. Mimeo report. Dhaka: IBRD.

Index